GALDRAMAL

A Practical Guide to Rune Magick and Spell Work

About the Author

André Jooste stands as a dedicated practitioner of magick, having traversed the realms of mysticism throughout his entire life. His profound expertise and unwavering commitment are particularly prominent in the domain of Galdr, a form of magick deeply rooted in Northern traditions. As a Vitki, which denotes a skilled sorcerer and Northern shaman, he has ventured deep into the heart of Nordic Folk Magick, embracing its ancient wisdom, symbolism, and rituals. In his journey along the winding path of magick, André Jooste delves into the realm of Sigils, symbols imbued with powerful intent and purpose. He crafts these symbols to manifest his desires and intentions, forging a connection with the ethereal forces that shape our world.

On the path of the Left Hand, André Jooste delves into the mystical, unconventional realms of magick. This unique approach challenges conventional norms and pushes the boundaries of the unknown. It's a path that calls upon the practitioner to embrace personal power, eschewing societal conventions and limitations. It is here that André finds the courage to explore and harness the hidden, transformative forces that dwell in the shadows.

A Practical Guide to
Rune Magick and Spell Work

André Jooste

Chicago, IL

Paperback ISBN: 978-1-964537-50-4
Hardcover ISBN: 978-1-964537-73-3
eBook ISBN: 978-1-968185-44-2

Library of Congress Control Number on file.

Published by:
Crossed Crow Books, LLC
518 Davis St, Suite 205
Evanston, IL 60201
www.crossedcrowbooks.com

Printed in the United States of America.
IBI

I dedicate this book to fifteen-year-old me, who, more than a quarter-century ago, picked up his first book on Northern Germanic runes.

"Unknowingly, you created a lifelong obsession and started unravelling our fate."

Table of Contents

Introduction

Welcome to *Galdramál: A Practical Guide to Nordic Rune Magick*, a journey into the rich tapestry of Old Norse mysticism. The term *Galdramál* originates from an Old Norse term denoting the "Speech of Galdr." However, the nuanced definition of *galdr* eludes easy categorization. In the Old Norse context, it signifies a spell or incantation intricately intertwined with actions like screaming, singing, or crowing. As you immerse yourself in the pages of this text, you'll gradually grasp the profound significance of sound in this mystical art, effectively making it, in essence, my "book of incantations" or "song of the crow," if you'd like.

This comprehensive guide explores the ancient craft of Nordic rune-specific magick, the activation of runes, and the intricate skill of crafting bind-runes. Together, we will embark on an immersive journey into the depths of runic magick, discovering how these ancient symbols can be wielded to manifest your innermost intentions and desires. Whether you are a newcomer or a seasoned practitioner, this book offers you a treasure trove of knowledge and techniques to unleash the innate potency of each rune and to skillfully weave them into powerful bind-runes.

While we embark on this enchanting odyssey into the world of runic magick, always keep in mind that the genuine essence of rune activation and bind-runes lies within the unique connection you establish with these symbols and your personal intentions. Armed with the wisdom and techniques shared in this book, you will unlock a world of boundless possibilities in your interactions with these ancient runes. May you embrace the transformative force of runes with reverence, wisdom, and a profound sense of responsibility. Let the radiant energy of the runes illuminate your path as you manifest your desires, setting forth on an extraordinarily magickal voyage.

Within Norse paganism, practitioners encounter a diverse array of spiritual avenues, encompassing interactions with deities, the exploration and utilization of runic symbols, and the practice of eclectic witchcraft involving herbs, potions, and various magickal arts. In this collaborative exploration, our primary focus will center on the art of rune craft, delving into its multifaceted dimensions. We shall traverse the spectrum, from the simplicity of folk magick, to the intricacies of high ceremonial rituals and the fascinating realm of divination.

To commence this exploratory journey, we must first undertake a comprehensive examination of the gods and spirits deeply ingrained in the Northern landscape. This thorough exploration shall furnish us with valuable insights into the cosmology of the Norse pantheon and the cultural backdrop against which these beliefs were interwoven into the fabric of daily life.

The Norse pantheon, a tapestry of rich and multifarious deities, embodies various aspects of life, nature, and the human experience. Odin, the Allfather and the god of wisdom, magick, and poetry, takes center stage. Thor, the mighty god of thunder, protection, and fertility, symbolizes strength and valor. Freyja, the enchanting goddess of love, fertility, and magick, graces us with her presence. Loki, the cunning trickster, adds an element of unpredictability and transformation to the divine ensemble.

These deities, alongside numerous others, fulfill distinctive roles within the Northern cosmology. Their stories resonate with the challenges, aspirations, and values of the people who once lived deeply immersed in this spiritual tapestry. Understanding the dynamics, personalities, and symbolic representations of these deities is pivotal as we embark on our runic journey, for they are intimately interwoven with runic lore and the magickal practices we will explore.

As we delve into the intricate world of rune craft, we shall traverse the history, symbolism, and applications of these ancient symbols. This journey encompasses their mundane use in writing and communication, as well as their profound role in magickal rituals and divination. We shall explore runic inscriptions, the runic alphabet, bind-runes, and *galdr,* or "runic chanting," to unlock their latent potential in spellwork and ritual.

Our voyage will also encompass the distinction between exoteric and esoteric rune craft, delving into the deeper, more ceremonial aspects where runic magick converges with the broader landscape of Western occultism. We will unearth the mysteries of runic divination, often referred to as "casting the runes," and explore how these ancient symbols can reveal insights into the past, present, and future.

Through this collective endeavor, our aim is to cultivate a profound appreciation for the intricate tapestry of Norse paganism while empowering those who seek to connect with the runes as a source of wisdom, magick, and spiritual transformation. By bridging the realms of history, mythology, and contemporary practice, we aspire to shed light on the enduring significance of Northern traditions in the modern world.

When embarking on a journey into the realm of magick, it is essential to commence by pondering the very essence of magick itself. What precisely is magick, and what sets Norse magick apart from other mystical practices?

Magick, in its purest form, can be distilled to the profound concept of "shaping reality in accordance with one's will." To comprehend this notion more deeply, we can dissect the Norse creation myth.

In this myth, Odin, the central figure and the source of inspiration, requires two key elements: *Vili,* signifying his will or intent, and *Ve,* symbolizing a sacred space. This myth underscores a fundamental principle of magick—that one needs only a sacred space and a magickal intent to bring about any desired outcome.

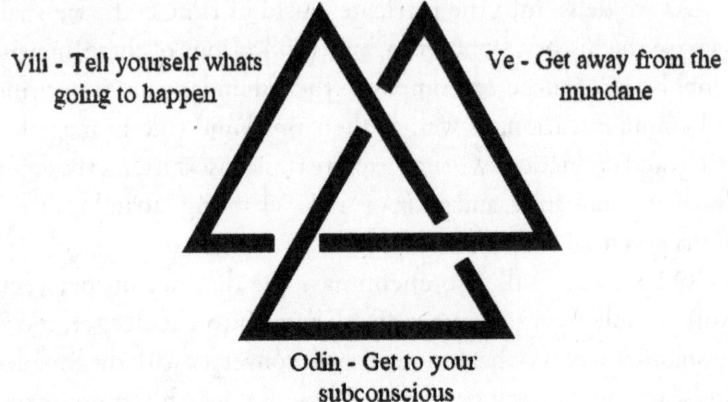

Here, "intent" refers to a profound awareness of one's true will, while a "sacred space" can manifest as the consecration of an altar, the establishment of a magickal circle, or even the creation of a grand temple. As we plumb the depths of Norse magick, we shall unveil its unique essence and its place within the broader tapestry of mystical practices.

That's magick in a nutshell.

Norse magick, a realm of mysticism deeply woven into the fabric of ancient Nordic cultures, reveals itself through a rich tapestry of practices and beliefs, manifesting through five primary branches:

1. ***Seiðr* (Spirit Work):** *Seiðr* (or Seidr) represents a form of Norse magick deeply entwined with shamanic traditions. Practitioners of seiðr would embark on journeys through altered states of consciousness, often facilitated by chanting, drumming, or meditation. These altered states allowed them to communicate with spirits, peer into the future, or influence the unfolding of events. Notably, in Norse society, women known as volur or seiðkonur held pivotal roles as seers and sorceresses. Seiðr encompasses the divinatory aspect often referred to as *spá*.
2. **Runes (Letters):** Runes form an Ancient Norse system of writing, with each symbol carrying both linguistic and

mystical significance. Runic magick revolves around the inscribing, carving, or vocalizing of runes to invoke their inherent powers. Each rune holds distinct meanings and can be employed for divination, protection, or the manifestation of intentions. The Elder Futhark stands as the most widely recognized runic alphabet in Norse magick.

3. ***Galdr* (Song Spells):** *Galdr* is the art of Norse incantation and chanting, a form of magick that harnesses specific vocalizations and rhythmic patterns to invoke spiritual forces, realize desired outcomes, or unlock hidden wisdom. Galdr can be employed for purposes ranging from healing and protection to the manipulation of the natural world. Rituals involving galdr often incorporate runic symbols to amplify their potency.
4. ***Útiseta* (Vision Quests):** *Útiseta,* colloquially known as "sitting out," is a practice embraced by Norse magicians. It entails a solitary soul's journey into nature, often amidst remote and desolate settings. Through deep meditation and a profound connection with the natural world, practitioners pursued communion with spirits, sought insight, or received guidance. Útiseta is a practice that involves communication with one's inner world, delving into the microcosms, while seiðr often focuses on the macrocosms.
5. ***Gand* (Elf Shot):** *Gand,* a lesser-known facet of Norse magick, centers on the utilization of staffs or wands adorned with runes and symbols. These tools serve as conduits for channeling and directing energy. Unlike some other forms of magick, gand involves sending energy outward toward a target, rather than receiving power. Gand practitioners (known as *Gandrmannen*) employ these implements for offense, protection, healing, or the enhancement of their magickal abilities.

In the realm of modern magick, these distinct branches often intermingle, blurring the lines between them. Most magickal workings encompass elements from all five facets, allowing practitioners to tap into the rich and multifaceted traditions of Norse magick which continue to resonate with those seeking its wisdom and power in the contemporary world.

In its simplest form, creating a potent ritual can be as straightforward as drawing a circle and declaring one's intent. This fundamental act holds the power to shape reality in alignment with one's will.

PROLOGUE

In the beginning, there existed but the void—a yawning abyss known as Ginnungagap, a realm as profound as it was unforgiving.

This chasm held dominion over all existence. Where its northern reaches bore the bitter name of Niflheim laid an expanse veiled perpetually in relentless ice and frost, a realm where the embrace of warmth dared not intrude. To the south, an infernal maelstrom named Muspelheim raged, a land of scorching flames and blistering heat, an incendiary crucible that knew no respite.

Within the frigid heart of Niflheim, an eerie stillness prevailed, and it was there that Hvergelmir lay—a spring of otherworldly origin from which numerous rivers known as *Élivágar* flowed ceaselessly. As these rivers ventured further from their glacial source, their essence, tainted and malevolent, congealed into formidable ice. This ice, unyielding and formidable, exhaled a toxic vapor that condensed into rime atop the frozen rivers. Layer upon layer, these thick strata of ice unfurled, painting the bleak landscape in a deadly embrace.

Yet, amidst the tumultuous expanse of Ginnungagap, there existed a curious respite—a windless pocket within the ceaseless clash of fire and ice. Here, the scorching breath of Muspelheim and the biting embrace of Niflheim found a brief cessation in their eternal strife. In this serene enclave, rime and scorching heat converged and melded, creating a unique moment of stillness—an interlude amidst chaos.

And it was within this calm interlude that the symphony of creation began.

This stark duality of fire and ice gave birth to a cataclysmic clash—an elemental collision of opposing forces that ignited the very core of existence. In the north, where the icy dominion gradually yielded to its fiery adversary, droplets formed—delicate, ephemeral, and bearing within them the secrets of creation. A low hum resonated through the void, a prelude to the grand cosmic overture that would follow. The steam began hissing, swirling with promise. As the great glaciers melted, rivers ran from them, merging, twisting, and coalescing into something completely foreign.

This something, born of fire and ice, came to be known as Ymir—an embodiment of primeval chaos and the progenitor of the frost giants.

Ymir, the colossal giant, slumbered, and from his slumber emerged a complex lineage: his left arm bore a male and female jötunn, while his legs begat further offspring.

To sustain himself, Ymir drank from the rivers of milk flowing from the celestial teats of the primordial cow, Auðumbla. This celestial cow, in turn, nourished herself by diligently licking salt from the rime-covered stones. Through her patient efforts, Auðumbla liberated a robust and handsome man named Buri. Buri, in turn, fathered Borr, who wed a jötunn named Bestla, resulting in the birth of three sons: Odin, Vili, and Vé—the gods destined to shape the cosmos.

Amidst this tumultuous backdrop, three enigmatic deities emerged as architects of destiny. Odin, the harbinger of fury and inspiration, took the leading role, his presence as formidable as the clash of fire and ice itself. Standing beside him was Vili, the embodiment of intent and the will to create, and Vé, the guardian of sacred spaces.

Unified in their purpose, they harbored the audacious intent to sculpt the nascent world from the very body of Ymir, embarking on a daring and audacious act of creation. With calculated ruthlessness, they executed their divine design.

From Ymir's tormented scream, the building blocks of reality emerged—Ymir's grotesque and formidable flesh hewed the rugged contours of the Earth, establishing a solid foundation for their grand design. The surging torrents of Ymir's blood were harnessed to shape the vast oceans and boundless seas, their depths teeming with both life and unfathomable mysteries. Ymir's colossal bones, unyielding and relentless, metamorphosed into towering mountains and rolling hills, defining the majestic landscapes that would cradle existence. The very skull of the fallen giant became the ethereal canvas upon which they painted the boundless tapestry of the sky, a realm of endless wonder and aspiration. From Ymir's tangled locks of hair, verdant and vibrant, sprouted the lush foliage of vegetation, a nurturing force providing sustenance and life. Finally, Ymir's enigmatic brain, a repository of ancient knowledge, became the wellspring from which they forged the ever-shifting, billowing clouds. These clouds bestowed beauty and enigma upon the world and imbued the winds that carried them with wisdom.

In this brutal and intricate symphony of creation, the formidable deities, Odin, Vili, and Vé, channeled their powers to forge the very world that would serve as the canvas for the myriad of creatures and tales in Norse mythology—a realm where gods, giants, and mortals would coexist and carve their destinies.

From the very inception of existence, death was intertwined with rebirth. As the glacier died, the river was born. As Ymir died, Midgard was formed. From the earliest notes of creation, death was woven into the tapestry of life—the song of creation, the song of magick itself.

This was creation in its purest form, a symphony where death and rebirth danced hand-in-hand, a profound song of genesis.

This is the world of Norse magick...

This is the world in which we find ourselves—amidst the cosmic clash of opposing forces, within the unforgiving embrace of Ginnungagap, the epic tale of creation unfolds. From the void's abyss, where fire and ice entwine, a world is born, shaped by gods and giants alike, and the ancient melody of magick weaves its intricate, eternal song.

The Nine Noble Virtues

The Nine Noble Virtues are a set of moral and ethical principles that are often associated with Norse and Germanic mythology. They provide guidance for living a noble and honorable life, according to the values of these ancient cultures. It's important to note that these virtues are modern interpretations and reconstructions, as historical sources on the exact ethical code of the Vikings and other Germanic peoples are limited. Here are the Nine Noble Virtues:

1. **Courage:** Courage is the foundation of all noble virtues. It means facing fear and adversity with bravery and determination. It involves taking risks and standing up for what is right, even in the face of danger.
2. **Truth:** Truthfulness and honesty are highly valued. To be noble is to be truthful in one's words and actions and to avoid deceit and falsehood.
3. **Honor:** Honor involves maintaining one's integrity, reputation, and self-respect. It means keeping one's word, fulfilling promises, and acting with dignity and respect toward others.
4. **Fidelity:** Fidelity refers to loyalty and faithfulness to one's family, friends, and community. It involves standing by those you care about in times of need and being a dependable ally.
5. **Discipline:** Discipline is the ability to control one's impulses and desires, to act with self-control and moderation. It involves making responsible choices and not yielding to destructive behaviors.
6. **Hospitality:** Hospitality is the act of welcoming and providing for guests and strangers with generosity and kindness. It reflects the importance of community and mutual support.
7. **Industriousness:** Industriousness emphasizes hard work, perseverance, and the value of productive labor. It involves using one's talents and resources wisely for the betterment of oneself and one's community.

8. **Self-Reliance:** Self-reliance is the ability to take care of oneself and one's responsibilities without becoming a burden to others. It encourages independence and resourcefulness.
9. **Perseverance:** Perseverance is the determination to endure and overcome challenges and obstacles. It involves resilience in the face of adversity and a commitment to personal growth and improvement.

These Nine Noble Virtues serve as a framework for those who seek to embrace the values of Norse and Germanic heritage. They are not exclusive to any particular religious or cultural group and can be adopted as a guide for personal ethics and behavior in a broader context. Keep in mind that interpretations and emphasis on these virtues may vary among individuals and communities.

Book of Songs

I grew and waxed in wisdom;
word following word, I found me words,
deed following deed, I wrought deeds
(*Poetic Edda*, "Hávamál," 140)

In line with numerous mythologies from various cultures, Norse mythology, too, emphasizes the power of the spoken word in the creation of the world. Within this rich tapestry of ancient beliefs, the world's genesis is attributed to the primal scream of Ymir, an enormous and primordial being. This thunderous cry echoed through the vast void, setting into motion the very fabric of existence.

Ymir, often referred to as the "first frost giant," emerged from the ice of Ginnungagap, the great chasm that separated the realms of fire and ice. His scream carried the raw essence of life, shaking the cosmos from its slumber. As his cry reverberated through the cosmic expanse, it sparked the cosmic elements into action.

From Ymir's scream, the very building blocks of reality took form.

Thus, in Norse mythology, as in many others, the word (in this case, a "primal scream"), served as the catalyst for the birth of the world. It resonates as a reminder of the profound connection between language, sound, and creation, echoing through time as a testament to the power of myth and the human imagination.

Ymir Equals Sound

The universe was sung into place. A great cosmic song; one of love, and one of death.

The name Ymir can have two roots in etymology. The first being "twin" or "hermaphrodite," derived from the theoretical Indo-European root-word *iemo,* meaning "twin." Quite adapt for a being that birthed all of creation.

But, more importantly for us from a magickal means is the second meaning...

The masculine name formation Ymir is mentioned in one of the *þulur,* the name lists Snorri's Edda, as a *heiti,* a synonymous name for "hawk." As such, we are in no doubt that the name is derived from *ymja,* "to scream," and may refer to the bird's shriek. The very closeness to the similarly derived noun *ymr,* "scream" or "noise, " makes it hard to miss the association and must have been evident to any Old Norse audience.

In the beginning was "the scream" that the "Völuspá" uses to introduce Ymir: "It was the dawn of time. When eagles screamed, holy water fell from the mountains of heaven..." (Verse 3)

Ymir is a being of the intangible, the invisible, and the inconceivable—or, in other words, of the abstract, the intellectual, and the spiritual. The giant nature informs this abstract "matter" as chaotic and threatening. This is the raw material of which the world is made. When the gods created the world, they took control of the raw material, ordered it, and made it conceivable and comprehensible to us.

They created the world by ordering and defining it in a comprehensible way. They proclaimed the world by transforming *Ymir*—"the scream"—into words. The scream is the raw material of words. Words are shaping the world.

Birds are often symbols of spirit, in Old Norse myths, too.

The spirit descends from heaven to become man. The scream is associated with birth and beginning, the language of babies, the first utterance that, through the process of divine creativity—the process of creating culture, will become words, language, runes, and the world as we know it.

Language and Magic: Exploring the Resonance of Words

Language, often considered the most powerful tool at humanity's disposal, has an inherent resonance with the realm of magick. Throughout history, various cultures and societies have attributed mystical qualities to words, believing in their ability to influence the world around them.

This connection between language and magick can be observed in practices such as spellcasting, incantations, and the use of curses and blessings. In this chapter, we will delve into the idea that words are magick in nature, exploring the concepts of "spelling" and "cursing" as manifestations of this belief.

Words as Incantations: The Art of Spelling

The concept of "spelling" is deeply rooted in the idea that words possess a magickal quality. To spell a word is to cast a linguistic enchantment, and this notion is evident in the very word "spell." In many cultures, incantations and rituals involve the repetition of specific words or phrases believed to possess the power to shape reality. These words are carefully chosen and imbued with intent, similar to a magician selecting the right ingredients for a potion.

Even the word "grammar" has magickal origins. It is believed to have been derived from the Old French word *gramaire,* which referred to a book of grammar and learning. Over time, *gramaire* evolved into *grimoire* and came to denote a book of magick spells and occult knowledge.

Thus, your grammar is your list of spells, your metaphysical rules.

In the realm of literature and storytelling, words are used to create entire worlds, breathing life into characters and landscapes. Writers are akin to sorcerers, weaving spells with their narratives, captivating readers and transporting them to different realms. The power of storytelling lies in the artful arrangement of words, invoking emotions and sparking the imagination.

The written word, too, has a magickal quality. Ancient civilizations considered the act of writing to be an act of creation. From the hieroglyphs of the Egyptians to the runic inscriptions of the Norse, writing was seen as a means to communicate with the divine. Words etched onto stone, parchment, or papyrus were believed to carry an enduring enchantment, preserving the thoughts and wisdoms of generations.

Every word we utter sends vibrations into the universe, transcending metaphysical speculation, while being grounded in empirical research. When we speak, we emit energy in the form of sound, a manifestation of energy itself.

These spoken words release energy into the universe, generating vibrations that resonate within us and the world, especially when imbued with emotion and intent. These vibrations possess the capacity to shape our reality, influencing our thoughts, emotions, and actions.

The potency of words is profound, subtly but enduringly affecting our psyche and worldview, thereby shaping our lived experiences. Words are more than mere symbols; they carry significant meaning that can either elevate or diminish us, depending on how we interpret them.

Choosing words deliberately becomes an act of empowerment itself. Words like *trust* and *know* convey confidence, while words like *hope* and *try* instill uncertainty.

Your words possess the enchanting power of spells, exerting a lasting influence on your individual experiences, transcending even this lifetime. By infusing a mystical element into our understanding of words, we highlight their transformative potential and the inherent power they hold.

Curses and Blessings: The Magic of Words in Action

The idea of "cursing" is another testament to the magickal resonance of words. A curse is not merely an expression of anger or frustration, it is seen as an invocation of harm or misfortune upon the recipient. This belief spans cultures and epochs, from ancient hexes and maledictions to modern-day expressions of ill-will.

The power of cursing lies in the belief that words have the capacity to shape reality. By uttering a curse, the speaker is, in essence, casting a spell, directing negative energy towards the target. This belief has led to the development of various protective measures (such as amulets and charms) designed to ward off curses and malevolent magick.

Conversely, blessings are positive invocations, where words are used to bestow goodwill and positive energy upon others. Blessings are found in religious rituals, ceremonies, and everyday expressions of goodwill. The belief in the efficacy of blessings is a testament to the idea that words can shape reality for the better, bringing luck, prosperity, and happiness to those who receive them.

The Influence of Language on Emotions and Behaviour

Beyond the realm of formal incantations and curses, everyday language has a profound impact on human emotions and behavior. Words can uplift, inspire, and motivate, just as they can wound, demoralize, and enrage. This emotional resonance of words reflects their inherent magickal quality.

Consider the power of a well-timed compliment or a heartfelt apology. Such words have the ability to mend relationships and heal emotional wounds, demonstrating the transformative potential of language. Conversely, hurtful words can scar deeply, leaving lasting emotional imprints.

The importance of language is evident in its role in shaping cultural norms and values. Through language, societies transmit knowledge, beliefs, and moral codes from one generation to the next. Words have the power to influence public opinion, drive social change, and shape the course of history. This influence is akin to the way a spell shapes the world according to the intent of the caster.

Language in the Digital Age: A Modern Perspective

In the digital age, the resonance of words is amplified through technology. Social media platforms, for instance, provide a virtual arena where words can be used as tools of empowerment or destruction. The speed at which information spreads online emphasizes the potency of language. In a world where a tweet can go viral within seconds, the impact of words is heightened.

The internet has also given rise to a new form of cursing, often referred to as "online harassment" or "cyberbullying." Individuals use words as weapons, hiding behind the anonymity of screens to launch verbal attacks on others. The consequences of such actions can be devastating, highlighting the real-world repercussions of words in the digital realm.

The belief that words are magick in nature is deeply ingrained in human history and culture. From the act of spelling, where words are carefully crafted to weave enchantments, to the use of curses and blessings, which seek to shape reality through language, the power of words is evident. Language influences emotions, behavior, and societal norms, reflecting its profound impact on human existence.

In a world where communication is more interconnected than ever, the resonance of words remains a potent force. Whether through storytelling, incantations, or everyday conversations, language continues to shape our understanding of the world and our place in it. Therefore, it is essential to recognize the power of words and use them responsibly, for they carry the potential for both magick and destruction.

The Importance of Poetry in Ancient Norse Society

In the annals of Ancient Norse society, poetry held a place of immense significance. To the Vikings and their predecessors, poetry was not merely an artistic pursuit, but a fundamental aspect of their culture—a means of preserving history, transmitting knowledge, and honoring their gods and heroes. In this book, we will explore the multifaceted importance of poetry in Ancient Norse society, delving into its role as a vehicle of oral tradition, a source of cultural identity, and a bridge to the mystical realms of Norse mythology.

Preservation of History and Knowledge

In the absence of a written language during much of their history, the Norse people relied heavily on oral traditions for the transmission of knowledge. Poetry became the primary medium through which this knowledge was preserved and passed down from one generation to the next. Skalds, the revered poets of Norse society, held the responsibility of memorizing and reciting the sagas, legends, and historical accounts that formed the collective memory of the Norse people.

The poetic form served as a mnemonic device, aiding in the retention and recitation of complex narratives. These poetic compositions were not only beautiful, but also functional, allowing the Norse to record their history and cultural heritage with remarkable accuracy. The *Poetic Edda* and the *Prose Edda,* two key literary works from this era, are prime examples of how poetry was used to encapsulate the wisdom, stories, and traditions of the Norse people.

Cultural Identity and Social Function

Poetry played a vital role in defining the cultural identity of the Norse people. The sagas and skaldic poems celebrated the heroic deeds of warriors, kings, and legendary figures, instilling a sense of pride and belonging in the community. These poems also served as a means of preserving the honor of individuals and clans, as a well-crafted poem could elevate a person's reputation for generations.

In addition to individual honor, poetry was an integral part of the social fabric of Norse society.

Skalds were highly respected and often served as court poets in the halls of chieftains and kings. Their compositions were not only a source of entertainment, but also a means of recording contemporary events, such as battles, alliances, and feuds. Through poetry, the Norse were able to navigate the complex web of social relationships and diplomacy that characterized their society.

The Connection to Norse Mythology

Perhaps one of the most captivating aspects of Norse poetry is its deep connection to the pantheon of Norse mythology. The Ancient Norse believed that poetry was a divine gift, granted to mortals by the god Odin himself. Odin, the Allfather, was not only the god of war and wisdom, but also the god of poetry and inspiration. He was said to have sacrificed an eye at Mímir's well in exchange for the knowledge of the runes, the mystical symbols that underpinned Norse poetry.

The magickal and spiritual dimensions of Norse poetry are evident in the concept of seidr (or seiðr), a form of sorcery practiced by the Norse, often associated with trance-like states and prophetic visions.

Poetry and seidr were intertwined, with skalds and seers alike using poetic incantations to access the wisdom of the gods and channel their power. The *Poetic Edda,* for example, contains verses that delve into the cosmology of the Norse universe, the creation of the world, and the impending *Ragnarök,* the end of the world.

In Norse myth and legend, an almost obsessive pursuit of knowledge and wisdom is one of the defining characteristics of Odin, the ruler of the group of gods known as the Æsir. It was this obsession, after all, that drove Odin to steal the "Mead of Poetry" from the giant, Suttung—an act of blatant theft he was able to commit by seducing Suttung's own daughter, Gunnlod. It was also this same obsession that led Odin to pierce his own side with a spear and hang himself from the branches of the world tree, Yggdrasil, where he hanged for nine days and nine nights in an act of ritual sacrifice in which Odin made an offering of himself to himself.

It was this act of self-sacrifice that allowed Odin to learn the secrets of the runes—though, his pursuit of knowledge also led Odin to learn even greater magick from other sources. As outlined in "Hávamál," one of the poems found in the *Poetic Edda,* Odin also learned nine powerful songs from his maternal uncle, the unnamed son of his grandfather, Bolthor. Odin's pursuits had also led him to acquire knowledge of eighteen charms, or powerful spells, not known to any man or woman.

The Eighteen Charms Known by Odin

In the last part of "Hávamál," Odin counts the eighteen charms that can protect mankind from trolls (*Poetic Edda*).

"Hávamál" verse 146

The first charm I know is unknown to rulers
or any of humankind;
help it is named,
for help it can give in hours of sorrow and anguish.

"Hávamál" verse 147

I know a second that the sons of men
must learn who wish to be leeches.

"Hávamál" verse 148

I know a third: in the thick of battle,
if my need be great enough,
it will blunt the edges of enemy swords,

their weapons will make no wounds.

"Hávamál" verse 149

I know a fourth:
it will free me quickly
if foes should bind me fast
with strong chains,
a chant that makes Fetters spring from the feet,
bonds burst from the hands.

"Hávamál" verse 150

I know a fifth: no flying arrow,
aimed to bring harm to men,
flies too fast for my fingers to catch it
and hold it in mid-air.

"Hávamál" verse 151

I know a sixth:
it will save me if a man
cut runes on a sapling' s Roots
with intent to harm; it turns the spell;
the hater is harmed, not me.

"Hávamál" verse 152

I know a seventh:
if I see the hall
ablaze around my bench mates,
though hot the flames, they shall feel nothing,
if I choose to chant the spell.

"Hávamál" verse 153

I know an eighth:
that all are glad of,
most useful to men:
if hate fester in the heart of a warrior,
it will soon calm and cure him.

"Hávamál" verse 154

I know a ninth:
when need I have
to shelter my ship on the flood,
the wind it calms, the waves it smoothes
and puts the sea to sleep.

"Hávamál" verse 155

I know a tenth:
if troublesome ghosts
ride the rafters aloft,
I can work it so they wander astray,
unable to find their forms,
unable to find their homes.

"Hávamál" verse 156.

I know an eleventh:
when I lead to battle old comrades in-arms,
I have only to chant it behind my shield,
and unwounded they go to war,
unwounded they come from war,
unscathed wherever they are.

"Hávamál" verse 157

I know a twelfth:
if a tree bear
a man hanged in a halter,
I can carve and stain strong runes
that will cause the corpse to speak,
reply to whatever I ask.

"Hávamál" verse 158

I know a thirteenth:
if I throw a cup Of water over a warrior,
he shall not fall in the fiercest battle,
nor sink beneath the sword,

"Hávamál" verse 159

I know a fourteenth, that few know:
if I tell a troop of warriors
about the high ones, elves and gods,
I can name them one by one.
(Few can the nit-wit name.)

"Hávamál" verse 160

I know a fifteenth:
that first Thjodrerir
sang before Delling's doors,
giving power to gods, prowess to elves,
foresight to Hroptatyr Odhinn,

"Hávamál" verse 161

I know a sixteenth:
if I see a girl
with whom it would please me to play,
I can turn her thoughts, can touch the heart
of any white armed woman.

"Hávamál" verse 162

I know a seventeenth:
if I sing it,
the young girl will be slow to forsake me.

"Hávamál" verse 163

I know an eighteenth that I never tell
to maiden or wife of man,
a secret I hide from all
except the love who lies in my arms,
or else my own sister.

To learn to sing them, Loddfafnir,
will take you a long time,
though helpful they are if you understand them,
useful if you use them,
needful if you need them.

"Hávamál" verse 164

The Wise One has spoken words in the hall,
needful for men to know,
unneedful for trolls to know:
hail to the speaker,
hail to the knower,

joy to him who has understood,
delight to those who have listened.

Knowledge of the Charms

The charms mentioned are often confused with runes because the runes have been mentioned just previously in the "Hávamál"; the "charms" do, in fact, mean songs/poems.

- **Help:** Offers assistance in moments of strife or grief, though the exact nature of this aid is unspecified.
- **Healing:** Can be used to heal physical injuries and provide relief from physical pain.
- **Protection:** Blunts the blades of enemies, rendering their weapons incapable of causing serious harm.
- **Escape:** Allows Odin to escape from any attempt to bind him.
- **Arrow Alteration:** Enables Odin to stop or alter the course of arrows in flight.
- **Spell Reflection:** Reflects spells or curses back upon the caster.
- **Fire Control:** Can extinguish any fire, regardless of size, with a simple chant.
- **Anger-Soothing:** Soothes feelings of anger and hatred.
- **Storm-Calming:** Calms the wind on a stormy sea.
- **Shapeshifting Curse:** Curses those with the ability to change shape, making it difficult for them to return to their true form or home.
- **Battle Blessing:** Blesses soldiers entering battle to ensure victory and safety.
- **Raising the Dead:** Allows Odin to raise the dead and communicate with them.
- **Child's Battle Protection:** Guarantees that a child sprinkled with water on their head will not fall in battle.
- **Name Knowledge:** Provides Odin with the knowledge of anyone he meets.
- **Dwarf's Chant:** A chant learned from the dwarf Thjodrerir,

which grants strength to gods, skill to elves, and wisdom to Odin.

- **Love Enchantment:** Rouses feelings of love and desire in women who attract Odin's interest.
- **Unwavering Love:** Ensures that a woman's love for Odin will remain steadfast and unchanging.
- **Mystery Charm**: A secret kept by Odin for himself, the exact nature of which is not disclosed.

The Skaldic Tradition

The skaldic tradition, with its intricate forms and *kennings* (metaphorical expressions), exemplifies the complexity and artistry of Norse poetry. Skalds were not only expected to craft verses of great beauty, but also to demonstrate their skill by composing poems with elaborate wordplay and metaphors. This tradition emphasized the importance of wit and creativity in the crafting of poetry, further underscoring its cultural significance.

One of the most celebrated skalds in Norse history was Snorri Sturluson, who authored the *Prose Edda.* Sturluson's work not only provided valuable insights into Norse mythology, but also served as a manual for aspiring poets, outlining the rules and techniques of skaldic composition. His efforts ensured the continuity of the skaldic tradition and the preservation of Norse poetry for future generations.

The importance of poetry in Ancient Norse society cannot be overstated. It served as a vessel for the preservation of history and knowledge, a means of forging cultural identity, and a bridge to the mystical realms of Norse mythology. Through poetry, the Norse people celebrated their heroes, recorded their sagas, and communed with their gods.

Today, the legacy of Norse poetry continues to captivate and inspire, not only as a historical artifact, but as a testament to the enduring power of language and storytelling. The skalds of old, with their verses of bravery and beauty, remind us that poetry has the ability to transcend time and connect us with the rich tapestry of human experience. In the words of the skalds themselves, "Words have power, words are magick." And, in the case of Ancient Norse poetry, this magick endures.

Galdr, the Magick Incantations of the North

In Norse mythology and the Old Norse language, *galdr* (pronounced "GAHL-dur") refers to a form of magick or sorcery associated with chanting, incantations, and spells. Galdr was a practice in which specific words, sounds, or phrases were chanted or sung in a ritualistic manner to invoke supernatural powers or influence the natural world.

Galdr was often performed by individuals known as *galdramenn* (or *galdralær*), who were skilled in the art of magickal incantations. These practitioners believed that, by reciting the right words with the correct intonation and rhythm, they could harness the magickal forces inherent in the spoken or sung words.

The use of galdr was not limited to any one aspect of Norse culture or mythology; it had a broad range of applications. It could be used for healing, protection, divination, influencing the weather, or even in battle to enhance one's prowess or weaken an opponent.

The concept of galdr is closely connected to the broader notion of *rúnar* (runes), as runes were often incorporated into galdr practices. Each rune had its own meaning and magickal significance, and Galdramenn would use them as part of their incantations.

Thus, galdr in Norse culture referred to a form of magickal practice involving the chanting or singing of specific words and sounds to invoke mystical or supernatural effects, making it an essential aspect of Norse magickal and mystical traditions. Galdr, seidr, and the runes are very intertwined—you sing a song to get into a trance while sending your intent into a sigil.

Eagles, crows, giants, and shamans all scream—all galdr!

Intent

The word is all that one needs in magick...that is, if your spoken intent is your true will.

Intention and focus play crucial roles in activating and harnessing the energies of the runes. When working with the runes, your intention sets the stage for the type of energy and guidance you seek, while your focus allows you to channel and direct that energy effectively. Here's a closer look at the importance of intention and focus in the process of rune activation:

- **Setting Clear Intentions:** Before engaging with the runes (or any magick), it's essential to set clear intentions for your work. Ask yourself what you hope to achieve or understand through your interaction with the runes. Clarify your goals, whether it's seeking guidance, personal growth, healing, or connecting with specific energies. Your intentions act as a roadmap, guiding your focus and shaping the energies you attract.
- **Directing Attention and Focus:** Once you've set your intentions, it's crucial to cultivate your focused attention during your rune practice. Concentration allows you to establish a strong connection with the rune you're working with. Direct your attention solely on the rune, its symbols, and its energetic presence. By immersing yourself fully in the present moment and the rune's energy, you create a receptive space for its vibrations to resonate within you.
- **Visualization and Imagination:** Visualization is a powerful tool to enhance your focus and intention during rune activation. As you hold the rune, close your eyes and visualize its symbols, colors, and energy. Imagine yourself merging with the essence of the rune, embodying its qualities. Visualize the rune's energy flowing through you, activating and aligning with your intentions. This visualization practice strengthens your connection with the rune's vibrations and helps manifest your desires.

- **Affirmations and Mantras:** Affirmations and mantras are verbal statements that reinforce your intentions and focus. As you work with a rune, repeat affirmations or mantras that resonate with its energy and your desired outcomes. For example, if you're working with the rune Ansuz, which represents communication and wisdom, you could repeat affirmations like "I am open to clear and authentic communication" or "I embrace the wisdom within me." These affirmations help align your conscious and subconscious mind with the energy of the rune, amplifying your intention.
- **Emotional Engagement:** Engaging your emotions adds depth and power to your intention and focus. Allow yourself to feel the emotions associated with your intentions as you work with the runes. If you're seeking healing, evoke a sense of love, compassion, and healing within yourself. If you're seeking strength, tap into feelings of empowerment and resilience. Emotionally engaging with the intentions infuses your work with genuine energy and aligns your emotional state with the energies of the runes.
- **Active Participation:** Approach rune activation as an active and engaged process. Avoid being passive or detached. Actively participate in the ritual by holding the rune, reciting affirmations, visualizing, and embodying its energy. Your active participation demonstrates your commitment and focus, allowing the runes to respond more effectively to your intentions.

Remember that intention and focus are ongoing practices. As you continue to work with the runes, refine your intentions and strengthen your focus. Trust your intuition and let the energy of the runes guide you in deepening your connection and amplifying the power of your intentions.

The Merseburg Charms: Some of the Oldest Fully Intact Word Charms

The *Merseburger Zaubersprüche* ("Merseburg Charms") are a pair of Old High German incantations or spells found in a manuscript known as the Merseburg Incantations, which dates back to the ninth and tenth centuries. These spells are among the earliest known examples of Germanic pagan poetry and provide insight into the religious beliefs and practices of the time.

The two Merseburg Charms are often referred to as the "First Merseburg Incantation" and the "Second Merseburg Incantation." Each of them serves a specific purpose and offers a glimpse into the spiritual world of the early Germanic peoples.

The First Merseburg Incantation is a healing spell that was likely used to treat injuries or ailments. It is a short verse that describes a scenario in which the goddesses Phol and Volla are invoked to heal a wounded horse. The spell is spoken with the intention of mending the horse's leg and restoring its mobility.

"Bone sprain,
blood sprain,
joint sprain too:
Bone to bone,
blood to blood,
joints to joints.
May they be glued."

The Second Merseburg Incantation, on the other hand, is a more complex charm. It involves the release of a captured warrior named Baldur from his bonds. In this spell, the goddesses Sunna (or Sinthgunt) and Friia (or Volla) are mentioned. The charm describes how these goddesses call upon the healing powers of the Earth and the sky to free Baldur from his chains, which may symbolize the liberation of a warrior or the breaking of a curse.

The Merseburg Charms are important not only for their historical and linguistic value, but also because they provide a window into the religious and magickal practices of the Germanic peoples during the early medieval period. They blend elements of mythology, healing, and incantation, offering unique insights into the beliefs and rituals of the time.

We can take the Merseburg Incantations and work any song spell in that form. For instance, rewriting a love spell in that vein would look like such:

Heart to heart,
soul to soul,
two as one,
we will grow.
Let our love be deep and true,
growing stronger,
me and you.

The above spell is really powerful and potent, but the Merseburg Incantations are the product of quite a few translations. Let's take a look at the exact form that the Ancient Norse would have used.

Ancient Norse poetry, a rich and diverse tradition, played a pivotal role in preserving the cultural and historical heritage of the Norse people. These poems were not just artistic expressions, but served as a means of transmitting knowledge, legends, and values from one generation to the next. Among the many forms of Ancient Norse poetry, some stand out for their unique structures and purposes. This text will explore various forms of Norse poetry, including "ljoðaháttr" and "galdralag," shedding light on their distinctive characteristics and cultural significance.

- **Ljoðaháttr:** *Ljoðaháttr,* often referred to as "song meter" in English, was a prevalent form of Norse poetry. It is characterized by its regular stanza structure, typically consisting of eight lines divided into two sets of four. Each line contains two stressed syllables, followed by an unspecified number of unstressed syllables. Ljoðaháttr is known for its alliteration and intricate wordplay. This form was frequently used to convey heroic deeds, myths, and historical events. The *Poetic Edda,* a collection of Old Norse poems, contains numerous examples of ljoðaháttr.

- **Galdralag:** *Galdralag,* or "spell meter," was a distinct form of Norse poetry used for magickal or incantatory purposes. This form of verse was employed in rituals, chants, and spells. Galdralag is characterized by its distinctive rhythm and repetitive structure. It often features a refrain or a repeated phrase that contributed to its mystical quality. Norse sorcerers and seers would use galdralag to invoke various powers or seek protection. This form of poetry was closely associated with shamanistic practices in Norse society.
- **Drápa:** *Drápa* was a complex and formal poetic genre that celebrated the achievements of kings and warriors. This form of poetry was highly structured and contained intricate kennings (metaphorical expressions) that required in-depth knowledge of Norse mythology and history to decipher. Skalds, the court poets of the time, used *drápa* to compose praise poems for their patrons, earning favor and prestige through their skillful craftsmanship.
- **Fornyrðislag:** *Fornyrðislag,* or "ancient words meter," was a versatile form of Norse poetry characterized by a fixed stanza structure and a particular emphasis on the first syllable of each line. This poetic form was often used to convey moral lessons, myths, and historical narratives. The "Hávamál," a section of the *Poetic Edda,* is an example of a poem composed in fornyrðislag, offering practical wisdom and ethical guidance.
- **Háttatal:** *Háttatal,* meaning "list of verse forms," is an extraordinary composition by the Icelandic poet Snorri Sturluson. In this work, Sturluson systematically describes and demonstrates various poetic forms, including ljoðaháttr, dróttkvætt, and galdralag, among others. Háttatal serves as a valuable reference for understanding the intricacies of Norse poetry and the techniques employed by skalds.

In conclusion, Ancient Norse poetry encompassed a wide range of forms, each with its unique structure and purpose. These poems were not only artistic expressions, but also vital means of preserving and transmitting Norse culture, history, and spirituality. The ljoðaháttr, galdralag, drápa, fornyrðislag, and háttatal are just a few examples of the rich tapestry of Norse poetry that continues to captivate scholars and enthusiasts alike, offering insights into the world of the Vikings and their enduring literary legacy.

The Use of Kennings in Norse Poetry

The use of kennings in Norse poetry is a distinctive and fascinating aspect of this literary tradition. Kennings are poetic devices in which a compound word or phrase is used to describe something in a more indirect or metaphorical way. These figurative expressions are rich in imagery and often draw upon the mythology, cultural references, and the nature of the Norse world. Kennings add depth and complexity to Norse poetry, making it both challenging and rewarding for readers and listeners. Here are some key points about the use of kennings in Norse poetry:

- **Metaphorical Descriptions:** Kennings allow poets to create vivid and imaginative descriptions by substituting a common word with a poetic circumlocution. For example, "whale-road" might be used as a kenning for the sea, emphasizing its vastness and potential dangers.
- **Cultural Significance:** Many kennings draw upon the cultural and mythological heritage of the Norse people. Norse mythology, with its gods, giants, and heroic figures, provided a rich source of inspiration for kennings. Poets often used kennings that referenced these mythological elements to convey deeper meanings.
- **Nature and Environment:** The Norse environment, with its rugged landscapes, fjords, and harsh weather, also influenced kennings. Terms like "snowshoes of the mind" (meaning

"poetry") or "fire of the eyebrows" (meaning "gold") demonstrate the connection between the natural world and poetic expression.

- **Variety of Kennings:** There is a wide variety of kennings in Norse poetry. Some are straightforward, while others are more cryptic and require cultural or historical knowledge to interpret. Skalds, the poets of the time, were known for their skill in crafting intricate and layered kennings.
- **Kennings in Different Forms:** Kennings were used in various forms of Norse poetry, including drápa, ljoðaháttr, and fornyrðislag. Skaldic poets, in particular, were renowned for their mastery of kennings, and their compositions often featured these figurative expressions prominently.
- **Preservation of Culture:** Kennings played a crucial role in preserving and passing down the cultural and historical knowledge of the Norse people. They were a way of encapsulating important concepts, stories, and values within the poetry, ensuring that these elements would endure through generations.
- **Riddle-like Quality:** Some kennings take on a riddle-like quality, challenging the audience to decipher their meaning. This added an element of intellectual engagement to the poetry and encouraged listeners to delve deeper into the verses.

In summary, kennings in Norse poetry were not merely decorative language, but integral components of the art form. They enriched the verses with cultural, mythological, and environmental references, providing readers and listeners with a deeper understanding of the themes and messages conveyed in the poetry. The use of kennings remains a distinctive and enduring feature of Norse literature, showcasing the creativity and linguistic prowess of the poets who crafted these masterpieces.

List of Examples of Kennings

Here are some examples of kennings from Norse poetry, along with their meanings:

- **Whale-Road:** Meaning "the sea." This kenning emphasizes the vastness and potential dangers of the ocean.
- **Serpent's Bed:** Meaning "ship." This kenning draws upon the image of a serpent resting in the water, symbolizing the ship's movement through the sea.
- **Sky-Candle:** Meaning "the sun." This kenning likens the sun to a candle in the sky, emphasizing its role as a source of light and warmth.
- **Wave-Horse:** Meaning "ship." This kenning highlights the idea of a ship riding the waves like a horse.
- **Battle-Sweat:** Meaning "blood." This kenning associates bloodshed in battle with the physical exertion and perspiration of warriors.
- **Tree of Ice:** Meaning "a glacier." This kenning conveys the image of a towering, frozen landscape.
- **Shield-Sun:** Meaning "a warrior's shield." This kenning suggests that the shield provides protection and radiates strength like the sun.
- **Corpse-Candle:** Meaning "sword." This kenning alludes to the deadly nature of swords in battle, likening them to a flickering candle extinguished in combat.
- **Gold's Tears:** Meaning "coins." This kenning reflects the idea that gold was often acquired through significant effort or even suffering.
- **Word-Hoard:** Meaning a poet's knowledge or wisdom. This kenning emphasizes the idea that a poet's words and stories are treasures of knowledge.
- **Sky-Vault:** Meaning "the heavens" or "the celestial dome." This kenning portrays the sky as a vast, arching structure.

- **Battle-Bale:** Meaning "wounds" or "injuries sustained in battle." This kenning conveys the idea that battle brings suffering and harm.
- **Ale of Poetry:** Meaning "mead." This kenning highlights the connection between poetic inspiration and the consumption of mead, a common practice in Norse culture.
- **Odin's Eye:** Meaning "the sun." This kenning associates the sun with Odin's all-seeing eye, symbolizing its watchful presence in the sky.
- **Raven-Feast:** Meaning "battle." This kenning suggests that a battlefield is where ravens gather to feed on the fallen warriors, emphasizing the carnage of war.

These examples showcase the imaginative and metaphorical nature of kennings in Norse poetry, where everyday objects and concepts are described in poetic and often mythological terms, adding depth and vividness to the verses.

Galdralag

Galdralag is a term used in Norse magickal traditions and refers to the rhythmic and melodic patterns of chanting or singing used in rune magick and spellcasting. It involves the vocalization of specific sounds, words, or verses to attune oneself with the energies of the runes and invoke their power.

Here are some key points about galdralag:

1. **Runic Chanting:** Galdralag involves chanting or singing specific sounds, words, or verses associated with the runes. Each rune has its own phonetic sound or name, and, by vocalizing these sounds, you tap into their vibrational energy. The rhythmic and melodic nature of the chant helps to enhance the focus and intention behind the magickal work.
2. **Runic Verses and Incantations:** In addition to chanting individual rune sounds, galdralag often incorporates the

use of runic verses or incantations. These verses are poetic expressions that embody the essence and meaning of the runes. They can be found in Ancient Norse texts, such as the "Hávamál" and other texts in the *Poetic Edda*. By reciting these verses, you align yourself with the wisdom and power contained within them.

3. **Connecting with the Runes:** Galdralag serves as a method to establish a deeper connection with the runes and their energies. Through the act of vocalizing the runic sounds and verses, you create a direct and intimate link between yourself and the runic forces. This connection allows you to tap into the inherent power and symbolism of the runes and channel it for various magickal purposes.
4. **Amplifying Intentions:** The rhythmic and melodic qualities of galdralag aid in focusing and amplifying intentions. By combining specific sounds, words, or verses with your intentions, you align your energy with the corresponding runic vibrations, enhancing the potency of your spell or magickal work. The repetition and resonance created through galdralag help to reinforce your intention and project it onto the world.
5. **Personal Expression:** While there are traditional forms of galdralag, it's important to note that personal expression and intuition play a role in adapting and developing your own unique style of runic chanting. You can experiment with different melodies, rhythms, and vocalizations to find what resonates best with you and enhances your connection with the runes.
6. **Practice and Mastery:** Galdralag, like any form of magick, requires practice and mastery. Regular practice of runic chanting helps to refine your vocalization skills, deepen your understanding of the runes, and strengthen your connection with their energies. As you become more proficient, you may find that galdralag becomes an intuitive and powerful tool in your magickal practice.

The "statement of magickal intent" intertwines deeply with galdralag. In practice, these two aspects are intricately entwined, as they share a fundamental purpose. An incantation, spell, charm, or enchantment serves as a mystical formula designed to set in motion a specific effect, whether it be directed towards oneself or others (or even objects). This formula can take the form of spoken words, songs, or chants, and may be enacted during intimate individual rituals, grand ceremonial magick, or in the tranquil moments of prayer and meditation.

The "statement of intent" represents the verbalized essence of one's actions or spells, acting as a compass and guiding the magickal working. A well-constructed spell typically commences with a clear statement of intent, often becoming an integral component of the incantation or utilized in the creation of bind-runes and various other sigils. In all magickal practices, the explicit articulation of intent stands as the bedrock upon which the entire endeavor is constructed.

A robust statement of intent often resembles an affirmation, serving as a positive and unequivocal declaration that outlines the purpose of the spell or other mystical activities. This declaration emanates from the will of the practitioner and should be both lucid and succinct. For instance, if one's objective is to augment their income, the statement of intent may be as straightforward as "My wealth increases."

It's crucial to note that magickal intent must scrupulously avoid the inclusion of words like "I wish," "I want," or "I hope." Expressing one's intention as "I wish for one million dollars" inevitably leads to a perpetual state of wishing without fulfillment. Magick invariably follows the path of least resistance, and a wish for one million dollars might materialize as an insurance payment or an inheritance.

Hence, careful consideration must be given to crafting the statement of intent, striking a balance between specificity and generality. For example, one might declare, "My wealth increases through my work," thereby setting a more direct and focused course for their magickal endeavor.

Poetry held a profound role in the social and religious life of the Nordic people. In the enchanting realm of Norse mythology, the Skáldskaparmál weaves a captivating tale of Odin's journey to acquire the sacred Mead of Poetry for Asgard. This mythological narrative stands as a resounding testament to the extraordinary significance that poetry held within the contemporary Scandinavian culture.

Indeed, poetry was celebrated as a divine gift from Odin, the venerable Allfather, and it served as a pivotal conduit for transmitting spiritual mysteries and concealed wisdom. The Old Norse poetic tradition, exemplified in revered texts like the "Hávamál," the rune poems, or the "Grimnismol," was inherently intertwined with the mystical and the magickal. Poetry and magick, from the very outset, existed as harmonious companions, each enhancing the other's power and resonance.

Nordic Poetic Structure

Old Norse poetry exhibited distinctive characteristics, setting it apart from more familiar poetic forms found in English literature. Rather than relying on end-rhyming, this poetic tradition was defined by the artful use of alliteration on specific stressed syllables. It was this masterful interplay of sound and meaning that rendered Old Norse poetry a mesmerizing and evocative medium for conveying the profound narratives, wisdom, and spiritual insights of the Nordic people.

1. **Alliteration:** Alliteration is the occurrence of the same letter or sound at the beginning of adjacent or closely connected words (Example: "I sing songs").
2. **Syllables:** Words are made up of letters, and those letters create syllable sounds. You can recognize a syllable by remembering that each one contains a vowel sound. For example, in the word computer, there are three syllables: com/pu/ter. The word bike, however, has only one syllable.

A single syllable may contain as little as just one letter, or as many as five.

3. **Counting Syllables:** You can check how many syllables a word has by putting your hand under your chin and saying a word. Each time your chin moves to make a vowel sound, count a syllable. For example, the word "difficult" moves your chin three times. Therefore, "difficult" has three syllables.
4. **Stressed Syllables:** In any language, we tend to stress or give prominence to certain syllables in words that we pronounce. We do so by pronouncing those syllables with stronger force, therefore making them sound louder than those syllables that we do not stress. In one-syllable words, finding the stress is easy, as the whole word is stressed; just alliterate the words as in the example "I sing songs." However, with two (or more)-syllable words (in English) it is a bit trickier. In Old Norse, the first syllable of multi-syllable words were always the stressed one, and, thus, always the one that you alliterated.
5. **Two-syllable Words:** A normal two-syllable word in English is generally stressed on the first syllable (Examples: ENGlish, WELcome, PRACtice). Unfortunately, English is sometimes a bit more complicated, as, in some two (or more) syllable words, the stress does not always fall on the first syllable. However, there are a few easy rules to help you out in most situations:

    a. **Rule 1:** If the first syllable of a two-syllable word is a single letter, the stress falls on the second syllable (Examples: aLONE, eSTATE, oFFENCE).
    b. **Rule 2:** If the first syllable of a two-syllable word is a prefix, the stress falls on the second syllable. Some prefixes include: be-, con-, de-, pro-, to-, ex-, ob-, re-, co-, mal-, in-, il-, etc. (Examples: toDAY, proMOTE, enJOY).

On Galdr

Galdr means not only "spell" or "incantation," but also "sing" or "chant."

In the Nordic creation myth, the world (or, actually, the universe) were created from the giant Ymir's body parts, the root of the proto-Norse *Ymir* can be traced back to mean "sound."

In various cultures around the globe, the world was called into existence by the word. Magick is the calling of your will into existence. Galdr is the word. Old Norse poetry has many metrical forms. *Galdralag* is the "magick spell metre," and, hence, your focus today.

But first, we have to understand *ljóðaháttr* (the metre of song).

On Ljóðaháttr

In Eddic poetry, the metric structures are generally simple and are almost invariably ljóðaháttr (ljodahattr). Because of its structure comprised of broken stanzas, it lends itself to dialogue and discourse.

Ljóðaháttr is composed out of three lines (or, sometimes, six) with four or more syllables per line. It works with alliteration—not with the end rhyming that we are familiar with in most modern poetry.

Each of the three lines work as follows: one always alliterates with two, two always alliterates with one, three always alliterates with itself.

Then, we might continue with another three lines also based on the above.

Example:

1. I sing songs
2. I send magick
3. We weave faith

On Galdralag

For galdralag (the magickal meter we use to talk about spells), we simply add a fourth line: one always alliterates with two, two always alliterates with one, three always alliterates with four, four always alliterates with three.

We can either stop here, or we can add a ljóðaháttr/galdralag stanza or up to four additional lines alliterating with line three.

Example:

1. I sing songs
2. I send magick
3. We weave faith
4. We work with wonder

Galdralag Cheat Sheet:

- Lines one and line two alliterate with each other.
- Lines three and four alliterate with each other.

Stressed Syllables:

- Line one usually has two lifts, could be between one and three.
- Line two usually has one lift, could be between one and three.
- Line three usually has three lifts, could be either two or three.
- Line four usually has three lifts, could be either two or three.

Guide on Starting a Galdralag Incantation:

I find the easiest way to write a quick galdralag is to break the poem down into its most basic structure. Here is a quick guide on forming a galdralag intention:

- Most galdralag poems only consists out of two alliteration pairs.
- Each pair has between two and six words that alliterate.
- At minimum, lines one and two only need two words that alliterate—one in each line.
- Lines three and four can be duplicated, so the second pair could be as little as only two words as well—both in each line.

Example:

For instance, this POEM
PULSATE as it grows
With MINIMAL MARKINGS
With MINIMAL MARKINGS

Let's further take you through my personal practice of quickly writing one. Sometimes you *need* an incantation by yesterday.

Let's say that you need an incantation to make money fast. First, I start by writing down a few words that convey my message (Example: money, wealth, etc.). Then, I find words that alliterate with those words. If I am really in a hurry, I even sometimes use an online alliteration dictionary.

I write down the alliterations that I think might by helpful in my poem.

Some examples include:

- money/model/motto/mother/modify
- wealth/welcome

So:

Mother of money,
Modify its growth,
Welcome increasing wealth,
We welcome increasing flow,

Apart from intent, galdralag can also be used for evocations.

Odin:

Odin, wise wanderer,
God of wind and wild,
Grant me thy megin,
Lend me thy megin.

Frey:

God of the good year
And giver of gold,
Wealth is fair weather,
You welcome no woes.

Homework

Now, take the gods Thor, Tyr, and Freyja and write a one-verse galdralag poem for each of them, using at least one kenning for the above god(dess).

Let's take the eighteen charms known to Odin and galdr them properly:

Help:

Sorrow is a storm,
Solemn is the saga,
Help is on the hedge,
The healthy have a helm.

Healing:

He who heeds,
Advise for healing,
Pain will pass,
As the pane gets painted.

Protection:

Battle-bale turned,
And blade grow blunt,
No harm to our house,
No harm to our heart.

Homework

Can you fill in the rest of the "charms" as authentic galdralag poems?

1. **Escape:**
2. **Arrow Alteration:**
3. **Spell Reflection:**
4. **Fire Control:**
5. **Anger Soothing:**
6. **Storm Calming:**
7. **Shapechanging Curse:**
8. **Battle Blessing:**
9. **Raising the Dead:**
10. **Child's Battle Protection:**
11. **Name Knowledge:**
12. **Dwarf's Chant:**
13. **Love Enchantment:**
14. **Unwavering Love:**
15. **Mystery Charm:**

Galdralag Examples

Money:

Mother of money,
Modify its growth,
Welcome increasing wealth,
Welcome increasing flow.

Love:

I take my stock,
In the stars that cross,
As my mate,
Was made for me.

Offense:

The currency of curses,
Curve the very curtain,
Delve into death,
Delve into her depths.

It's important to approach galdralag with respect and reverence, honoring the ancient traditions and cultural significance associated with the runes. As you explore and incorporate galdralag into your magickal work, let your intuition and connection with the runes guide you in discovering the unique expression of this practice that resonates with you.

Galdring the Runes

While it is common that the utterance of an incantation or the recitation of a galdralag is the customary means of engaging with these potent symbols, the art of rune magick is, in fact, a multifaceted endeavor that offers practitioners a variety of approaches.

One intriguing method for evoking the essence of the runes is through the sonorous vibrations of their very names. As the runes have their unique appellations, these names can be intoned. Such vocalizations breathe life into the runic symbols, connecting the practitioner with their inherent powers.

Moreover, for the creation of bind-runes, a more intricate and personalized approach can be employed. Instead of relying on traditional incantations or galdralag, a practitioner can craft a bind-rune by ingeniously weaving together the first syllables of the individual runes involved in its formation. This clever and nuanced technique allows for the creation of highly personalized symbols uniquely tailored to address specific intentions, desires, or needs. Thus, you, the Vitki, can galdr the name of the newly created bind-rune.

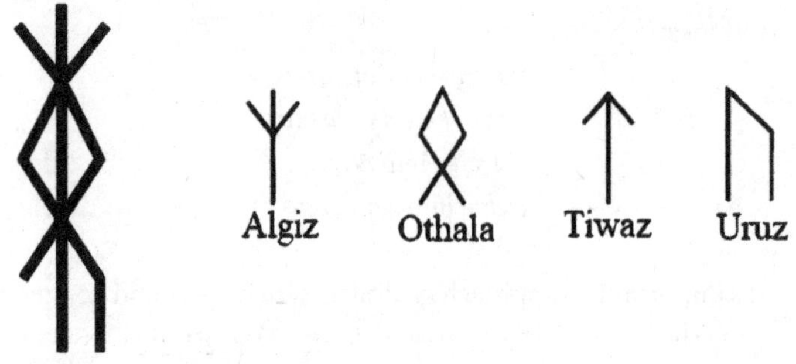

Al—Oth—Ti—Ur
New name: Aloftiur

In single-rune rituals where the intent is directly indicated by the rune and not as a custom form created by you, the Vitki, galdr sounds can be used instead of a detailed galdralag.

Galdr Sounds:

- ᚠ: *ffffffff* (a hissing f, like the crackle of flames)
- ᚢ: *uuuuuuuuuuu* (oo as in "moon." Prolonged, steady, forceful, like the lowing of a bull)

- ᛞ: *thu-thu-thu* (a deep, violent, explosive grunt, pronounced and cut off very sharply, repeated rather than prolonged)
- ᚨ: *aaaaaaa* (a as in "call," a steady rush of wind)
- ᚱ: *rrrrrrrrrrr* (a rolled r, as in the Scottish brogue or like the sound of a motor starting)
- ᚲ: *Keh-Keh-Keh* (the K sound is hit hard, volume tapering down like the sound of a sharply struck bell. The galdr-sound is neither prolonged like those of most of the runes, nor chopped off like that of thurisaz, but fades swiftly to a natural end.)
- ᚷ: *gggggggggg* (a deep growl, like the distant rumble of thunder or the growl of a large wild animal.)
- ᚹ: *wwwwwwwwww* (a soft, whispering w sound, like the wind rustling through leaves)
- ᚺ: *hhhhhhhhh* (a breathy h sound, like a sigh or the sound of wind passing through a small opening)
- ᚾ: *nnnnnnnnnnn* (a nasal n sound, like the hum of a chant or the drone of a distant engine)
- ᛃ: *yyyyyyyyyyy* (a soft y sound, like the murmur of a stream or the distant cry of a bird)
- ᛇ: *eh eh eh* (soft e sound, volume tapering down)
- ᛈ: *ppppppppp* (a popping p sound, like the crackling of a fire or the sound of raindrops on a surface)
- ᛉ: *zzzzzzzzzz* (a buzzing z sound, like the drone of bees or the distant murmur of a crowd)
- ᛊ: *ssssssssss* (a hissing s sound, like the sound of wind through tall grass or the whisper of waves)
- ᛏ: *ttttttttt* (a sharp t sound, like the striking of a drum or the tapping of a woodpecker)
- ᛒ: *bbbbbbbbbb* (a booming b sound, like distant thunder or the deep resonance of a drum)
- ᛖ: *eeeeeeeeee* (e as in "pet," a gentle and melodious sound, like the cooing of doves)
- ᛗ: *mmmmmmmmmm* (a humming m sound, like the drone of a chant or the gentle hum of machinery)

- ᛚ: *llllllllll* (a flowing sound, like the murmur of a brook or the rustling of leaves)
- ᛝ: *iiiinnnnnngggg* (a dragged out "ing" sound, repeated every time the sound fades out)
- ᛞ: *dddddddddd* (a deep, resonant d sound, like the thud of a drum or the beat of a heart)
- ᛟ: *oooooooooo* (o as in "go," a resonant and drawn-out sound, like the howling of wind or the distant roar of a lion)

Homework

Bookmark this page. After reading and studying the "Book of Runes," come back to this page.

Pick three runes from the Elder Futhark (or any system) and galdr them in the three ways described earlier in the chapter, namely by galdralag, sound, and, finally, by combing the three chosen runes into one bind-rune using the first syllable method.

Book of Spirits

In this sacred space,
out of this scream,
everything grew, not just the seen,
but also the unseen.

At the center of Norse cosmology stands *Yggdrasil,* the "World Tree."

Yggdrasil is an immense ash tree that connects and supports the various realms of the cosmos. It has three main roots, each of which extends into a different realm: one into Asgard (the realm of the gods), one into Midgard (the realm of humans), and one into Niflheim (the realm of ice and mist).

Yggdrasil is also inhabited by various creatures, including a serpent, an eagle, and a squirrel.

After killing Ymir, Odin and the other gods created an orderly universe made up of three levels. Although journeys between the different levels of the universe were possible, they were difficult and dangerous, even for the gods. The top or heavenly level contained Asgard, the home of the Æsir, and Alfheim, the place where the light or good elves lived. Valhalla, the hall where Odin gathered the souls of warriors who had died in battle, was also located on this level.

Connected to the upper level by the rainbow bridge Bifrost was the middle or earthly level. It contained Midgard, the world of men. Midgard was said to contain multiple realms, including Jötunheim, the land of the giants; Vanaheim, the home of the Vanir; and the primordial realms of ice, Niflheim, and fire, Muspelheim. A huge serpent called Jormungand encircled the middle world.

The bottom level consisted of the underworld of Svartalfaheim, the land of the dwarves, and Helheim, also known as "Hel," after Loki's daughter, Hel, who ruled there.

Realms

Each realm can and will add its own nuances to your magickal work. Their utilization is by no means necessary for a quick spell, but this method will strengthen your work accordingly. When setting up an altar, I draw the stave of the corresponding realm in the middle of the circle to symbolize Yggdrasil.

Its great branches reach all the realms:

Asgard: Asgard is the realm of the Æsir, the principal group of gods in Norse mythology. This realm is associated with the heavens and is characterized by grand halls, divine palaces, and celestial beauty. Odin, Thor, Frigg, and other major deities reside in Asgard.

Sphere of influence: Justice, Order, Civilisation, and War

Alfheim: Alfheim is the realm of the light elves, beings known for their beauty and radiance. It is considered a luminous and ethereal realm, distinct from the more earthly Midgard.

Sphere of influence: Ancestor Veneration, Nature, and Fertility.

Midgard: Midgard is the realm of humans—Earth. It is situated between Asgard and Niflheim, symbolizing the connection between the divine and the mortal. Midgard is where humans live and interact with the natural world.

Sphere of influence: Growth, Skills, and Intellect.

Jötunheim: Jötunheim is the realm of the giants (*jötnar* or "Frost Giants"). It is a vast and untamed wilderness inhabited by various giant clans. The giants are often portrayed as chaotic and unpredictable beings.

Sphere of influence: Transformation, Wisdom, and Baneful Magick.

Vanaheim: Vanaheim is the realm of the Vanir, another group of gods in Norse mythology. The Vanir are associated with fertility, agriculture, and natural forces. They initially warred with the Æsir, but later formed a truce and exchanged hostages.

Sphere of influence: Nature, Fertility, Sex, and Magick.

Niflheim: Niflheim is a realm of ice and mist, often associated with cold and darkness. It is one of the primordial realms in Norse cosmology and is the birthplace of Ymir, the first giant. Niflheim is inhabited by various frost giants and other sinister creatures.

Sphere of influence: Cold, Darkness, and Creation.

Muspelheim: *Muspelheim* is the opposite of *Niflheim;* it is a realm of fire and heat inhabited by jötnar. It is ruled by the fire giant Surtr. Muspelheim is often associated with chaos and destruction.

Sphere of influence: Fire and Other Destructive Forces.

Svartalfheim: Svartalfheim is the realm of the dwarves (*Svartálfar*). Dwarves are skilled craftsmen and blacksmiths, and they are known for creating powerful artifacts. This realm is often associated with underground caves and forges.

Sphere of influence: Crafting, Paranormal, and the Hidden.

Helheim: Helheim is the realm of the dead and is ruled by the goddess Hel. It is a place where souls of the deceased go after death, especially those who did not die in battle. Helheim is often depicted as a cold and gloomy realm.

Sphere of influence: Medicine, Disease, and Necromancy.

Norse cosmology is a rich and intricate system that reflects the worldview of the Ancient Norse and Germanic people. It is a universe filled with both divine and natural forces where the gods, giants, humans, and other beings all play their roles in the intricate tapestry of fate and destiny.

Animism

With the creation of our world, other worlds, and the universe at large, Odin and his brothers created both the seen and the unseen. The Norse world is animistic in nature.

Animism is a belief system and worldview that holds that everything in the natural world, not *just* living beings, possesses a spiritual essence or soul. It is characterized by the ideas that the world is alive with both consciousness and intention and that all things, from animals and plants to rocks and rivers, have a spiritual presence.

In the Norse context, animism was a fundamental aspect of the belief system. The Ancient Norse and Germanic peoples held a profound reverence for the natural world and believed that it was inhabited by a multitude of spirits or souls. These spirits were considered conscious and sentient, each with its unique characteristics and significance.

One of the key principles of Norse animism was the belief in the soul. According to this worldview, everything has a soul—not only humans, but also animals, plants, natural elements, and even celestial bodies. This belief in universal animation meant that the world was viewed as a dynamic living entity with a universal spiritual significance.

Ancestor worship was a central element of Norse animism. Ancestors were regarded as powerful spirits who had the ability to influence the living. Families would honor their ancestors in order to seek guidance and protection from them, maintaining a strong connection between the living and the deceased.

Land spirits were another integral part of the Norse animistic belief system. The land itself was considered to have a soul, and various natural features—such as mountains, forests, rivers, and lakes—were believed to be inhabited by spirits. These land spirits were to be respected and their favor sought in order to ensure a harmonious and fruitful relationship with the environment.

Animals, too, were believed to possess souls, and each species of animal had a unique spiritual significance. These animal spirits were often associated with specific deities or held symbolic meanings. The Norse people recognized the totemic power of animals and frequently integrated them into their mythology, rituals, and daily life.

The Norse pantheon, including deities such as Odin, Thor, and Freyja, was another essential aspect of animism. These gods were seen as having personal relationships with humans and other entities in the natural world. Interaction between humans and deities was an integral part of Norse animistic practices.

Nature worship was a central theme in Norse animism. The changing of seasons and the cycles of nature were celebrated in various rituals and festivals. This deep reverence for nature and its patterns reinforced the interconnectedness of all life forms and the importance of maintaining a harmonious relationship with the environment.

The worldview of Norse animism emphasized the dependence and interconnectedness of all things. Humans were considered just one part of a vast web of life, and the well-being of individuals and communities depended on maintaining a harmonious relationship with all living beings and spirits. This belief system profoundly influenced the way the Norse people interacted with their physical surroundings, as well as the spiritual world, that surrounded them.

Thus, we move through an unseen sea of souls every day... fragmented souls...as the soul consist out of four distinct parts.

The spirit work that follows can clearly be categorised as seidr. Seidr is a form of shamanism dealing with outside entities and trance work.

Seidr can be defined as "the gathering of power that is greater than your own."

Norse Parts of the Self: Fylgja, Hamingja, Hamr, and Hugr

The *fylgja* is also known as "the fetch"/"the follower." It is the essence of a person. The fylgja can travel away from the body in the form of an astral shape. Famous examples of fylgja are Odin's ravens, Huginn ("thought") and Muninn ("memory").

The fylgja can sometime even by divided into three related (but slightly different) concepts:

- **Mannsfylgja:** *Mannsfylgja* is a concept that involves a supernatural, animal-shaped spirit or being that is thought to accompany a person throughout their life. This spirit is often considered to be a representation of the individual's character or destiny. In some cases, it is believed that the mannsfylgja can even appear in the form of the person it accompanies.
- **Kynnfylgja:** *Kynnfylgja* is a term that is related to the concept of family or ancestral spirits. It is associated with a supernatural being or spirit that is tied to a particular family or lineage. This spirit is believed to protect and watch over the family members, often serving as a guardian or guiding force. The kynnfylgja is thought to have a connection to the ancestral roots of the family.
- **Aetterfylgja:** *Aetterfylgja* is a term that is similar to kynnfylgja in that it also pertains to ancestral spirits. The term is derived from *ætt*, which means "family" or "lineage." Aetterfylgja refers to a supernatural being or spirit that is associated with and represents the entire lineage of an individual. It is a broader concept than kynnfylgja and

> encompasses the entirety of one's familial heritage. It can also extend to a group or a fraternity that one belongs to, such as in the case of bears and beserkers or wolves and the ulfhednar—warrior brotherhoods in Norse tradition who were said to channel the spirit and strength of their totem animals in battle.

While *mannsfylgja, kynnfylgja,* and *aetterfylgja* are distinct terms, some interpretations suggest a connection between the individual's spirit and their changing personality over time.

The idea is that the fylgja is not a static entity, but can manifest or change its form based on the individual's personality, actions, and life experiences. In this interpretation, the fylgja is a dynamic being and evolves alongside the individual. As one's personality changes throughout their life, influenced by various experiences, challenges, and personal growth, the fylgja may reflect these changes by altering its appearance or characteristics. It's as if the spirit is a mirror of the person's inner self, adapting to the individual's journey through life.

This concept aligns with the broader Norse belief in destiny and the interconnectedness of individuals with their spiritual counterparts. It implies that the fylgja is not only a passive observer, but an active participant in the person's life, responding to the twists and turns of their fate. While the specific details and interpretations may vary, the fluidity of the fylgja in relation to the individual's evolving personality adds depth to the Norse understanding of the spiritual realm and the profound connection between the human and supernatural aspects of existence.

The concept of *hamingja* in Norse mythology holds a profound significance, encompassing two key aspects. First, it represents an individual's inherent potential and inclinations, akin to their "base stats." This encompasses both their natural strengths and weaknesses. It is akin to the unique set of attributes and tendencies that define a person. This notion of hamingja is often believed to be inherited within a family or lineage, passed down from one generation to the next.

In addition to this personal connotation, hamingja was also perceived as a form of female guardian spirit in Norse mythology. This guardian spirit was thought to accompany and influence the luck and happiness of an individual. A so-called "Lady Luck." As a result, the term hamingja was synonymous with happiness in Modern Icelandic.

When a person passed away, their hamingja was believed to be transferred to a cherished family member, thus remaining with a family for several generations and continuing to shape their fortunes. In certain cases, individuals could even lend their own hamingja to a friend, as exemplified by Hjalti Skeggiason's request to borrow Olaf II of Norway's hamingja before embarking on a perilous journey.

The hamingja often made its presence known during sleep, typically taking on the form of an animal. However, it could also manifest as the spirit of a slumbering person assuming an animal form, as seen in the saga of Hrólfr Kraki with Bödvar Bjarki.

In Norse mythology, hamingja encompasses two distinct concepts: first, it embodies the personification of an individual's or a family's good fortune and luck influencing their life path. Second, it pertains to the altered appearances of shapeshifters, reflecting the transformative aspects of these beings.

Scholars such as Andy Orchard and Rudolf Simek have drawn parallels between hamingja and the concept of fylgja, which is another form of guardian spirit. Hamingja could be passed down to descendants, members of a tribe embarking on perilous journeys, or even used to signify honor.

Over a person's lifetime, hamingja accumulates and can bestow wealth, success, power, and other positive attributes to those it accompanies, making it a pivotal element of Norse mythology and culture.

The *hamr* is your outer appearance—your physical form, your airs, and your presentation. The essence of the hamr can be manipulated by the *hugr* ("mind"). Examples of this are found in the Old Norse berserkir and úlfhéðnar, warriors who were thought to assume the hamr of a bear and wolf respectively through battle-frenzy (a function of *oðr*, or "inspiration"). Hamr can also be manipulated with the alteration of appearance.

The hamr is left behind after death.

The hugr is the mind, emotions, and will. This is the property of consciousness and agency. The hugr leaves the body upon death.

Animal Symbolism

While Norse mythology includes a variety of animals associated with the concept of fylgja, it's important to note that specific animals and their meanings might vary based on different interpretations and sources. However, here's a list of twenty animals often mentioned in connection with Norse fylgja and their general symbolic meanings. Please note that other parts of the soul might also take on these animal forms and that, in essence, one may have up to four animal soul companions:

- **Wolf:** Instinct, protection, strength.
- **Raven:** Wisdom, magick, prophecy.
- **Bear:** Introspection, inner strength, healing.
- **Deer:** Sensitivity, intuition, grace.
- **Boar:** Courage, determination, warrior spirit.
- **Eagle:** Vision, freedom, transcendence.
- **Fox:** Cunning, adaptability, intelligence.
- **Horse:** Power, journey, companionship.
- **Cat:** Independence, mystery, stealth.
- **Swan:** Elegance, transformation, inner beauty.
- **Salmon:** Wisdom, perseverance, transformation.
- **Owl:** Wisdom, clairvoyance, mystery.
- **Snake:** Rebirth, transformation, healing.
- **Hare:** Fertility, intuition, balance.
- **Squirrel:** Preparation, resourcefulness, gathering.
- **Otter:** Playfulness, joy, curiosity.
- **Falcon:** Precision, agility, focus.

- **Lynx:** Insight, patience, keen perception.
- **Moose:** Authority, self-esteem, endurance.
- **Walrus:** Adaptation, survival, resourcefulness.

Later, there will be a spell to find your fylgja. Some people know theirs from birth—maybe you have seen it or instinctually know of something being around all the time—for the rest, there is an easy meditative guide to find yours.

This "Svartebok" chapter can be used in two ways; on the mundane level, it can be viewed as an encyclopedia of Northern mythology. It is a piece to be studied by both beginners in this field and advanced practitioners as we cover the more obscure Germanic gods, as well as the "popular" ones.

Secondly, for the more magickally inclined, it can be viewed as a sort-of Northern Goetia (The Lesser Keys of Solomon), as all the gods are accompanied by a stave rune that can be viewed as a seal, according to Goetic Theurgy. A word to the wise: please practice the appropriate precautions, as most of these are not minor deities, but fully formed gods.

There is a divide between minor and major deities. Work alongside the gods, do *not* try to command them.

Gods of Northern Europe

Norse mythology comes from the northernmost part of Europe, Scandinavia: Sweden, Norway, Denmark, and Iceland. The mythology of this region is grim, shadowed by long, sunless winters. *This* is the world that formed the Norse Pantheon.

However, the darkness is laced with gleams of grandeur and sparks of humor. The myths depict a universe in which gods and giants battle among themselves in a cosmic conflict fated to end in the destruction of the world.

Norse mythology developed from the myths and legends of Northern peoples who spoke Germanic languages. It shares many features with the mythology of pre-Christian Germanic groups. When some of these groups spread into England and Scandinavia, they carried their myths with them.

As they converted to Christianity, their traditional beliefs faded. But Christianity did not take hold in Scandinavia until a later date, and the Norse version of Germanic mythology remained vigorous through the Viking era from about AD 750 to 1050. Modern knowledge of Norse mythology stems from medieval texts, most of them written in Iceland. Descendants of Norse colonists in that country maintained a strong interest in their heritage, even after becoming Christian.

A major source of information about Norse mythology is a book called the *Poetic Edda,* sometimes known as the "Elder Edda." It consists of mythological and heroic poems, including "Völuspá," an overview of Norse mythology from the creation to the final destructive battle of the world, *Ragnarök.* The unknown author who compiled the *Poetic Edda* in Iceland around 1270 drew on materials dating from between 800 and 1100.

Around 1222, an Icelandic poet and chieftain named Snorri Sturluson wrote the *Prose Edda,* or "Younger Edda," which interprets traditional Icelandic poetry for the audiences of his time. Part of the *Prose Edda* describes a visit by Gylfi, a Swedish king, to the home of the gods in Asgard. There, the king questioned the gods about their history, adventures, and fate.

Norse mythology is found in other Scandinavian texts as well. Many Norse poems refer to mythic events or figures. In the early 1200s, Icelanders started writing familial sagas about their ancestors and heroic sagas about legendary figures. Many of these sagas contain references to mythological subjects. Around the same time, a Danish scholar named Saxo Grammaticus wrote *The History of the Danish,* which begins with an account of their pagan gods and ancient heroes. Works by earlier Roman and medieval historians also include information about Germanic and Norse myths. In AD

98, for example, the Roman historian Tacitus wrote *Germania,* a description of the Germanic tribes that mentions some of their religious beliefs and customs.

Divided between the Æsir and the Vanir (and, sometimes, including the jötnar (giants), elves, dwarves, and other landveattir), these various other groups of beings acted as minor gods from time-to-time and place-to-place.

In various locations, there were small cults and sacred places devoted to them. I will feature them all, as the dividing line between these groups is less than clear.

The Æsir were gods of war and the sky. Chief among them was Odin, god of battle, wisdom, and poetry, who was regarded by the Vikings as the ruler of the deities and the creator of humans. The mighty Thor, warrior god of thunder, was ranked as the second-most important Norse deity. Tiwaz, an early Germanic sky god who became known as Tyr in Norse mythology, appears in some accounts as a son of Odin. Balder, also Odin's son, was a gentle, beloved god. Murdered, he descended to the underworld, only to return after a new world had been created. Loki, a cunning trickster, sometimes helped the other gods, but more often caused trouble, due to his spiteful and destructive nature. The sky goddess Frigg was Odin's wife and the patron of marriage, children, and households.

The Vanir were associated with the Earth, fertility, and prosperity. In the beginning, the Æsir and Vanir waged war against each other, perhaps reflecting an actual historical conflict between two cultures, tribes, or belief systems. Realizing that neither side could win, the two groups of gods made peace and together fought their common enemy, the giants. To ensure a lasting peace, some of the Vanir came to Asgard, the home of the Æsir, as hostages. Among them was Njord, the patron of the sea and seafaring. His twin children, Freyr and Freyja, were the most important Vanir, representing love, sexuality, and fertility. The giants' desire to capture Freyja was one cause of strife between the gods and the giants.

Northern Goetia

Angrboða

Etymology: Old Norse; "she who offers sorrow."

Female Jötnar.

Mother of the monsters, Fenrir, Jormungandr, Hel, and various jötnar in wolf form.

Consort to Loki, among others.

Attributes: Known as both a fierce warrior and witch, Angrboda grants both protection to her children and aids in baneful magick.

Audumla

Etymology: Old Norse; "hornless cow rich in milk."

The primeval cow.

Audumla (*Audhumla*) was born from rime at Ginnungagap. The primeval giant Ymir (*Aurgelmir*) lived on the milk that flowed from the cow's teats. Audumla also provided nourishment to Ymir's six-headed son.

Audumla received nourishment through licking a salty rime-stone until it was shaped into a man. This stone became Buri, grandfather of the Æsir gods Odin, Vili, and Vé.

Attributes: Helps in the creation of anything, sets things in motion.

Baduhenna

Etymology: The prefix of her name, *Badu,* can be roughly translated to *badwa,* which means "battle." The suffix *henna,* or *henaeis,* was often used to describe females.

Frisian (North Germany and Netherlands) goddess of war and storms.

Attributes: As a war goddess, she helps in strength of all sorts, as well as with weather magick.

Baldur (Baldre, Balder)

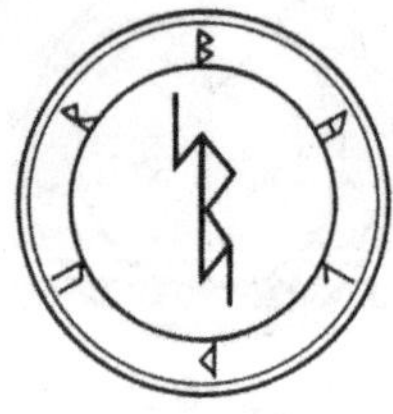

Etymology: Bealdor (Old English); "lord."

Æsir god of beauty, love, purity, peace, innocence, rebirth, and righteousness.

Son of Odin and Frigg, brother of Hodr. He is depicted as the god of beauty, purity, love, righteousness, and peace. To make sure he cannot die, Frigg goes to every single animal, plant, and race to make them swear an oath to not kill her son. Only, the simple mistletoe seems too unimportant for Frigg to ask an oath of. The gods make a game out of it and hit Baldur with anything they can think of *without* killing him. Loki deceives Hodr into throwing a spear of mistletoe at his brother. The branch hits Baldur and kills him, which makes Hodr the killer of his brother. Baldur is also described as the god of the sun, and, upon his death, he is associated with the Winter and Summer Solstices.

Attributes: Helps in work of beauty, peace, transformation, and the cyclical form of nature.

Beyla

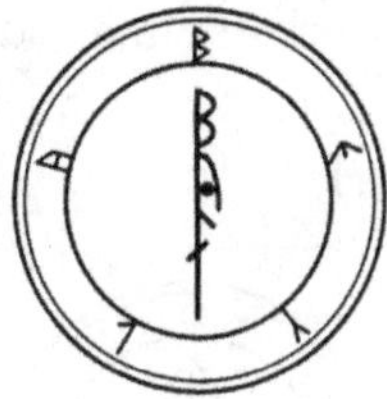

Etymology: Younger form of the Old Norse *Baunila* ("Little Bean").

Goddess of the Earth and bees.

Although a goddess herself, Beyla is servant to Freyja, goddess of fertility. She is often connected with Earth and known as the goddess of bees. She is wife to Byggvir, as well as a servant to Frey and Freyja.

It is also said that she is a personification of manure, providing the seeds in the earth with nutrition.

Attributes: Fertility magick, especially those surrounding bees.

Bil

Etymology: The etymology of the name Bil is uncertain, but it is thought to be connected to the moon's phases and the waning moon.

Ásynjur goddess of the waning moon.

Bil is not a goddess like others, but a human girl adopted by the god of the moon, Mani, who rescues her and her brother. She stays alive by eating Iduns apples, which give her longevity, and lives amongst the gods as an equal. Bil is a goddess destined to die in Ragnarök, mostly because she is, in reality, human and not a goddess. She is depicted riding a chariot across the sky, being constantly hunted by the wolf Hati. That is why she is seen only in the nighttime sky.

Attributes: Helps in work of fame and immortality.

Borr (Bor, Bör, Bur, Burr)

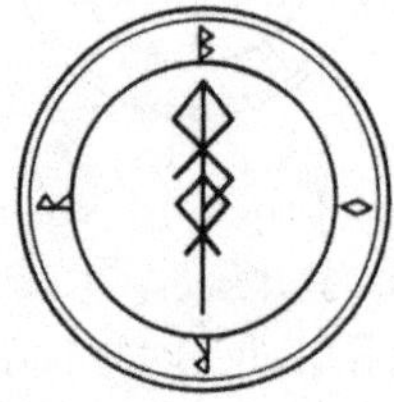

Etymology: Borr can be translated as "son."

There is not much known about this god and there are discussions about his looks. A lot of mythologists say that he was a god in the shape of a human, but others depict him as a giant. He is said to have existed even before the world was created. He is the son of Buri, who is known as the "father of all," but he is also the father of three sons: Odin, Vili, and Vé. He is married to a giant-woman named Bestla. He is not mentioned in many mythology texts, so there is still much to discover about him.

Bragi (Brage)

Etymology: Bragr (Old Norse); "poetry."

Æsir god of knowledge, poetry, music, and the harp. Patron of skalds.

Bragi—the one god always welcome in any realm he visits. He is a son of Odin and is seen as the god of poetry and fine arts. Unlike a lot of Norse gods, he is not a warrior. His talents lie in diplomacy and peace talks. It is said that he travels the nine realms talking and singing of peace and cooperation. He is husband to Idun, keeper of the gods' orchard and its golden apples, which keep the gods young and healthy. However, he is born out of selfish reasons. Odin wants the "Mead of Poetry," which is guarded by the giant Suttung and his daughter Gunnlod. They keep the mead in a cave, but Odin managed to get into the cave disguised as a snake. He presents himself to Gunnlod as a handsome lover and drinks all the Mead while staying with her for three nights. The product of these three nights of love is Bragi, who is sent to live with his father and, due to the Mead of Poetry, becomes the god of the golden tongue that he is.

Attributes: Bragi helps with poetry, inspiration, and public speaking. However, Bragi may also be called forth to help in politics and peace treaties.

Buri (Búri, Bori, Bure)

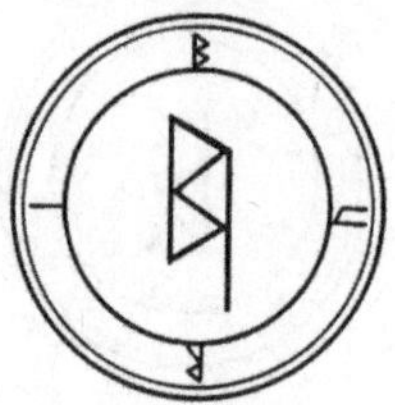

Etymology: Buri; "creator" or "father."

God of creation, ruler of prehistory, and the first god.

Buri is the father of all gods in Norse mythology, as he is depicted as the "father of all gods" or the "god of creation." There is not much information about him and the only time he is mentioned is in Snorri Sturluson's *Prose Edda.* This Edda tells of the birth of Buri in a very particular way. He had been licked out of a salt stone by a cow named Audhumla over three days. On the first day, she licked free his hair, then his head, and, on the third day, the rest of his body. There is no mention of a wife for Buri, but there is more known about his son Borr/Burr and his grandsons Odin, Vili, and Vé.

Attributes: Helps with creation in all its forms.

Byggvir

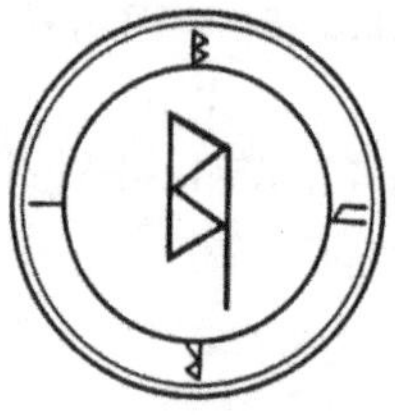

Etymology: Old Norse; "barley."

Agricultural god.

Byggvir is one of the many servants of the gods, more specifically Freyr. The only mention of him can be found in a stanza in the *Lokasenna.* He is husband to Beyla, as well as servant/maid to Freyja, and they are both said to be embodiments of agriculture and forestry. *Bygg* is an Old Norse word for "barley," which strengthens the connection to agriculture.

Attributes: Aids in fertility magick, especially vegetation.

Dagur

Etymology: "day," god of the daytime.

Dagur ("the day light") is the son of Delling ("dawn") and Nótt ("the night").

Attributes: Dagur helps in breaking through plateaus and obstacles.

Dellingr (Delling)

Etymology: Old Norse; "shining one."

Æsir god of the dawn.

Dellingr is, in Norse mythology, the god of dawn, or the personification of dawn. There are a few translations which say the name Dellingr means "the shining one." Like many other gods, his name is not often mentioned in many versions of the Edda. However, what is known is that he is the third husband of a giant-woman named Nótt (which means "night"), and together they have a son called Dagr (which translates to "day"). So, mythology has it that the dawn and the night gave birth to the day.

Attributes: Helps in enlightenment and self-realisation.

Dís

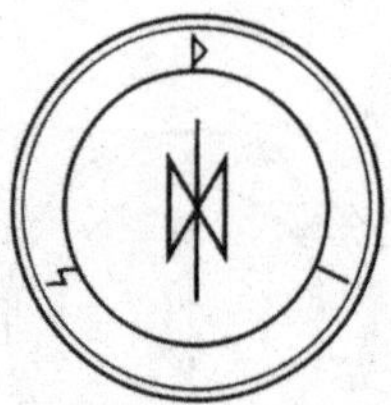

Etymology: Old Norse; "lady."

Female vættir/spirit.

A dís (plural: dísir) is a female deity, ghost, or spirit associated with fate who can be either benevolent or antagonistic toward mortals. The dísir may act as protective spirits of Norse clans. It is possible that their original function was that of fertility goddesses who were the object of both private and official worship called *dísablót* and their veneration may derive from the worship of the spirits of the dead. The dísir play roles in Norse texts that resemble those of fylgjur, valkyries, and Norns, so that some have suggested that dísir is a broad term including other beings.

Draugr

Etymology: Old Norse; "revenant," "undead man," or "ghost."

Undead.

The draugr (also called draug, dréag, draugar; draugur, dreygur, or draugen) is an undead creature from Norse mythology. Draugar live in their graves, often guarding treasure buried with them in their burial mound. They are reanimated corpses—unlike ghosts, they have a corporeal body with similar physical abilities as they possessed in life.

Attributes: The draugr can be called forth via necromancy as an undead minion tasked with the guarding of material and, in some cases, even ethereal possessions.

Eggþér (also Eggthér, or Egdir)

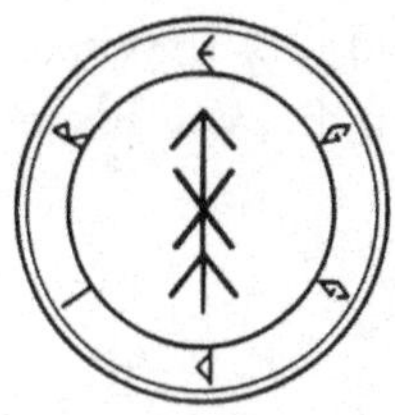

Etymology: Old Norse; edge-servant. The name comes from a compound formed with the word *egg* ("edge") attached to *þér* ("servant"). It could have denoted a "bearer of a sword" or "one who is servant of the sword," or simply "one who is a servant of the edge," as in the "edge" between civilisation and chaos, as the Ironwood is.

Jötunn.

He is the herder of the female jötunn (probably Angrboða) who lives in Járnviðr (Ironwood) and raises monstrous wolves. In the poem "Völuspá," Eggþér is described as sitting on a mound and joyfully striking his harp while the red rooster, Fjalarr, begins to crow to herald the onset of Ragnarök.

Attributes: Aids in Baleful magick, as well as controlling the "wolves."

Einherjar

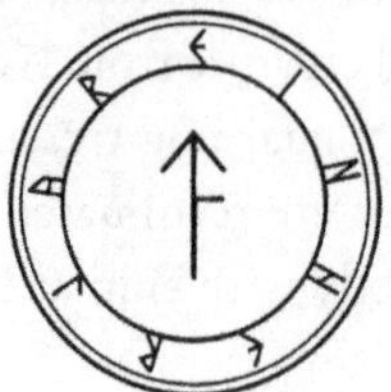

Etymology: literally "army of one" or "those who fight alone."

In Norse mythology, the einherjar (singular: *einheri*) are those who have died in battle and are brought to Valhalla by valkyries. In Valhalla, the einherjar eat their fill of the nightly-resurrecting beast Sæhrímnir, and valkyries bring them mead (which comes from the udder of the goat Heiðrún). The einherjar prepare daily for the events of Ragnarök, when they will advance for an immense battle at the field of Vígríðr.

Eir (Eil, Eira, Eyr, Eyra)

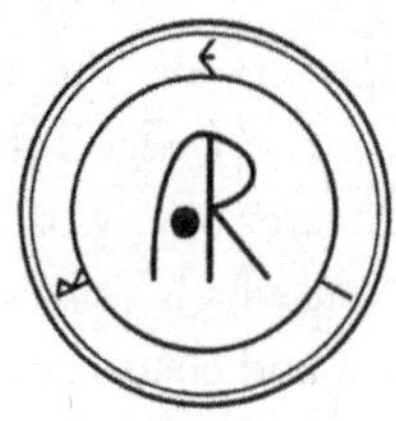

Etymology: Old Norse; "protection" or "help."

Ásynjur goddess of healing.

There are different references to Eir in the *Poetic Edda* and *Prose Edda*, which has led to much discussion as to whether she is a Norse goddess, a Valkyrie, or if these sources refer to two different figures. Either way, Eir is described as a figure of life and patron of all those who work in medicine. She is familiar with all treatments and is particularly skillful with herbs. She resides at the top of Lyfjaberg, the "healing mountain." If women climbed this mountain, then Eir healed them of any disease—and it is said that she was even capable of resurrecting the dead.

Attributes: Helps in all healing arts, as well as necromancy.

Ēostre (Eastre, Ostara)

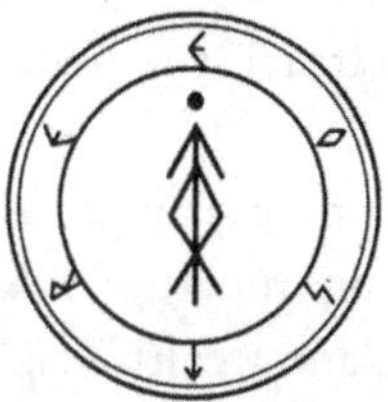

West Germanic goddess of spring, rebirth, and protector of fertility.

In most mythologies, Eostre is seen as a Western Germanic goddess. However, due to her connection with the Matronae, she may be connected to an even older goddess form.

Theories connecting Ēostre with records of Germanic Easter customs, including hares and eggs, have been proposed.

Attributes: Aids in work of fertility and rebirth.

Fafnir

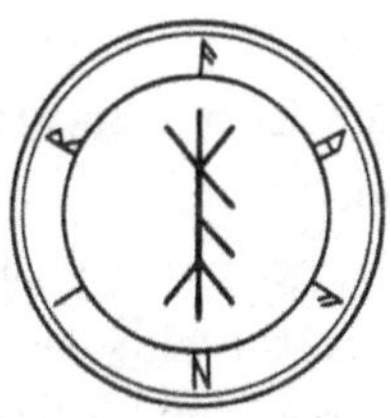

Dwarf/Dragon.

Fafnir was the son of Hreidmar and brother of Regin and Otter.

Originally, Fafnir was a dwarf who was able to shapeshift. After Fafnir gained possession of the treasure by killing his father, he drove his brother, Regin, away by changing himself into a dragon.

After being affected by the curse of Andvari's ring and gold, Fáfnir permanently became a dragon. The hero, Sigurd, killed Fafnir. Since his blood and heart contain magickal properties, Sigurd ate his heart, giving him greater strength, and the blood allowed him to understand the language of the birds. Some versions are more specific about Fáfnir's treasure hoard, mentioning the swords Ridill and Hrotti, the helm of terror and a golden coat of chainmail.

Attributes: Help in gaining strength and aids in the learning of the language of everything in nature. Also associated with greed, guarding what you have, and wealth magick.

Fenrir (Fenris-Wolf)

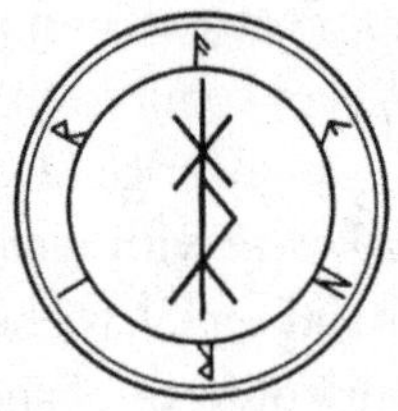

Etymology: "Fen-dweller."

Wolf Jötunn.

Fenrir was the offspring of Loki and the giantess Angerboda. Fenrir was also called Fenris, but Snorri Sturluson gave Fenrir another name, Vanargand.

Fenrir grew so rapidly and in such gigantic proportion that the gods feared it. And, for that, the gods bound him. When Ragnarök arrives, Fenrir will break free from his fetters.

Attributes: Helps in realising your power, growing from your differences, and aids in baneful magick.

Forseti (Forsete)

Etymology: Old Norse; "presiding one."

Æsir god of justice, peace, and truth.

Son of Baldr and Nanna.

Attributes: Aids in foresight and getting to the truth of a matter.

Freyja (Freya, Freja, Frey'a, Gefion, Horn, Mardal, Mardoll, Menglad, Menglod, Moertholl, Sessrymner, Syr, Vanadis)

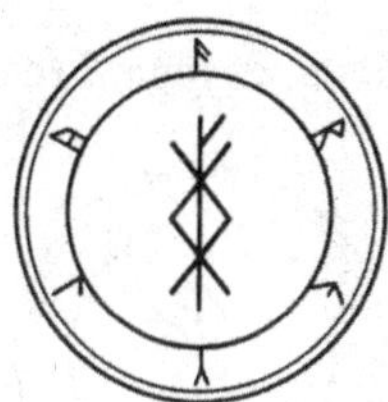

Etymology: Old Norse; "lady" or "mistress."

Vanir goddess of love, fertility, battle, and magick.

Freyja is the daughter of Njord, brother to Freyr and possible wife to Odin.

Attributes: Helps in fertility, love, beauty, and both benevolent and baneful magick.

Freyr (Frey, Fraig, Fro, Fricco, Ingun, Ingunnar-Frey, Ingvi-Frey, Sviagod, Yngri, Yngvi)

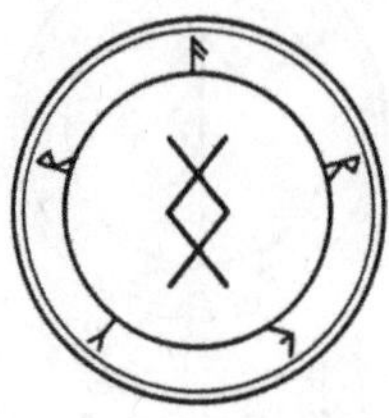

Etymology: Old Norse; "lord."

Vanir god of agriculture, prosperity, life, and fertility. King of the elves.

Son of Njord, brother to Freyja, and husband to Gerð.

Attributes: Helps in fertility magick and connection with the elves and ancestors.

Frigg (Frigga, Frig, Fri, Frija, Frygga, Frea, Fria, Frige, Holda)

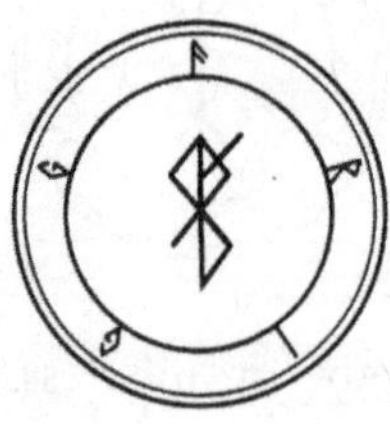

Etymology: Old Norse; "to love."

Ásynjur goddess of love, marriage, motherhood, fertility, family, and civilization, as well as a prophetess.

Consort to Odin.

Attributes: Helps in all magick surrounding the household and kitchen.

Gefjon (Gefjun, Gefion)

Etymology: Old Norse; "the giving one."

Goddess of knowledge.

Attributes: Aids in focus and academic learning.

Gerda (Gerd, Gerdhr, Gerðr)

Etymology: Garðr (Old Norse); "yard," "fenced-in," or "enclosure."

Jötunn.

Daughter of Gymir and wife to Freyr.

Attributes: Gerda is the personification of the "kept wife" and can be very helpful in restrictive magick.

Grendel

Jötunn.

Grendel and his mother dwelled in the underwater cave of a lake or the fen near the hall built by the Danish king, Hrothgar, called Heorot. Grendel usually came out of his lair at night and killed his unsuspecting victims while they slept. Grendel enjoyed not just killing, but the devouring of human flesh and drinking of their blood.

The Geatish hero Beowulf fought Grendel. Beowulf mortally wounded Grendel by ripping the monster's arm from his shoulder. Grendel fled back to his subterranean lair, where he died.

Attributes: Can be utilised in baneful magick.

Gullveig (Gollveig, Gulveig, Golveig-Heid, Gulveig-Hoder, Angerboda, Angerbohda, Aurboda, East Wind Hag, Heid, Heidr, Ljod, Midgard, Orboda, The Volva)

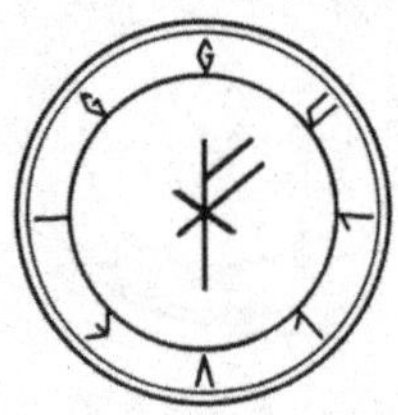

Etymology: "gold-drink" or "gold-drunk."

Vanir goddess.

Gullveig is a female figure in Norse mythology associated with the legendary conflict between the Æsir and Vanir. In the poem "Völuspá," she came to the hall of Odin (Hár), where she is speared by the Æsir, burnt three times, and, yet, thrice reborn. Upon her third rebirth, she began practicing seidr and took the name Heiðr.

Gullveig is sometimes held to be a personification of gold itself, purified through repeated smelting.

Scholars have variously proposed that Gullveig/Heiðr is the same figure as the goddess Freyja and that Gullveig's death may have been connected to corruption by way of gold among the Æsir (see: "Brisingamen Edda"). Other stories tell that Gullveig's treatment by the Æsir may have even led to the Æsir-Vanir War.

Attributes: Greed, money, but also ritual purification.

Garm (Garmr)

Etymology: Old Norse; "rag."

Jötunn; a ferocious hellhound that guards the gates of the underworld.

Hellhound. Garm was the giant hound that guarded the gate in Hel (world of the dead). Garm was very much like the three-headed Ceberus, who also guarded the Underworld in Greek myths).

Garm was bound by rope in Gnipa-cave or Gnipahellir.

Although Tyr had killed Garm at Ragnarök, the war-god died from his severe wounds that the hound had inflicted on him.

Attributes: Guarding and raising aggression.

Hati and Skoll

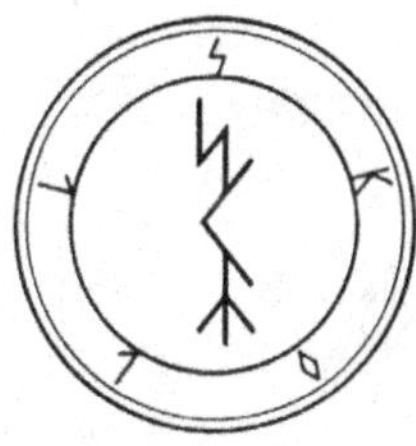

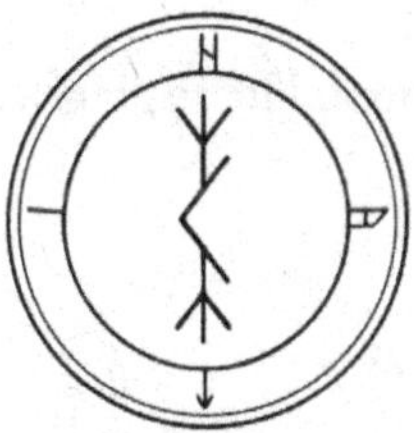

Etymology: Skoll (rough pronunciation: "SKOHL" *Sköll* (Old Norse), "One Who Mocks") and *Hati* (pronounced "HAHT-ee." *Hati* (Old Norse), "One Who Hates").

Jötnar.

Skoll and Hati were two giant wolves that pursued two heavenly bodies—Sol ("Sun") and Moon.

Skoll and Hati were descendants of the troll-wives or giantesses known as the *Iarnvidiur.*

One of the signs of the coming of Ragnarök was that Skoll would devour the goddess Sol and Hati would swallow the Moon. This would cause the nine worlds to suffer from a long winter.

Attributes: Bringing forth doom.

Heiðrún

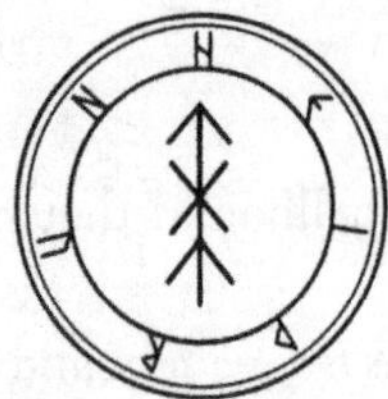

Etymology: Derived from Old Norse *heiðr,* meaning "bright" or "clear," and *rún,* meaning "secret lore," or "rune."

Vaettir.

In Valhalla, the einherjar eat their fill of the nightly-resurrecting boar (or other creature), Sæhrímnir, and valkyries bring them mead (which comes from the udder of the goat Heiðrún).

Attributes: Plenty.

Hoenir (Hoeni, Hœnir, Hone, Honer, Henir)

Etymology: The meaning of the name Hoenir (pronounced "HIGH-nir") is obscure and poses a mystery. Numerous interpretations have been suggested, including "sun god," "cloud god," "forest god," and "soul god."

The silent god. Æsir god.

Hoenir (Old Norse: *Hœnir*) is one of the original Æsir (gods of the principal pantheon) and is mentioned in the most important events in Norse mythology, such as the war between the Norse gods (the Æsir and the Vanir), the creation of human beings, and the "final battle," Ragnarök.

Hoenir gains validity as a significant god through his role in the creation story. When Hoenir, Odin, and Lodurr arrived at a beach and found two pieces of wood from which they create the first man, Ask, and the first woman, Embla, Hoenir was in charge of giving them senses, or a "spirit."

Attributes: Creation magick.

Heimdall (Heimdal, Heimdallr, Heimdalr, Heimdali)

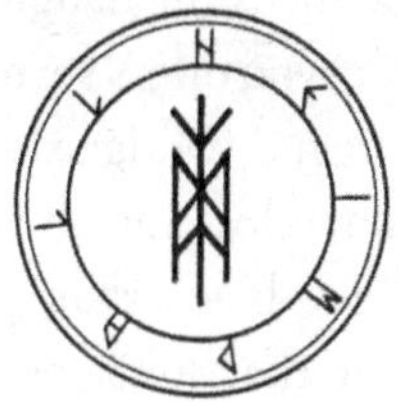

Etymology: The meaning and etymology of the name Heimdall (pronounced "HAME-doll") are unknown, but there have been numerous attempts at deciphering it. One proposal is "the one who illuminates the world." Heimdall is attested as having three other names: Hallinskiði, Vindlér, and Gullintanni, which means "the one with the golden teeth."

Æsir god and guardian of the gods.

Heimdall (Old Norse: *Heimdallr*) may just be one of the most popular gods in Norse mythology. He is certainly one of the strongest members of the Æsir (the gods of the principal pantheon). However, he is also a son of Odin and said to have nine mothers. Heimdall is blessed with a multitude of powers, including the gift of "foresight," or "second-sight," that allows him to see into the future, as well as overdeveloped senses (particularly hearing and sight.)

Attributes: Foresight and divination.

Hel (Hela)

Etymology: Old Norse; "that which hides."

Jötnar goddess of the dead. Ruler of Helheim the Norse underworld. Daughter of Loki.

In Norse mythology, Hel (or Hela) is the goddess of the dead, but she is not assigned to either the Æsir or Vanir gods—instead, she is one with the giants. She is the daughter of Loki and giantess Angrboða (Old Norse; "she who offers sorrow") and sister of Fenrir (Fenris-Wolf) and Jörmungand (Midgard's Serpent).

Hel is portrayed as fierce-looking, grim, and sinister. Her skin is half-normal and half blue-black that seems to be rotting, like that of a corpse, indicating that she is half-dead and half-alive at the same time. Depending on the source, she is either a vengeful goddess or a gentle one and she has been described as if half-plunged into the darkness of death, with the other half in the light of life.

Attributes: Personification of disease; can both heal and curse.

Hermod (Hermóðr, Heremod)

Etymology: Hermod (pronounced "HAIR-mode"), meaning "war-spirit."

Æsir messenger of the gods.

In Norse mythology, the deity Hermod (from the Old Norse *Hermóðr*) is considered the messenger of the gods. He was a great warrior and a member of the Æsir (the gods of the principal pantheon). He is also attributed with the titles, such as "Hermod the bold" and "Hermod the brave." He is the son of Odin and Frigg and brother to Balder and Hodr.

In the *Poetic Edda* (the oldest source for Norse mythology), Hermod is mentioned in the myth of Balder's death, when he volunteered to travel to the underworld (Helheim) in order to negotiate the release of his brother with the goddess of the dead, Hel. This odyssey took place over nine nights of complete darkness, whereupon he rode Odin's eight-legged horse, Sleipnir (Old Norse; "Slippy"), and crossed the echoing bridge, Gjallarbrú, in order to reach the underworld.

However, Hel would only relent if everyone and everything in creation shed tears of grief for Balder—only then would she release him. Hermod brought the message back to the Æsir. Everyone and everything wept over the passed god—except for one. Loki, disguised as a giantess, refused. Balder remained trapped in the underworld.

Attributes: Increasing courage.

Hlin (Hlín, Hlina)

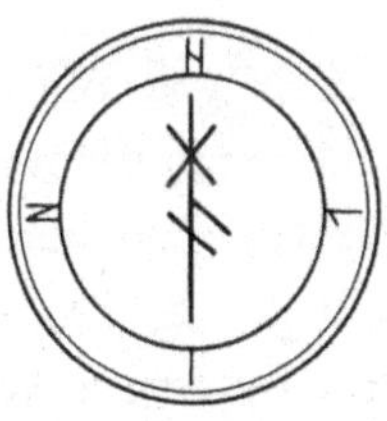

Etymology: Old Norse; "protector" or "protectress."

Ásynjur goddess of consolation and protection.

In Norse mythology, Hlin is the goddess of consolation and protection. She is one of the Ásynjur (female members of the Æsir. The *Æsir* refers to the gods of the principal pantheon in Norse mythology) and one of Frigg's three servants, along with goddesses Fulla and Gna.

Hlin is known for protecting and consoling mortals. She brings relief to mourners and is said to pour soothing comfort into their hearts to ease their grief and loss. Frigg tasked Hlin to listen to all prayers and to refer the pleas to Frigg. Hlin was responsible for protecting those whom Frigg wishes to help. He would advise Frigg on how to respond to these prayers and bring relief.

Some scholars believe that the reference to Hlin in the "Völuspá" may be another name given to the goddess Frigg herself.

Attributes: Helps in protection magick and the creation of protective amulets, as well as aiding in grief consoling.

Hodr (Höðr, Hod, Hothenus, Hodar, Hoder, Hodhr, Hodir, Hodur)

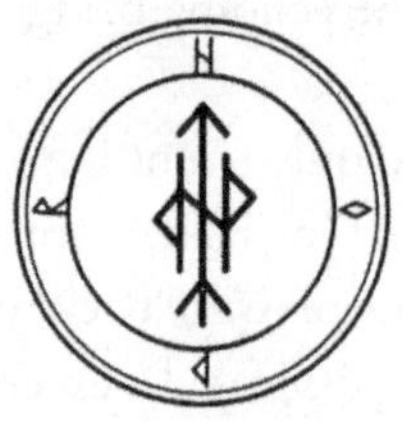

Etymology: Etymology: Hodr (pronounced "HO-der") from Old Norse *Höðr,* is made up of the noun *höð,* which means "fight" or "war." His name could then be linked to "fighter" or "warrior."

Æsir god of winter.

Hodr is a god of the Æsir (gods of the principal pantheon) in Norse mythology. He is the son of Odin and Frigg and brother to Balder and Hermod. Hodr was blind, but his physical strength was noteworthy, even for a god.

In the *Poetic Edda* (the oldest source for Norse mythology), the myth of Balder's murder by Hodr is one of the most famous in Norse mythology. After Balder foresaw his death in a dream, Frigg made everything in creation pledge not to harm him. The pledge was held so strongly that the Æsir amused themselves by throwing all manner of things at Balder, to no ill effect.

Loki grew jealous of Balder, a god so beloved that everything in creation had pledged not to harm him, so he searched for a way to hurt him. By deceiving Frigg, he discovered that one plant had not participated in the vow—the mistletoe plant had been overlooked. Loki tricked the blind god Hodr into throwing a mistletoe dart at Balder. When the dart struck, Balder fell dead. Vali then takes revenge and kills Hodr for this act, who joins his brother Balder in the underworld.

Attributes: Brawn over brains.

Hreasvelgr

Etymology: The Old Norse name Hræsvelgr has been translated as "corpse-swallower," or as "shipwreck-current."

Jötunn.

He is portrayed as the eagle-shaped originator of the wind.

Attributes: Weather magick.

Idun (Iðunn, Iduna, Idunn, Idunna, Ithun, Ydun)

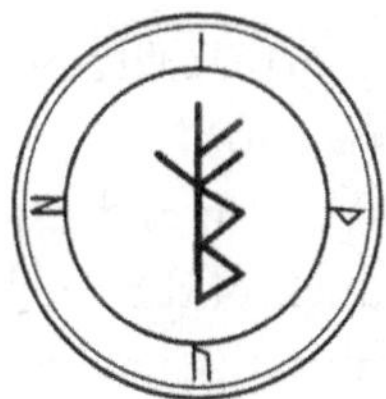

Etymology: Idun (pronounced "IH-dune") from the Old Norse *Iðunn,* which derived from *ið,* "again," and *unna,* "to love"), has been translated to "forever young" or "rejuvenating."

Ásynjur goddess of youth, spring, and rejuvenation.

Idun is described as the personification of spring, the goddess of youth and immortality, and, like, Bragi (her husband), a skald.

Few surviving texts refer to Idun, so her background is quite mysterious, but she does appear in several myths. The most notable explains how the gods never grow old and how they almost lost that source of life and eternal youth, which is described in the skaldic poem "Haustlöng" and retold in the *Prose Edda.*

In the myth, Idun never left her enchanted garden where only she could pick the apples that held the secret of everlasting youth. When the giant Thiazi captured Loki, Loki agreed to help capture Idun by leading her away from her garden for his release. Without the rejuvenating quality of the apples, the gods began to age and weaken. Loki, realizing he had to redeem himself, used Freya's feather-skin to transform into a falcon to rescue Idun.

Attributes: Beauty, youth, and immortality, but also music and carefreeness.

Irpa

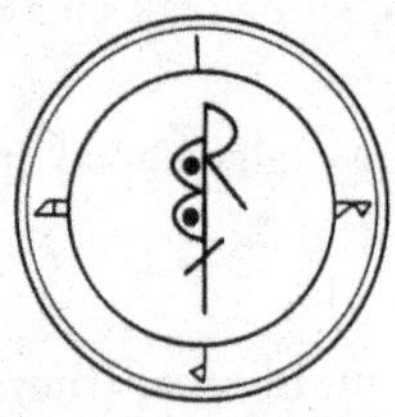

Etymology: Irpa is derived from the Old Norse *Jarpr,* meaning "brown."

Ásynjur goddess of the Earth.

Irpa is a member of the Æsir and sister to Thoregod. Irpa has been described as the goddess of the Earth.

Irpa appears in several myths, including "Njáls Saga," "Porleifs Pdttr Jarlsskdlds," and the "Jomsborg Viking Saga." In these tales, together, Irpa and Thoregod help the fleets of Haakon Sigurdsson and Sweyn Haakonsson in the battle of Hjorungarag by creating a hailstorm against the enemy fleet.

Attributes: Aids in Earth magick.

Iarnvidiur

Etymology: Járnviðr (Old Norse; "Ironwood").

Collective group of troll-wives.

This stanza is paraphrased by Snorri Sturluson in "Gylfaginning:"

> *Then spoke Gangleri: "What is the origin of the wolves?"*
>
> *High said: "A certain giantess lives east of Midgard in a forest called Ironwood. In that forest live trollwives called Iarnvidiur. The ancient giantess breeds as sons many giants and all in wolf shapes, and it is from them that these wolves are descended. And they say that from this clan will come a most mighty one called Moongarm. He will fill himself with the lifeblood of everyone that dies, and he will swallow heavenly bodies and spatter heaven and all the skies with blood. As a result the sun will lose its shine and winds will then be violent and will rage to and fro. Thus it says in Völuspá:*
>
> *In the east lives the old one, in Ironwood, and breeds there Fenrir's kind. Out of them all comes one in particular, sun's snatcher in troll's guise. He gorges the life of doomed men, reddens gods' halls with red gore. Dark is sunshine for summers after, all weathers hostile. Know you yet, or what?"* (Sturluson, *Prose Edda*).

Attributes: Baneful magick, lycanthropy.

Jörð

Etymology: Old Norse; *jǫrð* means "earth" or "land," serving both as a common noun ("Earth") and as a theonymic incarnation of the noun; "Earth-goddess."

Goddess of the Earth.

Mother of Þórr by Óðinn.

Attributes: Earth elemental powers.

Jörmungandr

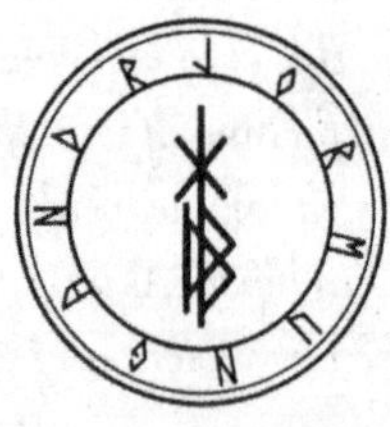

Etymology: The name Jörmungandr is a poetic title and consist of the prefix *jörmun-* and the word *gandr.* The prefix *jörmun-* denotes something huge, vast, or superhuman. The word *gandr* can mean a variety of things in Old Norse, but mainly refers to elongated entities and or supernatural beings—huge beast.

Giant serpent-shaped jötunn.

The World Serpent. The Midgard Serpent, called Jörmungand or Jörmungandr, was an offspring of Loki and the giantess Angerboda. Jörmungand symbolised evil.

Not only could Jörmungand kill its victim by crushing constriction, but the Midgard Serpent's venom was lethal, even against the gods. Jörmungand was Thor's most deadly enemy.

To confine the ever-growing serpent, Odin had Jörmungand thrown into the sea. However, Jörmungand grew so large that his entire body completely encircled the world.

At Ragnarök, Jörmungand escaped his underwater confinement. Thor managed to kill the evil serpent with the Mjollnir; but Thor succumbed to the deadly venom from Jörmungand.

Attributes: Evil, darkness, destruction, but also great magickal powers.

Kvasir

Etymology: The root *kvas-* in Kvasir likely stems from the Proto-Germanic base *kvass-*, meaning "to squeeze, squash, crush, bruise." Regarding this etymology, linguist Albert Morey Sturtevant comments that: "fluids may result from the crushing or pressing of an object."

God of inspiration.

In Norse mythology, Kvasir (Old Norse; [ˈkwasez̠]) was born of the saliva of the Æsir and the Vanir, two groups of gods. Extremely wise, Kvasir traveled far and wide, teaching and spreading knowledge. This continued until two dwarves, Fjalar and Galar, killed Kvasir and drained him of his blood.

Attributes: Inspiration and knowledge.

Landvættir

Land wights.

Landvættir are spirits of the land in Norse mythology and Germanic Neo-paganism. They protect and promote the flourishing of the specific places where they live, which can be as small as a rock or a corner of a field, or as large as a section of a country.

Attributes: Worship and sacrifice to the Landvaettir brings forth wisdom and abundance from the land.

Lofn (Lofna, Lofua, Lofe)

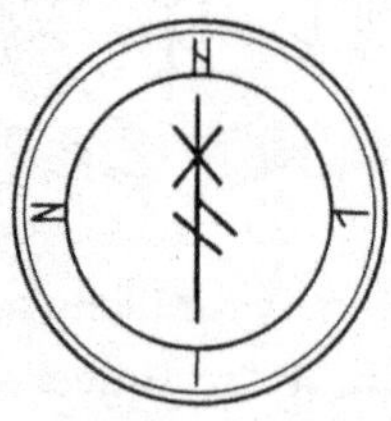

Etymology: Lofn (pronounced "LAW-ven"); "comforter" or "consoler," originates from the Old Norse word *Lof,* meaning "permission" or "praise."

Ásynjur goddess of marriage and forbidden love.

In Norse mythology, Lofn is described as a gentle and good goddess of marriage and "forbidden love." She is listed as a member of the Ásynjur (goddesses of the principal pantheon).

Lofn is mentioned in Snorri Sturluson's *Prose Edda* (an early thirteenth-century Icelandic manuscript): "She is so gentle and so good to invoke that she has permission from Odin and Frigg to arrange unions between men and women, even if earlier offers have been received and unions have been banned."

Attributes: Hand-fasting and strengthening love in the face of adversity.

Lodurr (Lóðurr, Lodur, Lóður, Lódurr, Lódur, Lóthurr, Lóthur, Lódhurr, Lódhur, Lothurr, Lothur, Lodhurr, Loðurr, Loður, Lodhur)

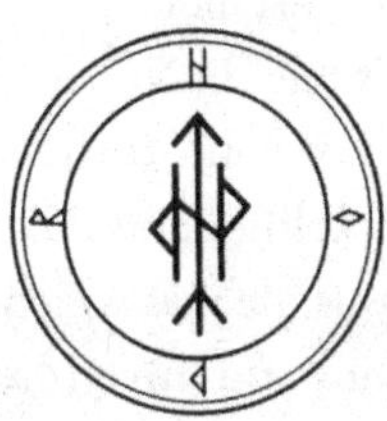

Etymology: The meaning of the name Lodurr (pronounced "LOAD-er") is unknown.

Few surviving texts refer to Lodurr, but he is mentioned in one of the most notable, the creation myth in the "Völuspá" (the first poem in the *Poetic Edda,* which is the oldest surviving text of Norse mythology). In the story, Lodurr, along with Odin and Hoenir, give life to Ask and Emba, the first humans. Odin gives them "breath" (*önd*), Hoenir the "spirit" (*öðr*), and Lodurr the "heat" (*lá*), sometimes translated as "blood."

Lodurr is also mentioned in two skaldic poems, which describe Odin as "the friend of Lodurr." However, besides the significant role in the creation myth and the mention in kennings, no other surviving texts mention the god Lodurr. Some scholars connect Loki to Lodurr.

Attributes: The fire within.

Loki (Loptr)

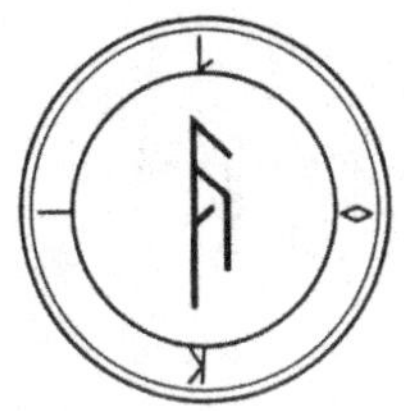

Etymology: The name Loki (pronounced "LOW-kee") has not yet, despite many attempts, been interpreted etymologically convincingly. One theory, however, is that the name is linked to the Old Norse *Lùka,* meaning "close." Some sources refer to Loki as Loptr. In Old Norse, *Loptr* means "air" or "wind."

Trickster and god of mischief.

Loki is the god of mischief in Norse mythology. He is the son of giants, Fárbauti and Laufey, consort to Sigyn (also called "Saeter"), and has two brothers, Helblindi and Býleistr, about whom little is known. Despite his origins, he was welcomed into the Æsir (gods of the principal pantheon) and mixed freely with the gods. He is considered by Odin as his own blood until Loki's jealousy led him to cause the death of Baldur. After this, the Æsir captured him and imprisoned him until the events of Ragnarök—here, Loki and Heimdall will kill each other during the great battle.

In most myths, Loki plays the instigator. He stirs up trouble where none existed. He then helps resolve the conflicts he created.

Attributes: Aids in illusion, fire magick, and shapeshifting.

Magni

Etymology: Derived from the Old Norse element *magn,* meaning "power," or "strength."

Æsir god of strength.

Son of Thor and the giant Járnsaxa.

Attributes: Physical strength.

Mani (Máni, Mane)

Etymology: The name Mani (pronounced "MAH-nee"), Old Norse; *Máni* means "moon" or "month."

Æsir god of the moon.

Mani is the god of the Moon in Norse mythology and a member of the Æsir (gods of the principal pantheon). Mani is mentioned in the *Poetic Edda* and the *Prose Edda,* both sources mention that he is the son of the giants Mundilfari and Glaur and brother of the sun goddess, Sol.

Since Mani pulled the chariot of the moon, Norse mythology explains lunar eclipses as a moment when Hati almost caught Mani. At the time of Ragnarök, Hati will catch and devour Mani.

Attributes: Moon, water, and emotional magick.

Mimir (Mim, Mímir)

Etymology: The name Mimir (Old Norse: *Mímir)* presents difficulties for historical linguists to interpret. According to some, it means "one who remembers" or "the wise one;" an alternative interpretation is "measure."

Æsir god of wisdom.

The giant Mimir is considered the wisest member of the Æsir (gods of the principal pantheon in Norse mythology). Mimir is the keeper of the *Mimisbrunnr* (Old Norse for "Mimir's Spring" or "Mimir's Fountain"), a spring located beneath the world tree, Yggdrasil, that gives wisdom to those that drink from it.

Attributes: Giver of wisdom.

Moongarm (*Mánagarm*)

Etymology: From Old Norse *Garmr,* from the word *garmr* (meaning "dog"), also referred to as Garm.

Wolf Jötunn.

Moongarm was the one of the offspring of one of the Iarnvidiur, the trollwives (giantesses) from Ironwood, east of Midgard. Her sons were all giants, but born in wolf form. Moongarm was the largest and the mightiest of these gigantic wolves. According to the "Völuspá," Moongarm was an offspring of Fenrir.

According to Snorri Sturluson, Moongarm was filled with the blood of all those who had died. He will swallow the heavenly bodies, spattering the sky and heaven with blood, causing the sun not to shine, and violent winds would rage unabated. For this reason, Moongarm was known as the "sun's snatcher."

It is believed that Skoll and Hati will swallow the horses that are drawing the sun and moon, or perhaps the personages driving the chariots, but Moongarm will swallow the heavenly bodies themselves.

Attributes: Destructive magick, herald of the apocalypse (inner or outer).

Nanna

Married to Baldr and mother to Forseti. Died because of Baldur's death.

Etymology: The etymology of the goddess Nanna, an Old Norse name deriving from Ancient Germanic *nanþi,* is uncertain. However, some researchers have hypothesized the derivation from the infinite term *nanna,* indicating "mother," while others theorize "the baldest" or "the daring."

Ásynjur goddess of joy and peace.

In Norse mythology, Nanna is one of the Ásynjur (goddesses of the principal pantheon), daughter of god Nep (sometimes referred to as Nepr), and wife of Baldur, with whom she has a son—Forseti. Nanna is referred to as the goddess of joy and peace.

In the *Poetic Edda* (the oldest source for Norse mythology), there is a myth of Baldur's death. Nanna was so overwhelmed, she died with grief and joined Baldur in the underworld (Helheim). Hermod, a son of Odin, travels to the underworld with the task of freeing Baldur from the world of the dead. But, unable to leave Helheim with Hermod, Nanna gives him a robe of linen for Frigg and a golden ring for Fulla.

Attributes: Unconditional love.

Nerthus (Nertous)

Etymology: The name Nerthus (pronounced "NUR-thus") is often identified with the Vanir deity Njörðr. Due to the reconstruction, Njörðr is Nerþus. This has led to various theories about the relationship between the two, including that their names indicate brother and sister deities, such as the Vanir gods Freyr and Freyja.

Vanir Earth goddess.

Nerthus is a fertility deity in Norse mythology and attested in the *Germania* (an ethnographic work of Germanic tribes written by Tacitus around the year AD 98). She is a member of the Vanir lineage and is referred to as "goddess of the Earth."

According to Tacitus, Nerthus was worshipped by Germanic tribes and described as *Terra Mater* (Latin for "Mother Earth").

Attributes: Nerthus is the personification of Earth.

Nidhogg

Etymology: Nidhogg (Old Norse; *Níðhöggr*, literally "Curse-striker" or "He Who Strikes with Malice").

Wyrm Jötunn.

Nidhogg was a giant worm that resided near the *Hvergelmir*, or "Roaring Kettle," one of three sacred wells. Nidhogg constantly gnawed at one of the roots of Yggdrasill that supported the world, Niflheim.

One of the signs that Ragnarök would arrive was when Nidhogg finally chews its way through one of the roots of Yggdrasill.

In the "Völuspá," Nidhogg was a dragon with wings. He would fly over the plains, carrying corpses. The great serpent enjoyed sucking on the bodies of the dead (*Poetic Edda*).

Attributes: Nidhogg is human death on a global scale. Nidhogg is the genocide and decay of civilization(s).

Njord (Njörðr, Njörd, Niördr Niord, Njorth, Nordur)

Etymology: Njord's name is spelled Njǫrðr in Old Norse. However, with spelling standardization, it can be presented in many ways, including Njörd and Njördr. The name derives from the proto-Germanic name "Nerþuz." The original meaning of the name is disputed, but researchers have suggested "strength."

Vanir god of sea, wind, fish, and wealth.

Njord is married to the giant Skaldi and father to goddesses Freyr and Freyja.

Njord is mainly known from the Edda (oldest source of Norse mythology), the "Ynglinga Saga," and other poems. In one myth, Njord and his children were exchanged for Hoenir and Mimir to secure a truce and end the Æsir-Vanir war. In the "Vafþrúðnismál" (third poem of the *Poetic Edda*), Njord is mentioned among the few who survive Ragnarök (the end of the world).

Attributes: Helps in wealth and weather magick.

Norns

Etymology: The origin of the term *Norn* is uncertain; it may derive from a word meaning "to twine," which would refer to their twining the thread of fate. Karen Bek-Pedersen suggests that the word *Norn*

has relation to the Swedish dialect word *norna* (*nyrna*), a verb that means "to secretly communicate." This relates to the perception of Norns as shadowy background figures who only reveal their secrets to people as their fates come to pass.

The name Urðr (Old English; *Wyrd*, "weird") means "fate." *Wyrd* and *urðr* are etymological cognates, which does not guarantee that *wyrd* and *urðr* share the same semantic quality of "fate" over time. Both Urðr and Verðandi are derived from the Old Norse verb *verða*, "to become," which is derived from Proto-Germanic *wurdiz*, from Proto-Indo-European *wrti-*, a verbal abstract from the root *wert-* ("to turn"). It is commonly asserted that, while Urðr derives from the past tense ("that which became or happened"), Verðandi derives from the present tense of *verða* ("that which is happening"). Skuld is derived from the Old Norse verb *skulu*, "need/ought to be/shall be"; its meaning is "that which should become," or "that needs to occur." Due to this, it has often been inferred that the three Norns are, in some way, connected with the past, present, and future respectively. However, it has been disputed that their names really imply a temporal distinction, and it has been emphasised that the words do not in themselves denote chronological periods in Old Norse.

The Norns are deities in Norse mythology responsible for shaping the course of human destinies.

In the "Völuspá," attested by Snorri Sturluson, the three primary Norns, Urðr (*Wyrd*), Verðandi, and Skuld, draw water from their sacred well to nourish the tree at the center of the cosmos and prevent it from rot. These three Norns are described as powerful maiden giantesses (Jötunns) whose arrival from Jötunheimr ended the golden age of the gods. The Norns are also described as maidens of Mögþrasir in the "Vafþrúðnismál."

Beside the three Norns tending Yggdrasill, pre-Christian Scandinavians attested to Norns who visit a newborn child in order to determine the person's future. These Norns could be malevolent or benevolent—the former causing tragic events in the world, while the latter were kind and protective.

Attributes: Fate, destiny, and works of divination.

Nótt

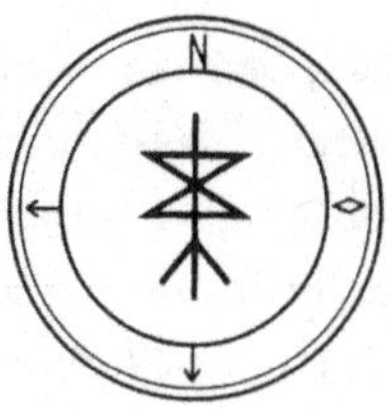

Etymology: Old Norse; "night."

Jötunn goddess of night.

Daughter of Narvi and mother of Auð, Jörð, and Dagur by Naglfari, Annar, and Delling respectively.

Nótt is a personification of the night in the Norse mythology. A goddess similar to her in Greek mythology is Nyx.

Nótt is called "night" by mankind, "darkness" by the gods, "unlight" by jötnar, and "joy-of-sleep" by the elves. She is black and swarthy, a daughter of the giant Narfi. She had three husbands.

Attributes: Darkness and the power of the black flame.

Nykr

Etymology: Held to derive from common Germanic ***nikwus*** or ***nikwis(i)***, derived from Proto-Indo-European word *neigw* ("to wash"). It is related to Sanskrit ***nénēkti***, Greek ***νίζω nízō***, and ***νίπτω níptō***, and Irish *nigh'* (all meaning "to wash" or "to be washed"). The form *nykr* appears in English and Swedish (*näck* or *nek*). The Swedish form is derived from the Old Swedish *neker*, which corresponds to

Old Icelandic *nykr* and *nykk* in Norwegian Nynorsk. In Finnish, the word is *näkki*. In Old Danish, the form was *nikke*, and in modern Danish and Norwegian Bokmål, it is *nøkk*.

Veattir.

The nykr (English: Neck; German: *Nix/Nixie/Nyx*; Dutch: *Nikker/Nekker*; Danish and Norwegian: *Nøkken*; Swedish: *Näcken*; Faroese and Icelandic: *Nykur*; Finnish: *Näkki*; Estonian: *Näkk*) are shapeshifting water spirits who usually appear in human form.

The Icelandic nykur is a horse-like creature. The modern Scandinavian names are derived from an Old Norse word, *nykr*, meaning "river horse." Thus, likely, the brook horse preceded the personification of the nykr as the "man in the rapids."

However, the English *knucker* is generally depicted as a wyrm or dragon, thus attesting to the survival of the other usage of *nuck* as any "water-being," rather than an exclusively humanoid creature.

These spirits have appeared in the myths and legends of all Germanic peoples in Europe. Although, they are perhaps most known in Norwegian and Scandinavian folklore. In recent times, such creatures have usually been depicted as human in shape (albeit, in many cases, shapeshifting).

Nykrs in folklore became water sprites who try to lure people into the water. The nkyrs are portrayed as malicious in some stories, but harmless and friendly in others.

Attributes: Like the Celtic selkies or Greek sirens, the nykrs should be venerated as Sea/Lakevaettir, but can also be called forth as either protectors of water journeys or minions to drown enemies.

Odin (Alfdaur, Alfadir, Bileygr, Glapsuidir, Othinn, Wodan, Wotan, Othin, Othinn, Othinus, Ouvin, Votan, Wode, Wodemus, Wodhen, Woden, Wodin, Wotam, Woutan, Wuotan...Odin has over 170 names)

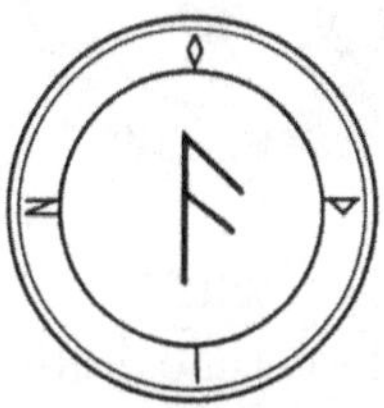

Etymology: Wōđanaz (Proto-Germanic); "lord of frenzy," or "leader of the possessed."

Æsir god of wisdom, war, magick, poetry, prophecy, victory, and death.

Son of Bestla and Borr. Sibling of Vili and Vé (Brothers). Father of Thor with Jörð and Baldr with Frigg.

Odin is a widely revered god in Germanic paganism.

Odin appears as a prominent god throughout the recorded history of Northern Europe.

Odin is frequently portrayed as one-eyed and long-bearded, wielding a spear named Gungnir or appearing in disguise wearing a cloak and a broad hat. He is often accompanied by his animal familiars—the wolves, Geri and Freki, and the ravens, Huginn and Muninn, who bring him information from all over Midgard—and he rides the flying, eight-legged steed Sleipnir across the sky and into the underworld.

Odin is also associated with the divine battlefield maidens, the valkyries, and overseeing Valhalla, where he receives half of those who die in battle, the einherjar, sending the other half to the goddess Freyja's Fólkvangr.

Attributes: Odin has such a wide area of coverage that he can help in most matters, but especially war, wisdom seeking, and rune magick.

Ran

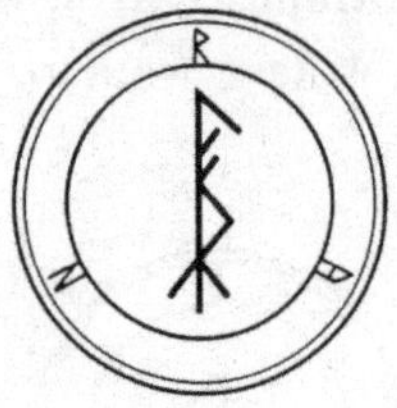

Etymology: Old Norse; *Rán*, "theft."

Ásynjur goddess of the sea and death.

In Norse mythology, Rán is a goddess and a personification of the sea. Rán and her husband, Ægir, a jötunn who also personifies the sea, have nine daughters who personify the waves. The goddess is frequently associated with a net, which she uses to capture sea-goers.

Attributes: Destructive nature of the sea.

Sæhrímnir

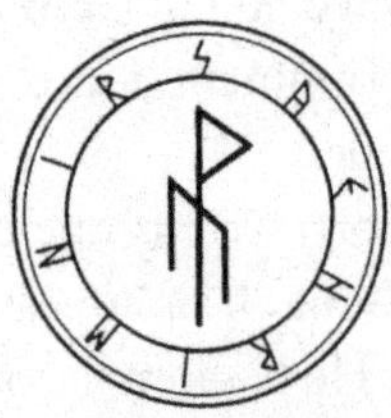

Etymology: It is commonly proposed to mean "sooty sea-beast" or "sooty sea-animal" (which may be connected to Old Norse *seyðir*, meaning "cooking ditch").

Vaettir.

In Valhalla, the einherjar eat their fill of the nightly-resurrecting boar (or other creature), Sæhrímnir, and valkyries bring them mead, which comes from the udder of the goat, Heiðrún.

Attributes: Plenty.

Sif

Etymology: Old Norse; "wife."

Ásynjur/jötunn goddess of harvest and the land.

Sif was a giantess, a goddess of grain and fertility, and one of the Ásynjur. She was the mother of Ull, god of archery, skiing, and single combat. Sif was Thor's second wife and Ull was his stepson.

Attributes: Help in providing and strengthening a positive outcome.

Sigyn (Siguna)

Etymology: Her name means "victory-giver."

Ásynjur goddess of fidelity.

In Norse mythology, one of the Ásynjur goddesses and the wife of Loki, the trickster fire god. By Loki, she had a son named Nari or Narfi. However, not much is known about Sigyn from the surviving literature, except in her connection to Loki's fate.

Attributes: Can aid in servitude, as well as faithfulness to a person, cause, or belief.

Skadi

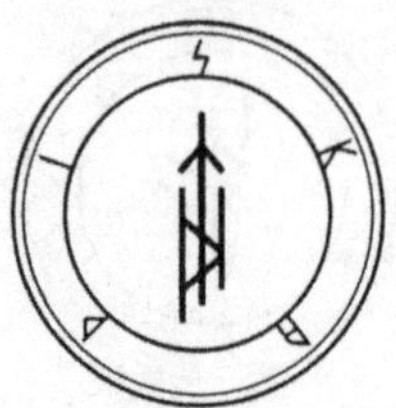

Etymology: Skaði (Old Norse); "shadow," "darkness," or "death."
Vanir/jötunn goddess of hunting and winter.
Njörðr's wife.
Attributes: Aids in hunting, shadow craft, and baneful magick.

Snotra

Etymology: Old Norse; "clever."
Ásynjur goddess of wisdom and prudence.
Attributes: Helps in work of purity.

Sol (Sól, Sunna)

Etymology: Old Norse; "Sun."
Goddess/personification of the Sun.

Wife to Glenr and sister of Mani.

Attributes: Hold all the qualities of the Sun.

Syn

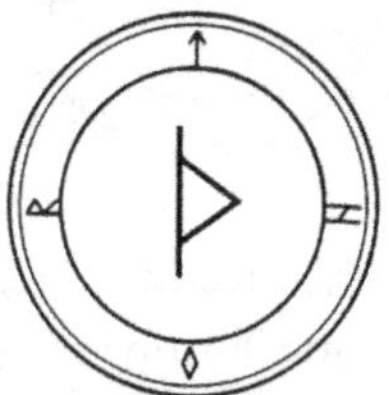

Etymology: Old Norse; "refusal."

Ásynjur goddess of defense and truth.

Attributes: Helps in legal defense.

Thor (þórr, þunor, Thunaer, Donar, Thur, Tor, Tror)

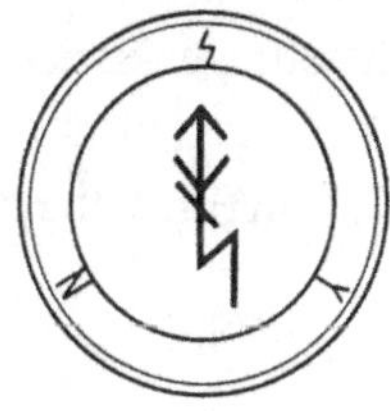

Etymology: The name "Thor" (*Þórr* in the Old Norse, *thunar* in Old Saxon) meant "thunder."

Æsir god of strength, protection, war, storms, thunder, and lightning. Son of Odin (Óðinn), god of thunder and battle. Consort to Sif.

Attributes: Strength, weather, fertility, and craftsmanship.

Tyr (Týr, Tiw, Tig, Ziu, Teu, Thingsus, Tiwaz, Ty, Tyw, Zio, Ziv, Ziw)

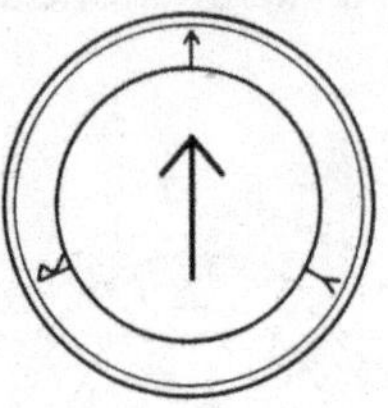

Etymology: The name "Tyr," meaning "a god," or even "the god," stemmed from the Proto Indo-European *dyeus-* by way of the Proto Germanic *Tiwaz,* meaning "god" or "deity."

Æsir god of war, justice in battle, victory, the skies, and heroic glory. In Old Norse sources, Týr is alternately described as the son of the jötunn, hymir, or of the god Odin ("Skáldskaparmál"; "Hymiskviða"). Lokasenna makes reference to an unnamed and otherwise unknown consort, perhaps also reflected in the continental Germanic record (see: "Zisa").

Attributes: Helps with courage, justice, and war.

Ullr (Auler, Holler, Oller, Ollerus, Uller, Ullerus, Ullr, Wuldor)

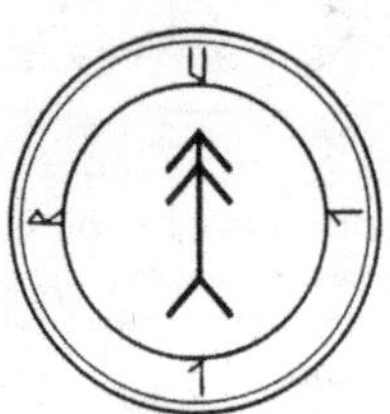

Etymology: Proto-Germanic *wulþuz* ("glory"), appears to have been an important concept, of which his name is a reflex.

Æsir god of justice, skiing, winter, hunt, and the duel.

Ullr is a god associated with archery. Although literary attestations of Ullr are sparse, evidence, including relatively ancient place-name evidence from Scandinavia, suggests that he was a major god in earlier Germanic paganism.

He further suggested that the god of rage, Óðr–Óðinn (Odin), stood in opposition to the god of glorious majesty, Ullr–Ullinn, in a similar manner to the Vedic contrast between Varuna and Mitra.

Attributes: Archery, glory, and doing things the right way.

Vali

Etymology: Váli (Old Norse); "the slain."

Æsir god of vengeance.

Váli is the son of the god Odin and the female jötun Rindr. Váli has numerous brothers, including Thor, Baldr, and Víðarr. He was born for the sole purpose of avenging Baldr and does this by killing Höðr.

In "Gylfaginning," a poem found in the *Prose Edda,* he is described as Loki's son. Here, the Æsir grants him the strength and rage of wolf, well-attested as being granted by Odin to warriors known as *ulfhednar,* which would make his son, Váli, a berserker and a possible origin for the ulfhednar legend.

Attributes: Vengeance and beserkers.

Valkyries

Etymology: Old Norse; "Choose of the Slain."

Female spirits, servants of Odin.

A valkyrie is one of a host of female figures who guide the souls of deceased Nordic soldiers in one of two paths. Selecting among half of those who die in battle go to Fólkvangr, Freyja's afterlife, the other half go to Odin's hall, called "Valhalla," sometimes accompanied by ravens and sometimes in conjunction with swans or horses.

Attributes: Helps in protective (and baneful) magick.

Vár

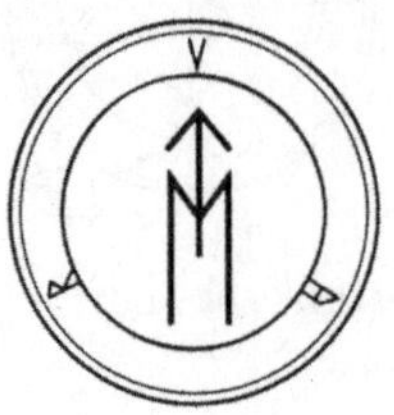

Etymology: Old Norse, meaning either "pledge" or "beloved."

Goddess of contracts.

Attributes: Aids in oaths and agreements.

Ve (Vé)

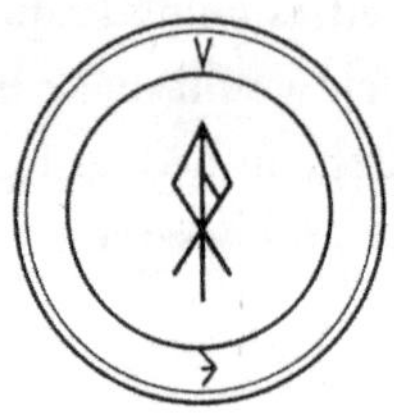

Etymology: Vé (or Véi) is cognate with Gothic *weiha* ("priest"), both stemming from Proto-Germanic *wīhōn,* itself from the adjective *wīhaz,* meaning "holy" (Gothic: *weihs,* Old High German: *wīh*). A related noun, *wīhan* ("sanctuary"), can also be reconstructed on the basis of Old Norse *vé* ("sanctuary;" Old English: *wēoh* ("idol"), and Old Saxon: *wīh* ("temple").

Æsir Earth god.

One of the three gods of creation. Brother of Óðinn and Vili.

Attributes: The sacred space, one of the key elements to all magick.

Vidarr (Víðarr)

Etymology: Old Norse; "wide ruler."

Æsir god of the forest, revenge, and silence.

Vidarr is described as the son of Odin and the jötunn Gríðr, and he is foretold to avenge his father's death by killing the wolf Fenrir at Ragnarök, a conflict he is described as surviving.

Vidarr upholds ritual silence in contemplation of his immense task.

Attributes: Revenge and focus on one goal.

Vili

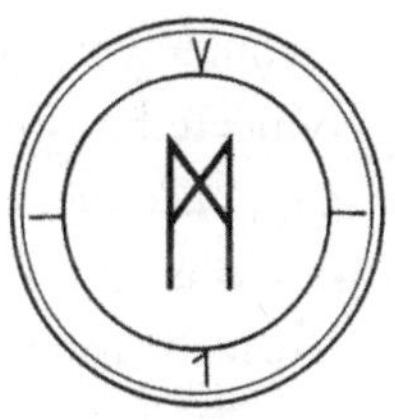

Etymology: Vili transparently means "will" in Old Norse. It stems from the Proto-Germanic noun *weljōn/weljan* ("will," "wish"; Century Gothic: *wilja,* Old English: *willa,* and Old High German: *willo*).

Æsir god.

One of the three gods of creation. Brother of Óðinn and Vé.

Attributes: Magickal intention, one of the key elements to all magick.

Vor

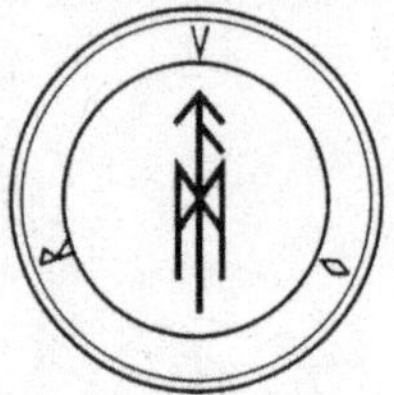

Etymology: Vör (Old Norse), "the careful one."

Ásynjur goddess of wisdom.

Attributes: Wise and inquiring—nothing can be concealed from her.

Ymir

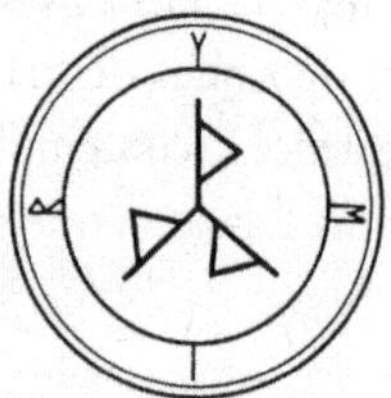

Etymology: Possibly derived from a word for "twin", this name has been folk-etymologically connected to Old Norse *ymja,* meaning: "to groan, whine, wail, scream, make noise."

Frost giant whose body was used to form the world. Formed by the drops of water that formed when the ice of Niflheim met the heat of Muspelheim.

Attributes: Aids in creation, but with huge sacrifice.

Yggdrasil

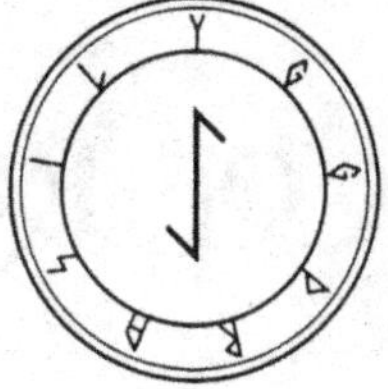

Etymology: Old Norse; "horse of the terrible one," referring to Odin's astral journey through the worlds.

Goddess of life. Tree of life. Connects the nine worlds.

Yggdrasil is a tree central to the Norse concept of the cosmos. The tree's branches extend into various realms and various creatures dwell on and around it.

Attributes: Aids in astral projection.

Book of Runes

I took up the runes, screaming,
I took them,
and then I fell back from there
(*Poetic Edda*, "Hávamál," 139)

Odin, the chief deity in Norse mythology, embarked on a momentous journey to gain profound knowledge and insight into the mysteries of the universe. He sought to attain the wisdom and power contained within the runes, which were considered a sacred and Ancient Norse writing system believed to embody the secrets of creation and existence.

To achieve his goal, Odin decided to undertake a self-imposed ordeal. He made his way to Yggdrasil, the cosmic world tree that connected the different realms of the Norse cosmology. As the tree's branches stretched far and wide, reaching into the heavens and down into the depths of the underworld, Odin chose one of its branches to hang himself from.

With great determination, Odin pierced himself with his own spear and suspended himself from the branch of Yggdrasil. This act of self-sacrifice and suffering was meant to demonstrate his commitment and willingness to endure extreme physical and mental anguish in his pursuit of esoteric knowledge.

For nine consecutive nights and days, Odin remained in this state of intense suffering and deprivation. He denied himself food and water, allowing himself to teeter on the brink of death. Throughout this grueling ordeal, Odin's mind was consumed with the desire to unravel the secrets of the universe and unlock the power of the runes.

As Odin neared the point of collapse and transcendence, the runes finally revealed themselves to him. They shimmered and glowed with a profound energy, manifesting before his eyes. In a moment of desperation and determination, Odin reached down and took hold of the runes, claiming them as his own.

By grasping the runes, Odin underwent a transformative experience. The immense knowledge and understanding of the runes' magickal and transformative properties flooded his being. He became infused with the ancient wisdom and cosmic insight they contained, gaining a deep comprehension of the fundamental principles of creation, existence, and the workings of the universe.

This acquisition of the runes bestowed upon Odin extraordinary powers and elevated his status as the Allfather, the supreme god of the Norse pantheon. He became synonymous with wisdom, magick, and the mystical arts. The sacrifice on Yggdrasil and the acquisition of the runes cemented Odin's position as a figure of great significance and a beacon of enlightenment in Norse mythology.

In summary, Odin's sacrifice on Yggdrasil, enduring extreme suffering while hanging from the tree's branches, granted him access to the runes. Through this act, he gained immense knowledge, understanding, and transformative power, solidifying his status as a wise and powerful deity in Norse mythology.

In rune magick, we do not only work with angular lines on pieces of wood. The runes are symbols and doorways to the rune deities, who are powerful, primordial entities in themselves. The runes can, thus, be used in conjunction with the above gods or by themselves.

The History and Origins of the Runes

Odin acquiring the runes has great significance within Norse cosmology. It is told in the "Hávamál," a poem found in the *Poetic Edda*, a collection of Old Norse poems. The narrative describes how Odin, the chief god in Norse mythology, sought knowledge and wisdom by sacrificing himself to gain the runes.

According to the "Hávamál," Odin hanged himself from the branches of Yggdrasil, the cosmic world tree, for nine nights and days. While hanging there, pierced by his own spear, he experienced intense suffering and self-sacrifice. He denied himself food and water, enduring extreme physical and mental anguish.

During this ordeal, Odin's aim was to attain esoteric knowledge and insight into the mysteries of the universe. He was seeking the wisdom and power contained within the runes, the Ancient Norse writing system believed to embody the secrets of creation and existence.

As Odin neared the brink of death, the runes revealed themselves to him. He reached down, taking them up, and claimed them as his own. This act granted him immense knowledge and understanding of the runes' magickal and transformative properties.

Through this self-sacrifice and the acquisition of the runes, Odin became the master of runes and the prime wielder of their powers. He gained the ability to use them for divination, magick, and communication with supernatural beings. Because Odin became associated with the runes, he was considered the god of wisdom, poetry, and magick in Norse mythology.

The story of Odin's acquisition of the runes emphasizes the importance of sacrifice and self-discovery in the pursuit of knowledge and wisdom. It illustrates the transformative power of the runes and their connection to the fabric of the cosmos, as embodied by Yggdrasil, the world tree.

This myth also reflects the reverence the Ancient Norse held for the written word and the symbolic significance they attributed to the runes. The runes were regarded as sacred symbols with mystical properties that could reveal hidden truths and grant their possessor extraordinary powers.

The history and origins of runes trace back to Ancient Germanic and Scandinavian cultures. Runes are an ancient writing system that was primarily used in the Germanic regions of Europe, including what is now present-day Scandinavia, Germany, and the British

Isles. The earliest runic inscriptions date back to the second century AD, but the origins of the runic script may be even older.

The word *rune* itself is derived from the Old Norse word *rún*, which means "secret" or "mystery." The early runic script consisted of a set of characters known as the Elder Futhark (*Fuþark*), which was composed of twenty-four symbols. The term *Futhark* is derived from the names of the first six characters: F, U, Þ, A, R, and K.

The exact origins of the runic script are still a subject of debate among scholars. One theory suggests that the runic script may have evolved from earlier Mediterranean writing systems, such as the Etruscan or the Latin alphabet. Another theory suggests that the runes developed independently within the Germanic cultures.

The runic script was primarily used for inscriptions on various objects, such as weapons, jewelry, tools, and runestones. These inscriptions served a variety of purposes, including recording names, commemorating individuals, conveying magickal or protective messages, and even providing instructions for rituals and divination.

The use of runes reached its peak during the Viking Age, from the eighth to the eleventh centuries, as the Norse seafarers explored and settled in different parts of Europe. During this time, the Elder Futhark underwent some regional variations, resulting in different runic alphabets, such as the Younger Futhark and the Anglo-Saxon Futhorc.

With the spread of Christianity and the Latin alphabet, the use of runes gradually declined. By the twelfth century, the Latin alphabet had become the dominant writing system in regions where runes were previously used. As a result, the knowledge and understanding of runes diminished over time.

However, the interest in runes revived during the nineteenth and twentieth centuries with the rise of Germanic nationalism and the Romantic movement. Scholars began to study and decipher runic inscriptions, leading to a better understanding of the runic script and its historical significance.

Today, runes are primarily associated with esoteric and divinatory practices. Many people use runic symbols for spiritual purposes, such as casting runes for guidance or creating runic talismans. The runic script continues to captivate people's imagination, serving as a connection to the Ancient Germanic and Scandinavian cultures of the past.

Different Runic Systems and their Histories

A "rune" is a letter in a set of related alphabets known as "runic alphabets" native to the Germanic peoples. Runes were used to write various Germanic languages (with some exceptions) before they adopted the Latin alphabet and for specialised purposes thereafter.

In addition to representing a sound value, runes can be used to represent the concepts after which they are named.

In the following pages, we will look at both the phonemic and ideographic meaning of the different European runic systems throughout the ages.

There are six (or seven) runic systems that can be classified as Germanic or Nordic, plus two major contemporary systems that we will look at in greater detail in the following chapter.

The six historical runic systems can be further divided into two classes: the first being the Elder Futhark (along with the Anglo-Frisian Futhorc) and the second being the Younger Futhark.

With the Elder Anglo-Frisian class, we find the Marcomannic rune set extending on them and trying to unite all the later-added sounds of the languages in that area (and time) into one writing system. Similarly, we find the medieval set (and the heavily Latin-inspired Dalecarlian runes) attempting the same years later with the Younger Futhark.

Thus, there are several runic systems that have been used throughout history, each with its own variations and historical context. Here are some of the major runic systems and a brief overview of their history:

1. **Elder Futhark (*Fuþark*):** The Elder Futhark is the oldest known runic alphabet and dates back between the second to

eighth centuries AD. It consists of twenty-four characters and was primarily used by Germanic tribes in Northern Europe. The word *Futhark* is derived from the first six letters: F, U, Þ, A, R, and K. It was used for various purposes, including inscriptions on stones, personal names, and divination.

2. **Anglo-Saxon Futhorc:** The Anglo-Saxon Futhorc, also known as the Anglo-Frisian Futhorc, was used by the Anglo-Saxons in England and Frisians in what is now the Netherlands from the fifth to the eleventh centuries. It is a derivative of the Elder Futhark, with some additional characters and modifications. The Anglo-Saxon Futhorc fell out of use with the Christianization of England.
3. **Marcomannic Runes:** Marcomannic runes are a runic script used by the Marcomanni, a Germanic tribe from ancient times. These runes have been found on various artifacts and inscriptions and are considered a subset of the Elder Futhark, which is the oldest known runic alphabet. The Marcomannic runes have distinct shapes and characters that set them apart from other runic scripts, reflecting the cultural and linguistic influences of the Marcomanni people. They provide valuable insights into the history and language of this Ancient Germanic tribe.
4. **Younger Futhark (*Fuþark*):** The Younger Futhark emerged during the Viking Age and was used predominantly in Scandinavia from the ninth to the twelfth centuries. It is a modified version of the Elder Futhark and contains sixteen characters. The Younger Futhark was primarily used for inscriptions on wood, metal, and other materials. It reflects linguistic changes in the Old Norse language.
5. **Medieval Runes:** During the Middle Ages, the use of runes declined, but runic inscriptions continued to appear in some contexts. These inscriptions often incorporated Latin letters and other symbols, reflecting the influence of the Latin alphabet and Christian culture.

6. **Dalecarlian Runes:** The Dalecarlian runes are a set of runes that emerged in the sixteenth century in the province of Dalarna, Sweden. They were mainly used for writing personal messages, carving inscriptions on furniture, or magickal purposes. The Dalecarlian runes have sixteen characters and are unique to that region.
7. **Contemporary Runic Usage:** In modern times, runes have experienced a revival and are used by some individuals for divination, magickal practices, and artistic purposes. Various contemporary runic systems and interpretations exist, often drawing inspiration from historical runic traditions.

Two contemporary systems stand out. One of the Armanen rune systems being purely used for esoteric means, while the other the modern Icelandic runes are purely linguistic in nature.

Exploring the Meanings and Symbolism of Each Rune in the Elder Futhark

(Between the Second and Eighth Centuries)

ᚠᚢᚦᚨᚱᚲᚷᚹᚺᚾᛁᛃᛇᛈᛉᛊᛏᛒᛖᛗᛚᛜᛞᛟ

The Elder Futhark (*Fuþark*), used for writing in Proto-Norse, consists of twenty-four runes that are commonly arranged in three groups of eight; each group is referred to as an *ætt* (Old Norse, meaning "clan," "group").

Aetts:	
Freya's Aett	ᚠᚢᚦᚨᚱᚲᚷᚹ
Hagall's Aett	ᚺᚾᛁᛃᛇᛈᛉᛊ
Tyr's Aett	ᛏᛒᛖᛗᛚᛜᛞᛟ

Most runic systems can be divided into three sets of runes.

The earliest known sequential listing of the full set of twenty-four runes dates to approximately AD 400 and is found on the Kylver Stone in Gotland, Sweden.

Despite popular belief, these are not yet "Viking runes," as there are still quite a few centuries (and other runic systems) before the so-called "Viking Age."

Most likely, each rune had a name chosen to represent the sound of the rune itself. The names are, however, not directly attested for in the Elder Futhark themselves.

Germanic philologists reconstruct names in Proto-Germanic based on the names given for the runes in the later alphabets attested in the rune poems and the linked names of the letters of the Gothic alphabet.

The Elder Futhark is the oldest known runic alphabet, consisting of twenty-four characters widely used by the Ancient Germanic peoples. Each rune has its own name, sound, and symbolic meaning. Here are the meanings and symbolism associated with each rune in the Elder Futhark:

Name: Fehu
Sound: "F"
Represents: Wealth, prosperity, and abundance.
Esoteric meaning: Cattle, which were a measure of wealth in ancient times.

Name: Uruz
Sound: "U"
Represents: The wild aurochs, an extinct species of large cattle.
Esoteric meaning: Strength, vitality, and physical power.

Name: Thurisaz
Sound: "Th"
Represents: A thorn or a giant.
Esoteric meaning: Protection, defense, and the ability to overcome obstacles.

Name: Ansuz
Sound: "A"
Represents: The breath of the divine.
Esoteric meaning: Communication, wisdom, and divine inspiration.

Name: Raidho
Sound: "R"
Represents: Travel, journeys, and personal growth.
Esoteric meaning: The wheel and the journey through life.

Name: Kenaz
Sound: "K"
Represents: A torch or a beacon of light.
Esoteric meaning: Knowledge, creativity, and illumination.

Name: Gebo
Sound: "G"
Represents: Partnerships, relationships, and gifts.
Esoteric meaning: The exchange of energy between individuals.

ᚹ

Name: Wunjo
Sound: "W"
Represents: The concept of a fulfilling and harmonious life.
Esoteric meaning: Joy, happiness, and contentment.

ᚺ

Name: Hagalaz
Sound: "H"
Represents: Chaos, disruption, and transformative forces.
Esoteric meaning: Hailstones and the destructive power of nature.

ᚾ

Name: Nauthiz
Sound: "N"
Represents: The concept of overcoming hardships and personal growth.
Esoteric meaning: Necessity and inner strength.

ᛁ

Name: Isa
Sound: "I"
Represents: Stillness, patience, and inner reflection.
Esoteric meaning: Ice and the need for self-control.

Name: Jera
Sound: "J/Y"
Represents: The concept of reaping what one has sown.
Esoteric meaning: Harvest, cycles, and rewards.

ᛇ

Name: Eihwaz

Sound: "Ea"

Represents: Perseverance, defense, and spiritual growth.

Esoteric meaning: The yew tree and endurance.

ᛈ

Name: Perthro

Sound: "P"

Represents: A dice cup and the concept of chance.

Esoteric meaning: Mystery, fate, and hidden knowledge.

ᛉ

Name: Algiz

Sound: "Z"

Represents: Protection, defense, and higher spiritual guidance.

Esoteric meaning: Elk or sedge plant.

ᛊ

Name: Sowilo

Sound: "S"

Represents: Energy, power, and the concept of personal transformation.

Esoteric meaning: The sun, success, and enlightenment.

Name: Tiwaz

Sound: "T"

Represents: Justice, honor, and self-sacrifice.

Esoteric meaning: The sky god Tyr and heroic deeds.

Name: Berkano
Sound: "B"
Represents: The birch tree and the concept of nurturing.
Esoteric meaning: Growth, fertility, and new beginnings

Name: Ehwaz
Sound: "E"
Represents: Partnership, trust, and harmony.
Esoteric meaning: Horses and teamwork.

Name: Mannaz
Sound: "M"
Represents: The concept of shared knowledge and co-operation.
Esoteric meaning: Humanity, community, and social connections.

Name: Laguz
Sound: "L"
Represents: Emotions, intuition, and the subconscious mind.
Esoteric meaning: Water and fluidity.

Name: Ingwaz
Sound: "Ng"
Represents: The god Ing and the concept of growth.
Esoteric meaning: Fertility, new beginnings, and inner potential.

Name: Dagaz
Sound: "D"
Represents: Breakthroughs, transformation, and enlightenment.
Esoteric meaning: Daybreak and the concept of awakening.

Name: Othala
Sound:"O"
Represents: The concept of heritage and family.
Esoteric meaning: Inheritance, ancestral wisdom, and home.

Rune	Name	Phoneme	Ideograph
ᚠ	Fehu	F	Cattle
ᚢ	Uruz	U	Aurochs
ᚦ	Thurisaz	Th	Thor
ᚨ	Ansuz	A	Odin
ᚱ	Raidho	R	Riding
ᚲ	Kenaz	K	Torch
ᚷ	Gebo	G	Gift
ᚹ	Wunjo	W	Joy
ᚺ	Hagalaz	H	Hail
ᚾ	Nauthiz	N	Need
ᛁ	Isa	I	Ice
ᛃ	Jera	J/Y	Harvest
ᛇ	Eihwaz	Ea	Yew
ᛈ	Perthro	P	Game Piece
ᛉ	Algiz	Z	Elk
ᛊ	Sowilo	S	Sun
ᛏ	Tiwaz	T	Tyr
ᛒ	Berkano	B	Birch
ᛖ	Ehwaz	E	Horse
ᛗ	Mannaz	M	Man
ᛚ	Laguz	L	Water
ᛜ	Ingwaz	Ng	Ing
ᛞ	Dagaz	D	Day
ᛟ	Othala	O	Home

Each rune carries its own energy and significance—they can be used for divination, meditation, or to invoke specific qualities or forces based on their meanings. Remember that interpretations can vary and different runic systems may assign slightly different meanings to the runes.

Homework

When learning about the runes, take a look at "twin runes." Twin runes are simply pairs of runes that follow one another in the natural order of the Futhark: Fehu and Uruz, Thurisaz and Ansuz, Raidho and Kenaz. Each pair represents a relationship—not always harmonious, but often filled with tension, progression, or challenge.

The first introduces a force, and the second either strengthens, tests, or transforms it. This pairing is not random—it's a rhythmic heartbeat in the runic row. The runes teach in sequence, and these "twins" reveal a layered understanding when read together—two forces dancing side-by-side, each influencing the other. To ignore their relationship is to miss a subtle, but potent aspect of runic work.

Runic Aett Structure

The aett structure, most notably prominent in the Elder Futhark (but can be utilised in most rune systems), enriches our comprehension of runic meanings. This enhanced understanding can subsequently be harnessed for practices like magick, bind-runes, and divination.

The First Aett—Freya's Aettir

The First Aett represents the life cycle.

- In Fehu, we see potential, ideas, concepts—a seed.
- In Uruz, we see ability, education—planting of the seed.
- In Thurisaz, we see movement, application—a seedling.

- In Ansuz, we see connection, a finished product—a grown plant.
- In Raido, we see reaction, changes caused by a product—the harvesting of the plant.
- In Kenaz, we see knowledge or results from the changes of a product—knowing what the processed plant is to be used for.
- In Gebo, we see outcome, benefits of the changes by a product—money from the sold plant.
- In Wunjo, we see wisdom, using the benefits to better the product—putting part of the money back from profits for more seed.

The Second Aett—Hagal's Aettir

The Second Aett represents the external forces that put themselves upon us. In most cases, these are not ruled by intelligence, but by the forces of nature.

- In Hagalaz, we have hail, an external force outside of our control. It is a neutral power.
- In Nauthiz, we have needs, external forces that drive us forward, like hunger, lust, and fear.
- In Isa, we have ice. It is how the world sees us. Its view is static and unchanged until exerted upon.
- In Jera, we have the cycle of time, as well as the external forces of entropy and its effect upon the world.
- In Eihwaz, we have the yew tree (Yggdrasil) and its apparent immortality, representing that of nature's own.
- In Pertho, we have the unknowable, or the energy of karma. It is the force of luck.
- In Algiz, we have protection by an external force.
- In Sowilo, we have a mentor or guide that encourages a feeling of safety.

The Third Aett—Tyr's Aettir

In the Third Aett, the last set of runes, are the internal forces that help us deal with the external forces of the Second Aett as we travel the path outlined in the First Aett.

- In Teiwaz, we have a rune of order, self-sacrifice, stability, lawfulness, and courage.
- In Berkana, we have the rune of "feminine energy."
- In Ehwaz, we have the rune that shows the duality of man in his ability to deal with the world.
- In Mannaz, we have the rune that represents intelligence, memory, rationality, and the traditions of mankind.
- In Laguz, we have not only the subconscious, but also that which is within it.
- In Inguz, we have the very essence of creativity and the act of creating.
- In Dagaz, we have a representative of the personal time you give to accomplishing goals.
- Lastly, Othila is our home turf, whether this is physically, emotionally, or spiritually.

Exploring the Meanings and Symbolism of Each Rune in the Anglo-Saxon Futhorc

(Between the Fifth and Eleventh Centuries)

ᚠᚢᚦᚩᚱᚳᚷᚹᚻᚾᛁᛄᛇᛈᛉᛋᛏᛒᛖᛗᛚᛝᛞᛟᚪᚫᚣᛠᛡᛣᚸᛢᛥ

The Anglo-Saxon Futhorc, used for writing Old English, consists of the twenty-four runes of the Elder Futhark, some slightly modified, and the addition of up to nine (number varies from source to source) completely new runes to accommodate the new language (as well as some extra esoterical concepts).

The terms "Anglo-Saxon runes" and "Anglo-Frisian runes"

are sometimes used interchangeably, but they can refer to slightly different historical and regional contexts. However, both terms are related and pertain to the runic script used in early medieval England and parts of Frisia.

Anglo-Saxon Runes

Anglo-Saxon runes primarily refers to the runic script used in early medieval England, especially during the Old English period. These runes were used to write Old English and they evolved from earlier runic scripts like the Elder Futhark. The name "Anglo-Saxon runes" highlights their use in England, where the Anglo-Saxons were a prominent Germanic group during this time.

Anglo-Frisian Runes:

Anglo-Frisian runes encompasses the runic scripts used in both early medieval England and parts of Frisia, which is a region in what is now the Netherlands and Germany. It recognizes the geographical and cultural connections between these regions and acknowledges that similar runic scripts were employed in both areas.

In essence, both terms refer to the same or closely related runic scripts used in early medieval Germanic-speaking regions, but the use of Anglo-Frisian runes acknowledges the broader regional context. These scripts have common features, as they evolved from the same runic traditions, but they may have had local variations and differences in usage within England and Frisia. The choice of terminology may depend on the specific historical or linguistic context being discussed.

Apart from slightly varied forms on certain runes, the meaning is the same as with most of the Elder Futhark runes.

Here follows a description of the new additions.

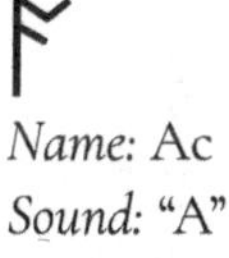

Name: Ac
Sound: "A"

Represents: The great oak tree.
Esoteric meaning: Wisdom, strength and endurance.

Name: Aesc
Sound: "Ae"
Represents: The ash tree.
Esoteric meaning: Yggdrasil, the "world ash," a connection to the divine.

Name: Yr
Sound: "Y"
Represents: The bow.
Esoteric meaning: Entrance to the underworld.

Name: Ear
Sound: "Ea"
Represents: The grave.
Esoteric meaning: The cold, earth, and death.

Name: Ior
Sound: "Ia"
Represents: Eel, amphibian or wyrm.
Esoteric meaning: The unknown or the supernatural; not here (earth), but not there (water).

Name: Calc
Sound: "K"
Represents: A chalice.
Esoteric meaning: Powerful magickal symbol.

Name: Gar
Sound: "G"
Represents: A spear.
Esoteric meaning: Weapon of the common soldier all the way to Odin himself, denotes keen perception and an unrelenting will of its owner.

Name: Cweorth
Sound: "Kw"
Represents: Fire.
Esoteric meaning: The fire within.

Name: Stan
Sound: "St"
Represents: Stone.
Esoteric meaning: Stones were known as the dwellings of spirits, from ancestors, to elves, dwarves, and trolls.

Rune	Name	Phoneme	Ideograph
ᚠ	Feoh	F	Wealth
ᚢ	Ur	U	Aurochs
ᚦ	Thorn	Th	Thorn
ᚩ	Os	O	God
ᚱ	Rad	R	Ride
ᚳ	Cen	C	Torch
ᚷ	Gyfu	G	Gift
ᚹ	Wynn	W	Joy
ᚻ	Haegl	H	Hail
ᚾ	Nyd	N	Need
ᛁ	Is	I	Ice
ᛄ	Ger	J	Year
ᛇ	Eoh	Eo	Yew
ᛈ	Peorth	P	Unknown/ Game Piece
ᛉ	Eohlx	X	Elk/Sedge
ᛋ	Sigel	S	Sun
ᛏ	Tiw	T	Tiw
ᛒ	Beorc	B	Birch
ᛖ	Eh	E	Horse
ᛗ	Mann	M	Man
ᛚ	Lagu	L	Lake
ᛝ	Ing	Ng	Ing
ᛞ	Daeg	D	Day
ᛟ	Edel	Oe	Estate
ᚪ	Ac	A	Oak

Rune	Name	Phoneme	Ideograph
ᚫ	Aesc	Ae	Ash Tree
ᚣ	Yr	Y	Bow
ᛠ	Ear	Ea	Grave
ᛡ	Ior	Eia	Eel
ᛣ	Calc	K	Chalice
ᚸ	Gar	G	Spear
ᛢ	Cweorth	Kw/Q	Fire
ᛥ	Stan	St	Stone

Exploring the Meanings and Symbolism of Each Rune in the Marcomannic Runes

(Eighth to Ninth Centuries)

ᚫᛒᚴᛞᛖᚠᚼᚺᛁᛯᛚᛗᚾᚱᛕᛉᚱᚳᛏᚢᛏᛉᛏ

The Marcomannic runes appeared in a treaty called *De Inventione Litterarum,* which attributes these runes to Marcomanni, hence the name. It's a merger of Elder Futhark and Futhorc runes. The manuscript was drawn up in the southern part of the Carolingian Empire around Bavaria. These runes are supposedly in use in the eighth and ninth centuries.

With the Marcomannic runes, we start to see the familiar Latin alphabet order and not always the Futhark. At this time, the format was still about 50/50.

The runes can be seen to have the same meanings as their Elder Futhark and Anglo-Frisian counterparts.

System: Marcomannic Runes

Rune	Name	Phoneme	Ideograph
ᚫ	Asch	A	Ash Tree
ᛒ	Birith	B	Birch Tree
ᚴ	Khen	Ch	Torch
ᛞ	Thorn	Th	Giant
ᛖ	Eho	E	Horse
ᚠ	Fehc	F	Cattle
ᛡ	Gibu	G	Gift
ᚻ	Hagale	H	Hail
ᛁ	His	I	Ice
ᛤ	Gilch	K	Money (as in "his cup overflows")
ᛚ	Lagu	L	Lake
ᛗ	Man	M	Man
ᚾ	Not	N	Need
ᚱ	Othil	O	Home
ᛈ	Perch	P	Game
ᛈ	Khon	Q	Same as *Gilch* (only linguistically different)
ᚱ	Rehit	R	Ride
ᛋ	Suhil	S	Sun
ᛏ	Tac	T	God

Rune	Name	Phoneme	Ideograph
ᚢ	Hur	U	Auroch
ᛏ	Helahe	X	Underworld
ᛉ	Huyri	Y	Protection
ᛏ	Ziu	Z	God of the Sword

Exploring the Meanings and Symbolism of Each Rune in the Younger Futhark

(Between the Ninth and Twelfth Centuries)

ᚠᚢᚦᚬᚱᚴᚼᚾᛁᛅᛋᛏᛒᛘᛚᛦ
ᚠᚢᚦᚭᚱᚴᚽᚿᛁᛆᛌᛐᛓᛙᛚᛧ

The Younger Futhark, a runic alphabet used in the Nordic countries during the Viking Age and the Middle Ages, is further divided into two main variations: the Long Branch (also known as the Danish runic script) and the Short Twig (also known as the Swedish-Norwegian runic script) variations. This division occurred for several historical and practical reasons:

1. **Geographical Distribution:** The primary reason for the division into Long Branch and Short Twig variations was the geographical distribution of the script. The Long Branch variant was primarily used in Denmark and some parts of Sweden, while the Short Twig variant was predominantly used in Sweden and Norway. The division reflects regional differences in runic usage and local preferences.

2. **Phonetic Changes:** Over time, the spoken language in the different regions evolved, leading to variations in pronunciation and phonetics. These phonetic changes influenced the way runes were used to represent sounds in words. As a result, some runes were adapted to better match the evolving language in specific regions.
3. **Linguistic Shifts:** Different regions of the Nordic countries underwent linguistic shifts, which led to variations in how sounds were represented by runes. This affected the choice of runes and their forms, contributing to the development of two distinct runic traditions.
4. **Local Influences:** Local cultural and historical factors also played a role in the development of these variations. The Long Branch and Short Twig scripts may have been influenced by neighboring regions, trade routes, and contact with other cultures, resulting in unique regional runic traditions.
5. **Time Period:** The division between the Long Branch and Short Twig variations did not occur simultaneously. It is believed that the Long Branch runes predate the Short Twig runes and they coexisted for a significant period before evolving into their respective forms.

The division into Long Branch and Short Twig variations allowed for a more localized adaptation of the runic script to better suit the linguistic and cultural characteristics of specific regions. This differentiation in runic forms reflects the dynamic nature of written language and its relationship with the spoken language in different parts of the Norse world during the Viking Age and the subsequent centuries.

For any attempt and purpose, they are esoterically treated as the same.

Name: Fe
Sound: "F"

Represents: Wealth, prosperity, and abundance.
Esoteric meaning: Cattle, which were a measure of wealth in ancient times.

ᚢ

Name: Ur
Sound: "U"
Represents: Rain or dross from iron.
Esoteric meaning: Iron dross is a byproduct of smiting. It is a mixture of iron and other impurities that form on the surface of molten iron as it is processed. It translates to "sudden danger" or "blessings."

ᚦ

Name: Thurs
Sound: "Th"
Represents: A thorn or a giant.
Esoteric meaning: An adversary, but also the ability to overcome obstacles.

ᚬ

Name: Oss
Sound: "O"
Represents: The breath of the divine.
Esoteric meaning: Communication, wisdom, and divine inspiration.

ᚱ

Name: Reid
Sound: "R"
Represents: Travel, journeys, and personal growth.
Esoteric meaning: The wheel and the journey through life.

ᚴ

Name: Kaun
Sound: "K"
Represents: Ulcher.
Esoteric meaning: Pain, burning within, stomach ulcers, tumors, and cancer.

Name: Hagall
Sound: "H"
Represents: Chaos, disruption, and transformative forces.
Esoteric meaning: Hailstones and the destructive power of nature.

ᚾ

Name: Nauthr
Sound: "N"
Represents: The concept of overcoming hardships and personal growth.
Esoteric meaning: Necessity, and inner strength.

ᛁ

Name: Isa
Sound: "I"
Represents: Stillness, patience, and inner reflection.
Esoteric meaning: Ice and the need for self-control.

ᛅ

Name: Ar
Sound: "A"
Represents: Plenty.

Esoteric meaning: A good year. Plentiful crops, but also abundance in skills and knowledge.

ᛋ ᛌ

Name: Sol
Sound: "S"
Represents: Energy, power, and the concept of personal transformation.
Esoteric meaning: The sun, success, and enlightenment.

ᛏ ᛐ

Name: Tyr
Sound: "T"
Represents: Justice, honor, and self-sacrifice.
Esoteric meaning: The sky god Tyr and heroic deeds.

ᛒ ᛓ

Name: Bjarkan
Sound: "B"
Represents: The birch tree and the concept of nurturing.
Esoteric meaning: Growth, fertility, and new beginnings.

ᛘ ᛙ

Name: Madr
Sound: "M"
Represents: The concept of shared knowledge and cooperation.
Esoteric meaning: Humanity, community, and social connections.

Name: Logr

Sound: "L"
Represents: Emotions, intuition, and the subconscious mind.
Esoteric meaning: Water and the concept of fluidity.

ᛦ ᛧ
Name: Yr
Sound: "Z" or "r"
Represents: Bow made from a yew tree.
Esoteric meaning: The entrance to the underworld, a death rune.

Rune	Name	Phoneme	Ideograph
ᚠ	Fe	F	Wealth
ᚢ	Ur	U	Dross/Rain
ᚦ	Thurs	Th	Giant
ᚬ ᚭ	Oss	O	God
ᚱ	Reid	R	Ride
ᚴ	Kaun	K	Ulcer
ᚼ ᚽ	Hagall	H	Hail
ᚾ	Naudr	N	Need
ᛁ	Isa	I	Ice
ᛅ	Ar	A	Plenty
ᛋ ᛌ	Sol	S	Sun
ᛏ ᛐ	Tyr	T	Victory
ᛒ ᛓ	Biarkan	B	Birch
ᛘ ᛙ	Madr	M	Man
ᛚ	Logr	L	Lake
ᛦ ᛧ	Yr	R (word ending)	Underworld

Exploring the Meanings and Symbolism of Each Rune in the Medieval Runes

(Twelfth to Fifteenth Centuries)

ᛆᛒᛍᛑᛂᚠᚵᚼᛁᚴᛚᛘᚿᚯᛔᚴᚱᛌᛐᚢᚡᚤᛧᛂᚯᚦ

The medieval runes, or the *futhork,* was a Scandanavian-based runic alphabet that evolved from the Younger Futhark after the introduction of "stung" (or "dotted") runes at the end of the Viking Age.

These stung runes were regular runes with the addition of either a dot diacritic or bar diacritic to indicate that the rune stood for one of its secondary sounds (so an "i" rune could become an "e" rune or a "j" rune when stung).

The medieval futhork was fully formed in the early thirteenth century. Due to the expansion of its character inventory, it was essentially possible to have each character in an inscription correspond to only one phoneme, something which was virtually impossible in Younger Futhark with its small inventory of sixteen runes.

The medieval runic system is the first in which the familiar Latin (ABC) format is a lot more prominent and not the futhark format of previous systems.

Runes in this set have the same meaning as the Younger Futhark counterparts, with stung runes retaining the original meaning and only changing the sound associated with said rune.

Rune	Name	Phoneme	Ideograph
ᛆ	Ar	A	Abundance
ᛒ	Bjarka	B	Birch
ᛍ		C	Stung version of Sol
ᛑ		D	Stung version of Tyr
ᛂ		E	Stung version of Is

Rune	Name	Phoneme	Ideograph
ᚠ	Fe	F	Wealth
ᚵ		G	Stung version of Kaun
ᚼ	Hagal	H	Hail
ᛁ	Is	I	Ice
ᛁ	Is used	J	Is is used
ᚴ	Kaun	K	Ulcer
ᛚ	Logur	L	Water-
ᛘ	Maðr	M	Man
ᚿ	Nauð	N	Need
ᚬ	Os	O	God
ᛔ		P	Stung version of Bjarka
ᚴ	Purely linguistic	Q/Kw	Purely linguistic
ᚱ	Reið	R	Riding
ᛌ	Sol	S	Sun
ᛐ	Tyr	T	Tyr
ᚢ	Ur	U	Dross
ᚡ		V	Stung version of Fe
ᚼ	Hagal used	X	Hagal used
ᚤ	Yr	Y	Yew; stung version of Ur
ᛍ		Z	Stung version of Sol
ᛆ		Ae	Stung version of Ar
ᚯ		Oi	Stung version of Os
ᚦ	Thurs	Th	Giant

Exploring the Meanings and Symbolism of Each Rune in the Dalecarlian Runes

(Sixteenth to Twentieth Centuries)

The Dalecarlian runes was a runic alphabet used in the Swedish province of Dalarna/Dalecarlia until the twentieth century, mainly to write the Elfdalian language. They developed from Younger Futhork during the sixteenth century and, over time, became increasingly mixed with letters from the Latin alphabet. This alphabet is also known as Elfdalian runes or dalrunes.

This alphabet was mainly inscribed into wood and stone on furniture, buildings, bowls, measuring sticks, etc. to write the names of the owners and/or makers. The earliest known inscription in Dalecarlian runes, for example, appears on a bowl from Åsen, a village in Älvdalen parish, and says "Anders has made (this) bowl anno 1596."

Dalecarlian runes have the same esoteric meaning as their Younger Futhark or medieval rune counterparts. Historically, though, they were mostly used as a writing system.

Rune	Name	Phoneme	Ideograph
ᚷ	Ar	A	Abundance
ᛒ	Birka	B	Birch
ᚲ	Knasol	C	Torch
ᚦ	Dors	D	Giant
ᛂ	Er	E	Purely linguistic
ᚠ	Fir	F	Wealth
ᚱ	Gir	G	Gift
ᚼ	Hagal	H	Hail
ᛁ	Is	I	Ice

Rune	Name	Phoneme	Ideograph
ᚴ	Kan	K	Ulcer
ᛚ	Lagh	L	Lake
ᛘ	Madhar	M	Man
ᚿ	Nadh	N	Need
ᚮ	Or	O	Purely linguistic
ᛔ	Pir	P	Purely linguistic
ᚱ	Re	R	Ride
ᛁ	Sol	S	Sun
ᛐ	Tir	T	Tyr
ᚢ	Ur	U	Auroch
ᛉ		Y	Purely linguistic
ᚼ		Ao	Purely linguistic
ᚯ		Aö	Purely linguistic
ᛦ		Ö	Purely linguistic

Numbers in Runic Systems

In runic writing systems, numbers were typically represented using a combination of runes or specific symbols for numerical values. The runic alphabets varied across different Germanic languages and regions, but some common elements existed.

Here's an example of how numbers might be represented in the Elder Futhark:

- **ᚠ (Fehu):** 1
- **ᚢ (Uruz):** 2
- **ᚦ (Thurisaz):** 3

- **ᚨ (Ansuz):** 4
- **ᚱ (Raido):** 5
- **ᚲ (Kenaz):** 6
- Etc...

It's easy to see that, with higher numbers, you may run into some problems; while it may still be possible, the numbers do tend to look a bit clumsy. Thus, most Vitkar use pentadic numerals.

Pentadic Numerals

Pentadic numerals are a notation for presenting numbers, usually by inscribing in wood or stone. The notation has been used in Scandinavia, usually in conjunction with runic calendars.

The notation is similar to the older Roman numerals for the numbers one to nine (I, II, III, IV, V, VI, VII, VIII, IX). Unlike the Roman notation, there are only symbols for numbers one (I) and five (U), protruding off the side of a vertical stroke, or stem, which has no numeric value by itself. In some inscriptions the notches are placed horizontally on a vertical stem, or *stav,* of the rune; in other inscriptions, the stave is horizontal and the I and inverted U rise off of it.

The number four is represented by four vertical lines on the horizontal stem, five is represented by what looks like a half-turned letter U, resembling the letter P in combination with the stem. Ten is represented by two turned Us opposing each other. More numbers (up to nineteen or twenty) can be represented by a combination of Is and Us branching off of a stem, similar to how Roman numerals are represented by combinations of Is and Vs.

The rune for ten is used interchangeably for zero and ten. This can still be confusing, but less than with previous systems. For example, it may not be possible to distinguish 1010 from 100.

1 2 3 4 5 6 7 8 9 0

Exploring the Meanings and Symbolism of Each Rune in the Armanen Runes

(Twentieth Century to Present Day)

The Armanen runes, also known as the Armanen Futhark, is a set of runic symbols developed by the Austrian occultist and mystic Guido von List in the early twentieth century. Von List claimed to have derived the Armanen runes from Ancient Norse and Germanic runic traditions, although their historical authenticity is highly debated among scholars.

After years of runes being used only as a writing method, Guido von List believed that the Armanen runes represented not only an alphabet, but also a system of esoteric knowledge and spirituality.

He associated each of these new runes with a specific cosmic or mythological concept, such as gods, natural forces, or virtues.

Von List claimed that the Armanen runes had deeper mystical meanings and could be used for divination, magick, and self-transformation, just like the runic sets of old.

The Armanen runic system consists of eighteen characters. Von List's runic sequence differs from the historical runic systems and he assigned new names to the runes based on his own interpretations.

Some of the runes in the Armanen Futharkh closely resemble those in the historical runic systems, but others have unique shapes and names.

It's important to note that the Armanen runes and Guido von List's esoteric teachings were embraced by various occult and neo-pagan groups, particularly within Germanic and Norse-inspired esoteric traditions. However, their historical accuracy and authenticity as an ancient runic system are widely disputed. Many experts consider the Armanen runes to be a modern creation, rather than a genuine historical tradition.

After an eye operation, Guido von List claimed to have had a vision where he saw the "original" set of runes. He believed that these runes were the runes that all other rune-rows were based on. Having eighteen runes in his set, he identified each of his runes with one of the eighteen spells in the "Hávamál" in the "Elder Edda." However, there was no evidence to support his claim.

In Norse myth and legend, an almost obsessive pursuit of knowledge and wisdom is one of the defining characteristics of Odin.

It was this obsession, after all, that drove Odin to steal the Mead of Poetry from the giant Suttung—an act of blatant theft he was able to commit by seducing Suttung's own daughter, Gunnlod.

It was also this same obsession that led Odin to pierce his own side with a spear and hang himself from the branches of the world tree, Yggdrasil, where he hanged for nine days and nine nights in an act of ritual sacrifice in which Odin made an offering of himself, to himself. It was this act of self-sacrifice that allowed Odin to learn the secrets of the runes—though, his pursuit of knowledge also led Odin to learn even greater magick from other sources. As outlined in "Hávamál," one of the poems to be found in the *Poetic Edda,* Odin acquired knowledge of eighteen charms, or powerful spells, not known by any other man or women.

And that is the basis of the Armanen Rune system, as von List believed that, along with each of their charms, there was a corresponding rune.

Name: Fa
Sound: "f"

Represents: Primal Fire
Esoteric meaning: The power of spirit and change, as well as the power of creativity.

Name: Ur
Sound: "u"
Represents: Resurrection
Esoteric meaning: Ur is a physician's rune and represents resurrection, eternity, and continuity.

Name: Dorn
Sound: "th"
Represents: Lightning and thunder.
Esoteric meaning: The thunderbolt. Symbolically, it stands for targeting goals, activity, and the phallus.

Name: Os
Sound: "o" as in "cold"
Represents: Mouth.
Esoteric meaning: Os represents the spiritual power that is gained through speech. The breath of the world, its voice. Strength that a person needs to rise up in power.

Name: Rit
Sound: "r"
Represents: Ritual (or Primal Laws).

Esoteric meaning: The orderliness in the world, the ritual, primal law, and things that are done correctly. Cynical events and rescue from an enemy.

ᚴ

Name: Ka
Sound: "k"
Represents: Yggdrasil.
Esoteric meaning: The World Tree.

Name: Hagal
Sound: "h"
Represents: Hail
Esoteric meaning: Due to its shape, Hagal is sometimes called the "mother rune," and is said that all other runes derive from its shape. It is a rune of enclosure, but contains a potential for growth.

Name: Not
Sound: "n"
Represents: Necessity of fate.
Esoteric meaning: This rune can be taken as the same idea as the Hindu concept of karma: what is done in this lifetime will determine our future existence.

ᛁ

Name: Is
Sound: "i" as in "piece"
Represents: Ego

Esoteric meaning: Just like our ego, this rune is one that is used to control ourselves. It represents the personal power of control, obedience, and our compelling will.

Name: Ar
Sound: "a" as in "aah"
Represents: Light
Esoteric meaning: Sunlight that washes away darkness, as well as denoting nobility and leadership.

ᛋ
Name: Sig
Sound: "s"
Represents: Sun Power
Esoteric meaning: Like Ar, this rune represents the power of the sun. The difference is that Sig is the power of the sun, whereas Ar is the power that the light of the sun contains. It is also a rune of success and victory.

Name: Tyr
Sound: "t"
Represents: Rebirth of the Sun god
Esoteric meaning: Tyr is a rune that has the power to make situations turn completely around. A rune of wisdom, spiritual understanding, and the power of generation.

Name: Bar
Sound: "b"
Represents: Birth

Esoteric meaning: Birth, but in a sense of the birth of the future life that is preordained for us. Modern versions of this rune say it stands for the power of becoming, as well as the power of creativity found in song.

ᛚ

Name: Laf
Sound: "l"
Represents: *Ã–rlog* (Primal Law)
Esoteric meaning: List said this rune stood for the concepts of defeat and the laws of nature. Today modern versions have this rune denoting life, water, and primal law.

Name: Man
Sound: "m"
Represents: Man (as in human, not gender)
Esoteric meaning: The second mother rune of this set, Man was used in Armanen tradition to represent birth. Modern versions say it stands for health, increase, maleness, and man (gender this time).

Name: Yr
Sound: "y" as in "tiny"
Represents: Death
Esoteric meaning: Anger, falsehood, error and the oppositions found in man (as in human, not gender).

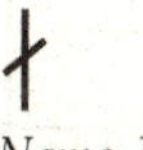

Name: Eh

Sound: "e," as in "every"
Represents: Duality (or possibly, even Horse)
Esoteric meaning: The rune Eh is said to symbolize duality, where a pair is bound by primal law, love, trust, and marriage.

Name: Gibor
Sound: "g"
Represents: Gift of life
Esoteric meaning: The giver of life and the gift of life itself. Cosmic consciousness and the divine principle.

Runic System: Armanen Runes

Rune	Name	Phoneme	Ideograph
ᚠ	Fa	F	Primal Fire
ᚢ	Ur	U	Resurrection
ᚦ	Thurs	Th	Thunderbolt
ᚬ	Os	O	Mouth
ᚱ	Rit	R	Ritual
ᚴ	Ka	K	Yggdrasil
ᛡ	Hagal	H	Hail
ᚾ	Nauth	N	Necessity of Fate
ᛁ	Is	I	Ego
ᛅ	Ar	A	Light
ᛋ	Sig	S	Sun
ᛏ	Tyr	T	Tyr
ᛒ	Bar	B	Birth
ᛚ	Laf	L	Primal Law
ᛘ	Man	M	Man

Rune	Name	Phoneme	Ideograph
ᛦ	Yr	Y	Death
ᚾ	Eh	E	Duality
ᛝ	Gibor	G	Gift of Life

Exploring Modern Icelandic Runes

(Twenty-First Century to Present Day)

ᛆᛒᛍᛑᛰᚠᚵᚼᛁᛃᚴᛚᛘᚿᚮᛔᛩᚱᛌᛐᚢᚡᚥᛪᛦᛎ

Icelandic Runic was created by Alexander R. as an adaptation of the runic script for Icelandic. He created it while researching if it was possible to write any modern language in runes. He thought that most languages cannot be written in runes, until he realised that Icelandic and medieval runes have a lot of similar letters.

The script is based on medieval runes, although vowels from Elder Futhark were added. This modern runic system is purely linguistic in origin.

Rune	Phoneme
ᛆ	A
ᛒ	B
ᛍ	C
ᛑ	D
ᛰ	E
ᚠ	F
ᚵ	G
ᚼ	H
ᛁ	I

Rune	Phoneme
ᛃ	J
ᚴ	K
ᛚ	L
ᛘ	M
ᚿ	N
ᚭ	O
ᛔ	P
ᛩ	Q
ᚱ	R
ᛌ	S
ᛐ	T
ᚢ	U
ᚷ	X
↕	Y
‡	Z
ᛆ	Ae
ᚯ	Ö

Connecting With the Energies and Vibrations of the Runes

Connecting with the energies and vibrations of the runes can be a profound and transformative experience. Here is a detailed guide to help you establish a deeper connection with the runes:

1. **Learn about the Runes:** Start by familiarizing yourself with the meanings, symbols, and associations of each rune. There are twenty-four runes in the Elder Futhark, which is the most used runic alphabet. Study their individual

interpretations, as well as their historical and mythological significance. Understanding the essence of each rune will deepen your connection with its energy.

2. **Create a Sacred Space:** Find a quiet and serene space where you can focus on the runes without distractions. You can create an altar or a designated area to honor the runes. Cleanse the space by smudging, lighting incense, or using other purification rituals. This will help create an atmosphere conducive to connecting with the energies of the runes.
3. **Ground and Center Yourself:** Before engaging with the runes, it's important to ground/center yourself. Take a few deep breaths, close your eyes, and focus on your breath. Feel your connection to the Earth beneath you. Visualize roots growing from your feet, grounding you to the core of the Earth. This practice will help you establish a stable and receptive state of mind.
4. **Choose a Rune:** Select a rune that you wish to connect with. You can draw one randomly from a bag or use a rune casting method, such as throwing the runes onto a cloth or tray and choosing the one that stands out to you. Alternatively, you can choose a specific rune based on your intentions or the guidance you seek.
5. **Meditate on the Rune:** Hold the chosen rune in your hands and observe its shape, symbols, and energy. Close your eyes and bring your awareness to the rune. Visualize its shape in your mind's eye. Begin to explore the rune's energy and vibrations. Notice any sensations, images, or thoughts that arise. Allow yourself to immerse in the rune's essence.
6. **Invoke the Rune's Energy:** To deepen your connection, you can recite the name and meaning of the rune out loud or internally. Repeat it several times, allowing the sound and vibration of the rune's name to resonate within you. This verbal invocation helps attune your energy to the specific qualities associated with the rune.

7. **Engage in Rune Divination:** You can also use the runes for divination or seeking guidance. As you draw a rune, pose a specific question or request for guidance in your mind. Reflect on the rune's meaning and how it relates to your query. Trust your intuition and the messages that come through. The more you practice, the stronger your connection will become.
8. **Journal and Reflect:** After your interaction with the rune, take a few moments to write down your experiences, insights, and any messages received. Journaling will help you integrate the energy of the rune and deepen your understanding of its significance in your life.
9. **Practice Regularly:** Connecting with the energies and vibrations of the runes is a continuous journey. Regular practice is essential for deepening your connection. Set aside dedicated time to work with the runes, whether it's daily, weekly, or as-needed. Consistency will enhance your sensitivity to the energies and allow for a more profound connection over time.

Remember that everyone's experience with the runes may vary, and it's essential to trust your intuition throughout the process. As you develop a personal relationship with the runes, they will become powerful tools for self-discovery, guidance, and spiritual growth.

Rune Poems

Some runic systems have poems assigned to themselves (well, two systems): the Younger Futhark (two sets of poems) and the Anglo-Saxon runes. It is uncertain whether the poems were of magickal inspiration, or simply a way of remembering the meaning of each rune. These poems provide descriptions and mnemonic verses for each of the runic characters in the runic alphabets used by the Norse people. Poems can easily be created for the other runic systems as well...magickal or not.

Please note that the poems are not in galdralag, but in a lot simpler form.

The Norwegian Rune Poems

The Norwegian Rune Poems for the Younger Futhark in the Original Old Norse

ᚠ **Fé**
vældr frænda róge;
føðesk ulfr í skóge.

ᚢ **Úr**
er af illu jarne;
opt løypr ræinn á hjarne.

ᚦ **Þurs**
vældr kvinna kvillu;
kátr værðr fár af illu.

ᚬ **Óss**
er flæstra færða
fǫr; en skalpr er sværða.

ᚱ **Ræið**
kveða rossom væsta;
Reginn sló sværðet bæzta.

ᚴ **Kaun**
er barna bǫlvan;
bǫl gørver nán fǫlvan.

ᚼ **Hagall**
er kaldastr korna;
Kristr skóp hæimenn forna.

ᚾ **Nauðr**
gerer næppa koste;
nøktan kælr í froste.

ᛁ **Ís**
kǫllum brú bræiða;
blindan þarf at læiða.

ᛅ **Ár**
er gumna góðe;
get ek at ǫrr var Fróðe.

ᛌ **Sól**
er landa ljóme;
lúti ek helgum dome.

ᛐ **Týr**
er æinendr ása;
opt værðr smiðr blása.

ᛓ **Bjarkan**
er laufgrønstr líma;
Loki bar flærða tíma.

ᛙ **Maðr**
er moldar auki;
mikil er græip á hauki.

ᛚ **Lǫgr**
er, fællr ór fjalle
foss; en gull ero nosser.

ᛧ **Ýr**
er vetrgrønstr viða;
vænt er, er brennr, at sviða.

Modern English Translations

ᚠ **Fe**
Wealth is a source of discord among kinsmen;
the wolf lives in the forest.

ᚢ **Ur**
Dross comes from bad iron;
the reindeer often races over the frozen snow

ᚦ **Thurs**
Giant causes anguish to women;
misfortune makes few men cheerful.

ᚬ **As**
Estuary is the way of most journeys;
but a scabbard is of swords.

ᚱ **Reidh**
Riding is said to be the worst thing for horses;
Reginn forged the finest sword.

ᚴ **Kaun**
Ulcer is fatal to children;
death makes a corpse pale.

ᚼ **Hagall**
Hail is the coldest of grain;
Christ created the world of old.

ᚾ **Naudhr**
Constraint gives scant choice;
a naked man is chilled by the frost.

ᛁ Isa
Ice we call the broad bridge;
the blind man must be led.

ᛆ Ar
Plenty is a boon to men;
I say that Frodi was generous.

ᛌ Sol
Sun is the light of the world;
I bow to the divine decree.

ᛐ Tyr
Tyr is a one-handed god;
often has the smith to blow.

ᛓ Bjarkan
Birch has the greenest leaves of any shrub;
Loki was fortunate in his deceit.

ᛙ Madhr
Man is an augmentation of the dust;
great is the claw of the hawk.

ᛚ Logr
A waterfall is a river which falls from a mountain-side;
but ornaments are of gold.

ᛦ Yr
Yew is the greenest of trees in winter;
it is wont to crackle when it burns.

The Icelandic Rune Poems

The Icelandic Rune Poems for the Younger Futhark in the Original Old Norse

ᚠ **Fé**
er frænda róg
ok flæðar viti
ok grafseiðs gata
aurum fylkir.

ᚢ **Úr**
er skýja grátr
ok skára þverrir
ok hirðis hatr.
umbre vísi

ᚦ **Þurs**
er kvenna kvöl
ok kletta búi
ok varðrúnar verr.
Saturnus þengill.

ᚬ **Óss**
er algingautr
ok ásgarðs jöfurr,
ok valhallar vísi.
Jupiter oddviti.

ᚱ **Reið**
er sitjandi sæla
ok snúðig ferð
ok jórs erfiði.
iter ræsir.

ᚴ Kaun
er barna böl
ok bardaga [för]
ok holdfúa hús.
flagella konungr.

ᚼ Hagall
er kaldakorn
ok krapadrífa
ok snáka sótt.
grando hildingr.

ᚾ Nauð
er Þýjar þrá
ok þungr kostr
ok vássamlig verk.
opera niflungr.

ᛁ Íss
er árbörkr
ok unnar þak
ok feigra manna fár.
glacies jöfurr.

ᛅ Ár
er gumna góði
ok gott sumar
algróinn akr.
annus allvaldr.

ᛋ Sól
er skýja skjöldr
ok skínandi röðull
ok ísa aldrtregi.
rota siklingr.

ᛏ **Týr**
er einhendr áss
ok ulfs leifar
ok hofa hilmir.
Mars tiggi.

ᛒ **Bjarkan**
er laufgat lim
ok lítit tré
ok ungsamligr viðr.
abies buðlungr.

ᛘ **Maðr**
er manns gaman
ok moldar auki
ok skipa skreytir.
homo mildingr.

ᛚ **Lögr**
er vellanda vatn
ok viðr ketill
ok glömmungr grund.
lacus lofðungr.

ᛦ **Ýr**
er bendr bogi
ok brotgjarnt járn
ok fífu fárbauti.
arcus ynglingr.

Modern English Translations

ᚠ **Fé**
Wealth
Source of discord among kinsmen
and fire of the sea
and path of the serpent.

ᚢ **Úr**
Shower
Lamentation of the clouds
and ruin of the hay-harvest
and abomination of the shepherd.

ᚦ **Thurs**
Giant
Torture of women
and cliff-dweller
and husband of a giantess.

ᚬ **Óss**
God
Aged Gautr
and prince of Ásgardr
and lord of Vallhalla.

ᚱ **Reid**
Riding
Joy of the horsemen
and speedy journey
and toil of the steed.

ᚴ **Kaun**
Ulcer
Disease fatal to children

and painful spot
and abode of mortification.

ᚼ Hagall
Hail
Cold grain
and shower of sleet
and sickness of serpents.

ᚾ Naud
Constraint
Grief of the bond-maid
and state of oppression
and toilsome work.

ᛁ Iss
Ice
Bark of rivers
and roof of the wave
and destruction of the doomed.

ᛅ Ár
Plenty
Boon to men
and good summer
and thriving crops.

ᛋ Sól
Sun
Shield of the clouds
and shining ray
and destroyer of ice.

ᛏ Tyr
God with one hand

and leavings of the wolf
and prince of temples.

ᛒ **Bjarken**
Birch
Leafy twig
and little tree
and fresh young shrub.

ᛘ **Madr**
Man
Delight of man
and augmentation of the earth
and adorner of ships.

ᛚ **Lögr**
Water
Eddying stream
and broad geysir
and land of the fish.

ᛦ **Yr**
Yew
Bent bow
and brittle iron
and giant of the arrow.

The Anglo-Saxon Rune Poems

The Anglo-Saxon Rune Poems in their Original Old English

ᚠ **Feoh**
byþ frofur fira gehwylcum;
sceal ðeah manna gehwylc miclun hyt dælan
gif he wile for drihtne domes hleotan.

ᚢ Ur
byþ anmod ond oferhyrned,
felafrecne deor, feohteþ mid hornum
mære morstapa; þæt is modig wuht.

ᚦ Ðorn
byþ ðearle scearp; ðegna gehwylcum
anfeng ys yfyl, ungemetum reþe
manna gehwelcum, ðe him mid resteð.

ᚩ Os
byþ ordfruma ælere spræce,
wisdomes wraþu ond witena frofur
and eorla gehwam eadnys ond tohiht.

ᚱ Rad
byþ on recyde rinca gehwylcum
sefte ond swiþhwæt, ðamðe sitteþ on ufan
meare mægenheardum ofer milpaþas.

ᚳ Cen
byþ cwicera gehwam, cuþ on fyre
blac ond beorhtlic, byrneþ oftust
ðær hi æþelingas inne restaþ.

ᚷ Gyfu
gumena byþ gleng and herenys,
wraþu and wyrþscype and wræcna gehwam
ar and ætwist, ðe byþ oþra leas.

ᚹ Wenne
bruceþ, ðe can weana lyt
sares and sorge and him sylfa hæfþ
blæd and blysse and eac byrga geniht.

ᚻ Hægl
byþ hwitust corna; hwyrft hit of heofones lyfte,
wealcaþ hit windes scura; weorþeþ hit to wætere syððan.

ᚾ Nyd
byþ nearu on breostan; weorþeþ hi þeah oft niþa bearnum
to helpe and to hæle gehwæþre, gif hi his hlystaþ æror.

ᛁ Is
byþ ofereald, ungemetum slidor,
glisnaþ glæshluttur gimmum gelicust,
flor forste geworuht, fæger ansyne.

ᛄ Ger
byþ gumena hiht, ðonne God læteþ,
halig heofones cyning, hrusan syllan
beorhte bleda beornum ond ðearfum.

ᛇ Eoh
byþ utan unsmeþe treow,
heard hrusan fæst, hyrde fyres,
wyrtrumun underwreþyd, wyn on eþle.

ᛈ Peorð
byþ symble plega and hlehter
wlancum [on middum], ðar wigan sittaþ
on beorsele bliþe ætsomne.

ᛉ Eolh-secg
eard hæfþ oftust on fenne
wexeð on wature, wundaþ grimme,
blode breneð beorna gehwylcne
ðe him ænigne onfeng gedeþ.

ᛋ Sigel
semannum symble biþ on hihte,
ðonne hi hine feriaþ ofer fisces beþ,
oþ hi brimhengest bringeþ to lande.

ᛏ Tir
biþ tacna sum, healdeð trywa wel
wiþ æþelingas; a biþ on færylde
ofer nihta genipu, næfre swiceþ.

ᛒ Beorc
byþ bleda leas, bereþ efne swa ðeah
tanas butan tudder, biþ on telgum wlitig,
heah on helme hrysted fægere,
geloden leafum, lyfte getenge.

ᛖ Eh
byþ for eorlum æþelinga wyn,
hors hofum wlanc, ðær him hæleþ ymb[e]
welege on wicgum wrixlaþ spræce
and biþ unstyllum æfre frofur.

ᛗ Man
byþ on myrgþe his magan leof:
sceal þeah anra gehwylc oðrum swican,
forðum drihten wyle dome sine
þæt earme flæsc eorþan betæcan.

ᛚ Lagu
byþ leodum langsum geþuht,
gif hi sculun neþan on nacan tealtum
and hi sæyþa swyþe bregaþ
and se brimhengest bridles ne gym[eð].

ᛝ Ing
wæs ærest mid East-Denum
gesewen secgun, oþ he siððan est
ofer wæg gewat; wæn æfter ran;
ðus Heardingas ðone hæle nemdun.

ᛟ Eþel
byþ oferleof æghwylcum men,
gif he mot ðær rihtes and gerysena on
brucan on bolde bleadum oftast.

ᛞ Dæg
byþ drihtnes sond, deore mannum,
mære metodes leoht, myrgþ and tohiht
eadgum and earmum, eallum brice.

ᚪ Ac
byþ on eorþan elda bearnum
flæsces fodor, fereþ gelome
ofer ganotes bæþ; garsecg fandaþ
hwæþer ac hæbbe æþele treowe.

ᚫ Æsc
biþ oferheah, eldum dyre
stiþ on staþule, stede rihte hylt,
ðeah him feohtan on firas monige.

ᚣ Yr
byþ æþelinga and eorla gehwæs
wyn and wyrþmynd, byþ on wicge fæger,
fæstlic on færelde, fyrdgeatewa sum.

ᛡ **Iar**
byþ eafix and ðeah a bruceþ
fodres on foldan, hafaþ fægerne eard
wætre beworpen, ðær he wynnum leofaþ.

ᛠ **Ear**
byþ egle eorla gehwylcun,
ðonn[e] fæstlice flæsc onginneþ,
hraw colian, hrusan ceosan
blac to gebeddan; bleda gedreosaþ,
wynna gewitaþ, wera geswicaþ.

Modern English Translations

ᚠ **Feoh**
Wealth is a comfort to all men;
yet must every man bestow it freely,
if he wish to gain honour in the sight of the Lord.

ᚢ **Ur**
The aurochs is proud and has great horns;
it is a very savage beast and fights with its horns;
a great ranger of the moors, it is a creature of mettle.

ᛞ **Thorn**
The thorn is exceedingly sharp,
an evil thing for any knight to touch,
uncommonly severe on all who sit among them.

ᚩ Os
The mouth is the source of all language,
a pillar of wisdom and a comfort to wise men,
a blessing and a joy to every knight.

ᚱ Rad

Riding seems easy to every warrior while he is indoors
and very courageous to him who traverses the high-roads
on the back of a stout horse.

ᚳ Cen

The torch is known to every living man by its pale,
bright flame;
it always burns where princes sit within.

ᚷ Gyfu

Generosity brings credit and honour, which support
one's dignity;
it furnishes help and subsistence
to all broken men who are devoid of aught else.

ᚹ Wynn

Bliss he enjoys who knows not suffering, sorrow nor
anxiety,
and has prosperity and happiness and a good enough
house.

ᚻ Haegl

Hail is the whitest of grain;
it is whirled from the vault of heaven
and is tossed about by gusts of wind
and then it melts into water.

ᚾ Nyd

Trouble is oppressive to the heart;
yet often it proves a source of help and salvation
to the children of men, to everyone who heeds it betimes.

ᛁ Is

Ice is very cold and immeasurably slippery;

it glistens as clear as glass and most like to gems;
it is a floor wrought by the frost, fair to look upon.

ᛄ Ger

Summer is a joy to men, when God, the holy King of Heaven,
suffers the earth to bring forth shining fruits
for rich and poor alike.

ᛇ Eoh

The yew is a tree with rough bark,
hard and fast in the earth, supported by its roots,
a guardian of flame and a joy upon an estate.

ᛈ Peordh

Peorth is a source of recreation and amusement to the great,
where warriors sit blithely together in the banqueting hall.

ᛉ Eolh

The Eolh-sedge is mostly to be found in a marsh;
it grows in the water and makes a ghastly wound,
covering with blood every warrior who touches it.

ᛋ Sigel

The sun is ever a joy in the hopes of seafarers
when they journey away over the fishes' bath,
until the course of the deep bears them to land.

ᛏ Tir

Tiw is a guiding star; well does it keep faith with princes;
it is ever on its course over the mists of night and never fails.

ᛒ Beorc
The poplar bears no fruit; yet without seed it brings forth suckers,
for it is generated from its leaves.
Splendid are its branches and gloriously adorned
its lofty crown which reaches to the skies.

ᛖ Eh
The horse is a joy to princes in the presence of warriors.
A steed in the pride of its hoofs,
when rich men on horseback bandy words about it;
and it is ever a source of comfort to the restless.

ᛗ Mann
The joyous man is dear to his kinsmen;
yet every man is doomed to fail his fellow,
since the Lord by his decree will commit the vile carrion to the earth.

ᛚ Lagu
The ocean seems interminable to men,
if they venture on the rolling bark
and the waves of the sea terrify them
and the courser of the deep heed not its bridle.

ᛝ Ing
Ing was first seen by men among the East-Danes,
till, followed by his chariot,
he departed eastwards over the waves.
So the Heardingas named the hero.

ᛟ Ethel
An estate is very dear to every man,
if he can enjoy there in his house
whatever is right and proper in constant prosperity.

ᛞ Dæg
Day, the glorious light of the Creator, is sent by the Lord;
it is beloved of men, a source of hope and happiness
to rich and poor,
and of service to all.

ᚪ Ac
The oak fattens the flesh of pigs for the children of men.
Often it traverses the gannet's bath,
and the ocean proves whether the oak keeps faith
in honourable fashion.

ᚫ Æsc
The ash is exceedingly high and precious to men.
With its sturdy trunk it offers a stubborn resistance,
though attacked by many a man.

ᚣ Yr
Yr is a source of joy and honour to every prince and knight;
it looks well on a horse and is a reliable equipment
for a journey.

ᛡ Ior
Ior is a river fish and yet it always feeds on land;
it has a fair abode encompassed by water, where it
lives in happiness.

ᛠ Ear
The grave is horrible to every knight,
when the corpse quickly begins to cool
and is laid in the bosom of the dark earth.
Prosperity declines, happiness passes away
and covenants are broken.

Rune Poem Comparison:

Rune	Younger Futhark		Anglo-Saxon
	Norwegian Poems	*Icelandic Poems*	*Old English Poems*
ᚠ ᚠ	**Fe** Wealth is a source of discord among kinsmen; the wolf lives in the forest.	**Fé** Source of discord among kinsmen and fire of the sea and path of the serpent.	**Feoh** Wealth is a comfort to all men; yet, must every man bestow it freely if he wish to gain honour in the sight of the Lord.
ᚢ ᚢ	**Ur** Dross comes from bad iron; the reindeer often races over the frozen snow.	**Úr** Lamentation of the clouds and ruin of the hay-harvest and abomination of the shepherd.	**Ur** The aurochs is proud and has great horns; it is a very savage beast and fights with its horns; a great ranger of the moors, it is a creature of mettle.
ᚦ ᚦ	**Thurs** Giant causes anguish to women; misfortune makes few men cheerful.	**Thurs** Torture of women and cliff-dweller and husband of a giantess.	**Thorn** The thorn is exceedingly sharp, an evil thing for any knight to touch, uncommonly severe on all who sit among them.

Rune	Younger Futhark		Anglo-Saxon
	Norwegian Poems	*Icelandic Poems*	*Old English Poems*
ᚬ ᚭ ᚩ	**As** Estuary is the way of most journeys; but a scabbard is of swords.	**Óss (God)** Aged Gautr and prince of Ásgardr and lord of Vallhalla.	**Os** The mouth is the source of all language, a pillar of wisdom and a comfort to wise men, a blessing and a joy to every knight.
ᚱ ᚱ	**Reidh** Riding is said to be the worst thing for horses; Reginn forged the finest sword.	**Reid (Riding)** Joy of the horsemen and speedy journey and toil of the steed.	**Rad** Riding seems easy to every warrior while he is indoors and very courageous to him who traverses the high-roads on the back of a stout horse.
ᚴ ᚳ	**Kaun** Ulcer is fatal to children; death makes a corpse pale.	**Kaun** Disease fatal to children and painful spot and abode of mortification.	**Cen** The torch is known to every living man by its pale, bright flame; it always burns where princes sit within.

Rune	Younger Futhark		Anglo-Saxon
	Norwegian Poems	*Icelandic Poems*	*Old English Poems*
ᚷ	**Hagall** Hail is the coldest of grain; Christ created the world of old.	**Hagall** Cold grain and shower of sleet and sickness of serpents.	**Gyfu** Generosity brings credit and honour, which support one's dignity; it furnishes help and subsistence to all broken men who are devoid of aught else.
ᚹ	**Naudhr** Constraint gives scant choice; a naked man is chilled by the frost.	**Naud** Grief of the bond-maid and state of oppression and toilsome work.	**Wynn** Bliss he enjoys who knows not suffering, sorrow nor anxiety, and has prosperity and happiness and a good enough house.
ᚼ ᚾ ᚻ	**Isa** Ice we call the broad bridge; the blind man must be led.	**Iss** Bark of rivers and roof of the wave and destruction of the doomed.	**Haegl** Hail is the whitest of grain; it is whirled from the vault of heaven and is tossed about by gusts of wind and then it melts into water.

Rune	Younger Futhark		Anglo-Saxon
	Norwegian Poems	*Icelandic Poems*	*Old English Poems*
ᚼ	**Ar** Plenty is a boon to men; I say that Frodi was generous.	**Âr** Boon to men and good summer and thriving crops.	**Nyd** Trouble is oppressive to the heart; yet often it proves a source of help and salvation to the children of men, to everyone who heeds it betimes.
ᛁ	**Sol** Sun is the light of the world; I bow to the divine decree.	**Sól - Sun** Shield of the clouds and shining ray and destroyer of ice.	**Is** Ice is very cold and immeasurably slippery; it glistens as clear as glass and most like to gems; it is a floor wrought by the frost, fair to look upon.
ᛄ	**Tyr** Tyr is a one-handed god; often has the smith to blow.	**Tyr** God with one hand and leavings of the wolf and prince of temples.	**Ger** Summer is a joy to men, when God, the holy King of Heaven, suffers the earth to bring forth shining fruits for rich and poor alike.

Rune	Younger Futhark		Anglo-Saxon
	Norwegian Poems	*Icelandic Poems*	*Old English Poems*
ᛇ	**Bjarkan** Birch has the greenest leaves of any shrub; Loki was fortunate in his deceit.	**Bjarken** Leafy twig and little tree and fresh young shrub.	**Eoh** The yew is a tree with rough bark, hard and fast in the earth, supported by its roots, a guardian of flame and a joy upon an estate.
ᛈ	**Madhr** Man is an augmentation of the dust; great is the claw of the hawk.	**Madr** Delight of man and augmentation of the earth and adorner of ships.	**Peordh** Peorth is a source of recreation and amusement to the great, where warriors sit blithely together in the banqueting-hall.
ᚨ	**Logr** A waterfall is a River which falls from a mountain-side; but ornaments are of gold.	**Lögr** Eddying stream and broad geysir and land of the fish.	**Eolh** The Eolh-sedge is mostly to be found in a marsh; it grows in the water and makes a ghastly wound, covering with blood every warrior who touches it.

Rune	Younger Futhark		Anglo-Saxon
	Norwegian Poems	*Icelandic Poems*	*Old English Poems*
ᛉ	**Yr** Yew is the greenest of trees in winter; it is wont to crackle when it burns.	**Yr (Yew)** Bent bow and brittle iron and giant of the arrow.	
ᛋ ᛌ			**Sigel** The sun is ever a joy in the hopes of seafarers when they journey away over the fishes' bath, until the courser of the deep bears them to land.
ᛏ ᛐ			**Tir** Tir is a guiding star; well does it keep faith with princes; it is ever on its course over the mists of night and never fails.

Rune	Younger Futhark		Anglo-Saxon
	Norwegian Poems	*Icelandic Poems*	*Old English Poems*
ᛒ ᛓ ᛒ			**Beorc** The poplar bears no fruit; yet without seed it brings forth suckers, for it is generated from its leaves. Splendid are its branches and gloriously adorned its lofty crown which reaches to the skies.
ᛖ			**Eh** The horse is a joy to princes in the presence of warriors. A steed in the pride of its hoofs, when rich men on horseback bandy words about it; and it is ever a source of comfort to the restless.

Rune	Younger Futhark		Anglo-Saxon
	Norwegian Poems	*Icelandic Poems*	*Old English Poems*
ᛘ ᛚ ᛗ			**Mann** The joyous man is dear to his kinsmen; yet every man is doomed to fail his fellow, since the Lord by his decree will commit the vile carrion to the earth.
ᛚ			**Lagu** The ocean seems interminable to men, if they venture on the rolling bark and the waves of the sea terrify them and the courser of the deep heed not its bridle.
ᛝ			**Ing** Ing was first seen by men among the East-Danes, till, followed by his chariot, he departed eastwards over the waves. So the Heardingas named the hero.

Rune	Younger Futhark		Anglo-Saxon
	Norwegian Poems	*Icelandic Poems*	*Old English Poems*
ᛟ			**Ethel** An estate is very dear to every man, if he can enjoy there in his house whatever is right and proper in constant prosperity.
ᛞ			**Dæg** Day, the glorious light of the Creator, is sent by the Lord; it is beloved of men, a source of hope and happiness to rich and poor, and of service to all.
ᚨ			**Ac** The oak fattens the flesh of pigs for the children of men. Often it traverses the gannet's bath, and the ocean proves whether the oak keeps faith in honourable fashion.

Rune	Younger Futhark		Anglo-Saxon
	Norwegian Poems	*Icelandic Poems*	*Old English Poems*
ᚫ			**Æsc** The ash is exceedingly high and precious to men. With its sturdy trunk it offers a stubborn resistance, though attacked by many a man.
ᛦ ı ᚣ			**Yr** Yr is a source of joy and honour to every prince and knight; it looks well on a horse and is a reliable equipment for a journey.
ᛡ			**Ior** Ior is a river fish and yet it always feeds on land; it has a fair abode encompassed by water, where it lives in happiness.

Rune	Younger Futhark		Anglo-Saxon
	Norwegian Poems	*Icelandic Poems*	*Old English Poems*
ᛠ			**Ear** The grave is horrible to every knight, when the corpse quickly begins to cool and is laid in the bosom of the dark earth. Prosperity declines, happiness passes away and covenants are broken.

Runic Astral Planes

Astral travel, also known as astral projection, is a phenomenon in which one's consciousness leaves the physical body and travels to other realms or dimensions. It's important to note that astral travel is a subjective experience and the perspectives on it vary widely. Some people believe it is a spiritual journey, while others view it as a product of the imagination or altered states of consciousness. If you're interested in exploring astral travel, here are some general guidelines:

1. **Prepare Your Mind:** Begin by focusing on a specific rune that holds significance for you. Concentrate on its symbolism and energy. Practice meditation or deep breathing exercises to calm your mind and attune yourself to the energies associated with the chosen rune.
2. **Create a Relaxing Environment (the *Ve*):** Choose a quiet and comfortable space where you won't be disturbed. Dim the lights and eliminate potential distractions, creating an

environment that resonates with the spiritual essence of the chosen rune.

3. **Choose the Right Time:** Select a time that aligns with the energies of the chosen rune. Consider the historical or mythological associations of the rune for guidance.
4. **Physical Comfort:** Lie down in a comfortable position, allowing the energy of the rune to envelop you. Ensure that your body is completely relaxed, using progressive muscle relaxation.
5. **Focus on Your Breath and the Rune:** Concentrate on your breathing, using it as a rhythmic guide to synchronize with the spiritual vibrations of the chosen rune. Direct your focus towards the rune, envisioning it as a portal to the astral realm.
6. **Reach the Hypnagogic State:** Transition into a hypnagogic state while maintaining your concentration on the rune. Feel its energy guiding you towards the threshold between wakefulness and the astral realm.
7. **Visualization:** Picture the chosen rune transforming into a gateway, inviting you to enter the astral home of rune spirits. Visualize yourself crossing this threshold with intention and respect.
8. **Energy Work:** Engage in energy work, imagining the rune's energy enveloping you and facilitating the separation of your consciousness from the physical body.
9. **Intent and Willpower:** Clearly state your intention to journey into the astral realm guided by the energies of the chosen rune. Harness the willpower associated with the runic symbolism.
10. **Be Patient:** Allow the spiritual journey to unfold, recognizing that the rune serves as a spiritual guide. Be patient and open to the experiences that may manifest.
11. **Keep a Journal:** Record your experiences, emphasizing the interactions with rune spirits and any insights gained during your astral journey through the chosen rune's portal.

Brief Guidance on a Hypnagogic State

The hypnagogic state, also known as the hypnagogic phase, is a transitional state of consciousness that occurs between wakefulness and sleep. It represents the onset of the sleep cycle and is characterized by various sensory experiences, such as vivid imagery, hallucinations, and a sense of floating or falling. This state is often accompanied by a shift in perception and a feeling of detachment from the physical body.

Key features of the hypnagogic state include:

1. **Vivid Imagery:** Individuals in the hypnagogic state often experience vivid and sometimes dream-like images. These can range from ordinary scenes to more fantastical or abstract visuals.
2. **Hypnagogic Hallucinations:** Some people may experience auditory hallucinations, such as hearing voices or sounds. These hallucinations can be quite vivid and may seem intensely real.
3. **Floating or Falling Sensations:** There is a common sensation of floating, flying, or falling, which adds to the dream-like quality of the experience.
4. **Transitional Consciousness:** The hypnagogic state marks the transition from full wakefulness to the deeper stages of sleep. It is a brief period that occurs as the mind and body prepare to enter the sleep cycle.
5. **Hypnagogic Jerks:** Some individuals may experience sudden muscle contractions or jerks known as hypnagogic jerks or sleep starts during this phase.

Rune Spirits

Runes are portals to powerful spirits. It is important to cultivate a relationship through direct experience.

Homework

Take one rune every night and meditate on it, then go to the rune's astral plane. Write down your surroundings upon returning; if you met the spirit of that rune, write down his demeanour and attributes.

I have used the Elder Futhark here as an example, but please do explore other runic sets as well.

1. **Fehu (ᚠ):** Fehu is a prosperous merchant with a golden touch. They have a hearty laugh and a generous heart, always willing to share their wealth with those in need. He dwells in a lavish manor adorned with opulent decor, surrounded by lush gardens and a river filled with gleaming fish.
2. **Uruz (ᚢ):** Uruz is a powerful and rugged warrior. Their physique is a testament to their strength and resilience. They have a brave spirit and an unwavering determination to overcome any obstacle. Uruz resides in a remote mountain fortress. His home is built from stone and surrounded by untamed wilderness with a breathtaking view of towering peaks.
3. **Thurisaz (ᛏᚺ):** Thurisaz is a sentinel standing at the gates of protection. He is both fierce and vigilant, ready to confront any threat with a sharp mind and a strong defense. His abode is a wooden cabin nestled among the trees with a tall watchtower to survey the surrounding wilderness.
4. **Ansuz (ᚨ):** Ansuz is a wise sage, often found with a quill and parchment, recording ancient knowledge and imparting wisdom to those who seek it. They have a voice that resonates with clarity and divine inspiration. Ansuz lives in a hidden library of ancient tomes and scrolls. The library is a vast chamber filled with countless books, with a soft, otherworldly light that bathes the room.
5. **Raido (ᚱ):** Raido is a skilled traveler who is always on a journey of discovery. He embodies the spirit of movement, both physical and spiritual, and has a knack for guiding others on their paths. His home is a cozy cottage near a

crossroad. Maps and globes adorn the walls, and the space is filled with the artifacts of their adventures.

6. **Kaunan (ᚲ):** Kaunan is a healer with gentle hands and a nurturing presence. They use the warmth of their heart to bring comfort and well-being to those in their care. Her home is a tranquil sanctuary with herbs, medicinal plants, and soothing streams where visitors seek solace.
7. **Gebo (ᚷ):** Gebo is a diplomat, fostering harmonious relationships between individuals and communities. He has an open heart and a spirit of generosity, always striving to find balance in exchanges. Gebo lives in a grand estate with beautifully manicured gardens. The halls are adorned with tapestries symbolizing unity, and their dining room is often filled with diverse guests.
8. **Wunjo (ᚹ):** Wunjo is a joyful bard, bringing happiness and harmony through music and art. Their laughter is infectious, and their creative spirit uplifts those around them. Musical instruments, paintings, and sculptures fill the space of his home, creating an atmosphere of endless celebration.
9. **Hagalaz (ᚺ):** Hagalaz is a force of nature, often appearing as a giant, stormy figure. He represent the transformative power of destruction and creation, reminding us that change is inevitable. Hagalaz resides on a remote, storm-swept island. His home is the mountain itself, constantly shaped and reshaped by the tempestuous weather.
10. **Nauthiz (ᚾ):** Nauthiz is a stoic hermit teaching the valuable lessons of endurance and self-discipline. They guide individuals through the challenges of life, helping them find inner strength. Nauthiz lives atop a snow-covered mountain. Their dwelling is a simple, solitary cabin where seekers of wisdom brave the harsh conditions to find inner strength.
11. **Isa (ᛁ):** Isa is an ice mage, dwelling in the frozen realms of introspection. They represent stillness and the power of meditation, guiding seekers to find clarity within the frozen silence. Isa resides in a crystalline ice palace at the

heart of a frozen tundra. The palace is a serene, silent haven, illuminated by the gentle glow of ice crystals.

12. **Jera (ᛃ):** Jera is a farmer, tending to the cycles of growth and harvest. They understand the importance of patience and the rewards that come with the passage of time. His home is a charming farmhouse and the land around it is filled with ripening crops.
13. **Eihwaz (ᛖᛁ):** Eihwaz is a wise tree standing in an ancient forest, deeply rooted in the earth and reaching toward the heavens. An embodiment of the balance between the material and the spiritual, offering stability and growth. In the vast hollowed tree trunk, seekers come to meditate and connect with the earth.
14. **Perthro (ᛈ):** Perthro is a mysterious oracle veiled in secrets and hidden truths. They reveal the unknown and guide those who seek insight into the mysteries of fate. Perthro can be found in a dimly lit, mysterious chamber.
15. **Algiz (ᛉ):** Algiz is a guardian with raised arms, offering protection and guidance to those in need. They provide a shield against harm and instill courage in those who stand by their side. The dwelling is fortified, with tall walls and watchtowers, offering protection to all who seek refuge.
16. **Sowilo (ᛋ):** Sowilo is a radiant sun deity, illuminating the path with clarity and warmth. They bring enlightenment and energy, dispelling darkness and doubt. The palace of light is on a mountain top. It is made of glistening crystal and overlooks a vast, sun-kissed landscape.
17. **Tiwaz (ᛏ):** Tiwaz is a noble warrior, upholding principles of justice and honor. They represent sacrifice for a greater cause and the courage to face challenges head-on. The noble warrior lives in a disciplined martial training camp. The surroundings are meticulously organized, and the camp is a place of honor and discipline.
18. **Berkano (ᛒ):** Berkano is a nurturing mother, providing comfort and support to all in her care. She symbolizes

fertility, growth, and the cycles of life. The nurturing mother resides in a cozy cottage surrounded by a vibrant, flourishing garden. The air is filled with the scent of blooming flowers and nurturing herbs.

19. **Ehwaz (ᛖ):** Ehwaz is a swift and graceful horse, carrying those who ride with purpose and partnership. They symbolize collaboration and the power of working together. Ehwaz lives in a spacious, well-kept stable.
20. **Mannaz (ᛗ):** Mannaz is a philosopher, seeking to understand the depths of human nature and relationships. They represent the potential for self-awareness and enlightenment. In a forest clearing, a small house is a contemplative space filled with books and symbols of self-awareness.
21. **Laguz (ᛚ):** Laguz is a tranquil mermaid, dwelling in the depths of emotion and intuition. They guide seekers through the waters of the subconscious, encouraging reflection and insight.
22. **Ingwaz (ᚾᚷ):** Ingwaz is a fertile field, representing the potential for growth and abundance. They signify a period of gestation and the promise of a bountiful harvest.
23. **Dagaz (ᛞ):** Dagaz is a radiant dawn, bringing a new beginning and enlightenment. They symbolize the transformation from darkness to light and the eternal cycle of day and night.
24. **Othala (ᛟ):** Othala is a wise ancestor, guarding the ancestral homelands and traditions. They represent heritage, inheritance, and the connection to one's roots. Othala lives in a historical homestead surrounded by ancient forests and stone circles. Their abode is a place of heritage, tradition, and deep-rooted connection to the past.

Historical Runic Magick

There is evidence that, in addition to being a writing system, runes historically served magickal purposes. This is the case from the earliest epigraphic evidence of the Roman to the Germanic Iron

Age, with non-linguistic inscriptions and the alu word (more in "Book of Spells"). An erilaz appears to have been a person versed in runes, including their magick applications (approximately fifth to seventh century).

In medieval sources, notably, the "Sigrdrífumál" poem found in the *Poetic Edda*, "victory runes" are instructed to be carved on a sword, "some on the grasp and some on the inlay, and name Tyr twice."

In the early modern period and more recent history, related folklore and superstition is recorded in the form of the Icelandic magickal staves. In the early twentieth century, Germanic mysticism coined new forms of "runic magick," some of which were continued or developed further by contemporary adherents of Germanic Neopaganism. Modern systems of runic divination are based on Hermeticism, classical Occultism, and the *I Ching*.

Historically, it is known that the Germanic people used various forms of divination and means of reading omens.

Tacitus (*Germania* 10) gives a detailed account (AD 98):

> *They attach the highest importance to the taking of auspices and casting lots. Their usual procedure with the lot is simple. They cut off a branch from a nut-bearing tree and slice it into strips. These they mark with different signs and throw them at random onto a white cloth. Then the state's priest, if it is an official consultation, or the father of the family, in a private one, offers prayer to the gods and looking up towards heaven picks up three strips, one at a time, and, according to which sign they have previously been marked with, makes his interpretation. If the lots forbid an undertaking, there is no deliberation that day about the matter in question. If they allow it, further confirmation is required by taking auspices.*

The inscription on the Kylver Stone ends with a stacked bind-rune combining six Tiwaz runes used to invoke the god Tyr and four Ansuz runes to invoke the Æsir.

The Ansuz and Tiwaz runes in particular seem to have magkical significance in the early Elder Futhark period.

The "Sigrdrífumál" instruction of "name Tyr twice" is reminiscent of the double or triple-"stacked Tyr" bind-runes (found on Seeland-II-C or the Lindholm amulet in the ᚨᚨᚨᚨᚨᚨᚨᚨᛉᛉᛉᛝᛝᛝ-ᛒ-ᛗᚢᛏᛏᛏ sequence, which, besides stacked Tyr, involves multiple repetition of Ansuz, but also triple occurrence of Algiz and Naudiz).

Many inscriptions also have apparently meaningless utterances interpreted as magickal chants, such as "ᛏᚢᚹᚨᛏᚢᚹᚨ" (Vadstena bracteate), "ᚨᚨᚦᚢᚨᚨᚨᛚᛁᛁᚨ" (DR BR42), or "ᚷᚨᚷᚨᚷᚨ" (Kragehul I).

ᚨᛚᚢ is a charm word appearing on numerous artifacts found in Central and Northern Europe dating from the Germanic Iron Age. The word is the most common of the early runic charm words and can appear either alone or as part of an apparent formula. The origin and meaning of the word are matters of dispute, though a general agreement exists among scholars that the word either represents amulet magick or is a metaphor for it.

A few Viking Age rings with runic inscriptions of an apparently magickal nature were found, among which was the Kingmoor Ring. The phrase "runes of power" is found on two rune stones in Sweden: DR 357 from Stentoften and DR 360 from Björketorp. Runestones with curses include: DR 81 in Skjern, DR 83 in Sønder Vinge, DR 209 in Glavendrup, DR 230 from Tryggevælde, DR 338 in Glemminge, and Vg 67 in Saleby.

The most prolific source for runic magick in the *Poetic Edda* is the "Sigrdrífumál," where the valkyrie Sigrdrífa (Brynhild) presents Sigurd with a memory-draught of ale that had been charmed with "gladness runes" (stanza 5):

Biór fori ec þer / brynþings apaldr!
magni blandinn / oc megintíri;
fullr er hann lioþa / oc licnstafa,
godra galdra / oc gamanruna.

Beer I bring thee, tree of battle!
Mingled of strength and mighty fame;

Charms it holds and healing signs,
Spells full good, and gladness-runes.

She goes on to give advice on the magickal runes in seven further stanzas. In all instances, the runes are used for actual magick (apotropaic or ability-enhancing spells) rather than for divination:

- **Sigrúnar:** "victory runes" (stanza 6, presumably referring to the "t" rune named for Tyr, with runes to be carved on the sword hilt).
- **Ølrunar:** "Ale-runes" (stanza 7, a protective spell against being bewitched by means of ale served by the host's wife; naudiz is to be marked on one's fingernails and laukaz on the cup).
- **Biargrunar:** "birth-runes" (stanza 8, a spell to facilitate childbirth).
- **Brimrunar:** "wave-runes" (stanza 9, a spell for the protection of ships, with runes to be carved on the stem and on the rudder).
- **Limrunar:** "branch-runes" (stanza 10, a healing spell, with runes to be carved on trees "with boughs to the eastward bent").
- **Malrunar:** "speech-runes" (stanza 11, the stanza is corrupt, but apparently referred to a spell to improve one's rhetorical ability at the thing).
- **Hugrunar:** "thought-runes" (stanza 12, the stanza is incomplete, but clearly discussed a spell to improve one's wit).

The *Poetic Edda* also seems to corroborate the magickal significance of the runes found in the "Hávamál," where Odin mentions runes in contexts of divination, healing, and necromancy a number of times:

- "Certain is that which is sought from runes / That the gods so great have made / And the Master-Poet painted" (79).
- "Of runes heard I words, nor were counsels wanting / At the hall of Hor" (111).

- "Grass cures the scab / and runes the sword-cut" (137).
- "Runes shalt thou find / and fateful signs" (143).
- "If high on a tree / I see a hanged man swing / So do I write and color the runes / That forth he fares / And to me talks" (158).

One oft-cited source for the practice of runic divination (*dubious—discuss*) is found in Snorri Sturluson's "Ynglinga Saga," where Granmar, the King of Södermanland, travels to the Temple at Uppsala for the seasonal blót. "There, the chips fell in a way that said that he would not live long;" original text: *Féll honum þá svo spánn sem hann mundi eigi lengi lifa* (*Heimskringla*, Chapter 38).

Another source is in the *Vita Ansgari*, the biography of Ansgar, the Archbishop of Hamburg-Bremen, which was written by a monk named Rimbert, in which he details the custom of casting lots by the Norse pagans (Chapters XXVI–XXX). The chips and the lots, however, can be explained respectively as a *blótspánn* ("sacrificial chip") and a *hlauttein* ("lot-twig"), which, according to Foote and Wilson, would be "marked, possibly with sacrificial blood, shaken and thrown down like dice, and their positive or negative significance then decided" (*The Viking Achievement*, 401).

Egil's Saga features several incidents of runic magick. The most celebrated is the scene where Egil discovers (and destroys) a poisoned drink prepared for him by cutting his hand and carving runes on the drinking horn, painting the runes with blood.

Types of Runic Magick

Time to get a little more practical and try our hands at crafting runes ourselves. Here, we will concentrate on the three main types of rune magick:

1. Single-Rune Forms
2. Runic Bands
3. Bind-Runes

Of course, you can add to the spells or even combine the types of runic magick into one grander ritual.

Single-Rune Form Rituals

Runes are not just mere letters or even representations of concepts, but full-blown spirits in their own right. Invoking/evoking a separate god will definitely add to the power and megin of a spell, but it is not always necessary or even conducive to your outcome. Let's explore the world of single-rune form magick by going through the Elder Futhark. Spell can obviously be written for any of the runes, in any of the systems.

Earlier, we discussed the runes in more detail, here we take just the Elder Futhark for an example and see how they can and should be employed into runic magick. This is not a comprehensive list but a list of the most common outcomes if a single rune is to be employed.

ᚠ

Calling forth Audumla, Frey, Freya, Njord, or any form of wealth magick.

ᚢ

Healing, strength, and returning to a primitive state.

ᚦ

Calling Thurs, powers beyond your power, curses, strength, and great energy.

ᚨ

Wisdom, poetry, communication, and art; great for wind magick and vision quests.

ᚱ

Traveling, both to protect and to increase swiftness.

ᚲ

A torch to illuminate the darkness, helps in works of knowledge seeking. In later futharks, it can be seen as meaning "ulcher." Thus, it is great in a variety of curses.

ᚷ

Sacrifice, a gift for a gift from the gods.

ᚹ

Victory and ensuring pleasant surroundings.

ᚺ

Can be used destructively, a curse from nature.

ᚾ

Help in surviving hardship.

ᛁ

Seeing through the veil.

Bringing forth a desired result.

ᛇ

Grants physical and spiritual endurance; in shamanistic works, it helps bridge the gap between the seen and the unseen worlds.

ᛈ

Creating pleasurable circumstances.

ᛉ

Protection magick.

ᛊ

Divine justice, lending power from the sun.

ᛏ

Victory rune, battle magick.

ᛒ

Love, marriage, and home magick.

ᛖ

Strengthening a bond, couple, deal, or relationship.

ᛗ

Amplifying the best qualities of mankind.

ᛚ

Working with the waters of the unseen.

Fertility and works of finance.

Working within a time frame, completion.

Ancestor magick.

The Correct Way to Write in Runes

Runes were not meant to be written in a letter-for-letter translation, but as a phonetic system. Thus, each runic set had its own language or languages that you should use in writing it.

- Elder Futhark—Proto-Norse.
- Marcomannic runes—Proto-Germanic.
- Anglo-Saxon runes—Old English.
- Younger Futhark—Old Norse.
- Medieval runes—North Germanic languages.
- Dalecarlian runes—Elfdalian language.
- Contemporary Icelandic runes—Made to fit most modern languages.
- Armanen runes—Purely twentieth-century esoterica.

In order to correctly write a phrase in runes, we need to translate it into the corresponding spoken language.

For example, if we wanted to translate a phrase to Younger Futhark runes, we first translate it into Old Norse, then into phonics, and finally into runes.

In summary, the translation process would look like this: English—Old Norse—Phonics—Younger Futhark.

In historical contexts, the inscription of runes exhibited a distinctive absence of punctuation or spaces between words. Moreover, duplicate runes were systematically reduced to a singular representation. This unique approach emerged as a pragmatic response to the inherent difficulty and laborious nature of carving additional and superfluous letters into stone surfaces.

Runic Bands

Inscriptions of a runic band containing two or more runes is the oldest form of rune magick ever found.

These spells can be further divided into two categories:

1. Literal runic bands
2. Figurative rune bands

Literal Rune Bands

With literal rune bands, the Vitki writes out quite literally what he wants. You can use a direct English to rune translation or translate the phrase into the appropriate language (e.g. Old Norse for Younger Futhark, Elfdalian for Dalecarlian runes, etc.).

Example:

> "by writing these runes a hundred dollars is mine"
> ᛒᚢᚱᛁᛏᛁᛝᚷᛏᚺᛇᛋᛇᚱᚢᛝᛇᛋᚨᚺᚢᛝᚦᚱᛇᚦᛟᛚᛚᚨᚱᛋᛁᛋᛗᛁᛝᛇ
> (direct English to Younger Futhark translation)

Figurative Rune Bands

With figurative bands, a handful of appropriate runes are selected, and their spirits will be actively called upon in the inscription of those runes. It can definitely be accompanied by galdr—even a simple galdr of resonating the rune name as one carves it...and even writing some rune three times to summon the god/spirit. In various cultures, the act of writing the name of a spirit three times and then knocking onto the object three times again is a quick way to summon said spirit.

The phrase "knock on wood" is a superstition or folk belief that has its origins in various cultures and it is often used to ward off bad luck or to prevent something negative from happening.

Historians suggest that the practice of knocking on wood may have its roots in pagan traditions. It was believed that spirits or supernatural beings inhabited trees, and, by knocking on wood, a person could seek protection or good luck from these spirits.

e.g. ᚠᚠᚠᚷᚹᛃᛈᛇᚾ:·

Bind-Runes

Bind-runes are created by combining two or more runes together to create a ligature of runes.

Bind-runes can be divided into both types and forms.

The two types are the same in the case of runic band spells—literal and figurative.

Further, both types can be divided into:

- Stacked Runes
- Linear Staves
- Radial Bind-Runes/Galdrastafir

Literal Bind-Runes

With literal bind-runes, much like literal runic bands, start out by physically writing out the name or phrase. From there, you can shape your planned bind-rune into one of three forms.

Figurative Bind-Runes

Simply choose the runes from any set that you want your bind-rune to represent or qualities that you want it to possess.

In this example, we will take Courage, Strength, and Wisdom. We will be working in the Elder Futhark. So, we use Tiwaz, Uruz, and Ansuz.

Historically, it was uncommon for more than three runes to be combined, but there is technically no limit to the number of runes you can bind.

Stacked Runes

This is the most common bind-rune and it's made with two (or three) runes that share the same axis.

The modern Bluetooth symbol is a prime example of a stacked bind-rune.

In magick, they are used to manifest your will and your reality. As with all the forms, both literal and figurative runes can be made into any form.

1. Take your name/phrase/selected runes and write them down. If it is quite a lengthy phrase, you may omit the vowels. This is an optional step, but it will make lengthy bind-runes a lot easier, at least on the eyes.
2. Time to translate your name/phrase/spell into runes. This may be done into any runic set, or even into a combination of different sets. This can be a direct English (or any language) to rune translation. Or, if you want it as "Viking"

as possible, translate the phrase into Old Norse and then rewrite it into Younker Futhark runes, as that would be the most Viking Age-appropriate method.

3. Once that you have your phrase in runes, take away all the duplicate runes.
4. ...and now, for the artistic endeavour—stack all the runes that were left over from your deletion stage onto each other in a visually pleasing way...there is obviously more than one way to rearrange runes in this fashion.

Example of a simple runic signature for a certain "John Doe."

1. Take your word or name (Optionally, translate the word/phrase into Old Norse. As this is a name, we will skip this stage).

JOHN DOE

2. Optionally, delete all the vowels, especially useful in longer phrases.

JHND

3. Translate into runes.
4. Stack the runes.

Linear Staves

We can find this type in Scandinavian runic inscriptions. A series of runic letters are written in a specific order along a common axis.

In magick, they are used to attack a problem directly.

Example of a simple runic signature for a certain "John Doe."

1. JOHN DOE (Optionally, translate the phrase into Old Norse. As this is a name, we will skip this stage).
2. If you'd like, delete all the vowels; this is especially useful in longer phrases.

JHND

3. Translate into runes.
4. Draw a vertical line and write down all the above runes in accordance with that axis.

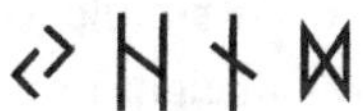

Radial Bind-Runes

We can find inspiration for this type of bind-rune in the Icelandic staves, or Galdrastafir. Each rune or combination of runes stems from a common centrepoint. The famous *Vegvisir* is a prime example of a Galdrastafir.

In magick, they are used in defensive spells and/or amulet creation.

It is worth noting that most Galdrastafir were historically created with a blend of medieval and Dalecarlian runes, as well as primstavs, Malachim, and Alchemy symbols. The runes are often in cipher or Lønnrunerform.

With radial bind-runes, we first have to decide the number of prongs used, which can be three or more. However, that said, the most common is four, six, or eight-pronged (with eight being the clear winner).

A prong may consist of a single rune or a bind-rune on its own. Therefore, an eight-pronged radial rune may be as complex as having eight bind-runes or as simple as just having eight single runes...or one rune used on all eight prongs.

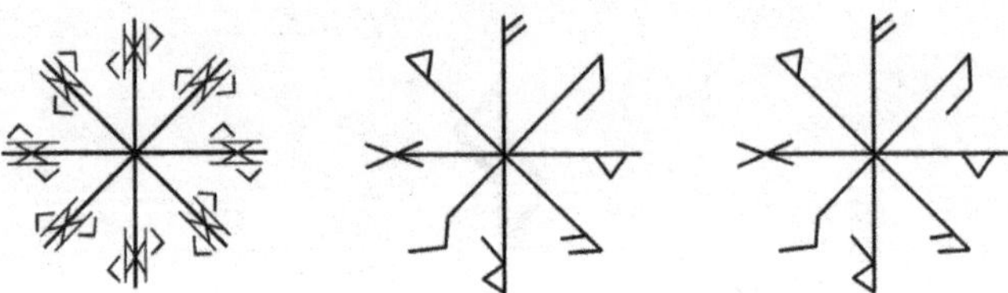

Let's do an example of a simple figurative radial rune for wisdom and courage. We will be using the Elder Futhark for this example. Using the rune Tiwaz for "courage" and Ansuz for "wisdom"...or using a bind-rune consisting out of Tiwaz and Ansuz.

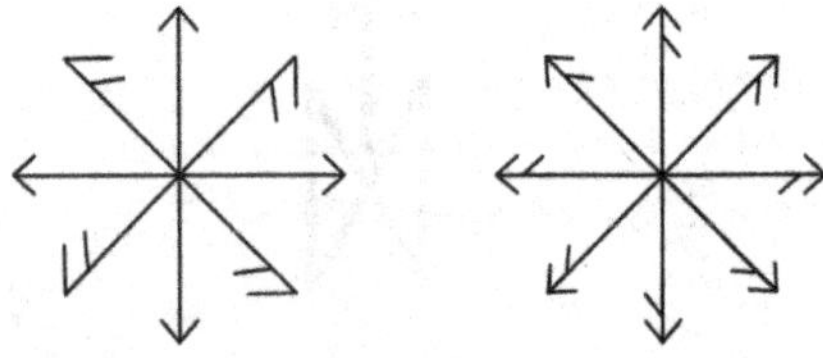

Real Galdrastafir is a type of radial rune system used from the sixteenth century onwards, frequently using Christian or kabballic magick formulas, alchemy, and astrological symbols, alongside Nordic runes of that time.

Lønnruner or Cipher Runes: The Secret Runic Alphabet

Lønnruner means "secret runes" in Norwegian. It was a way to encode runic messages (another method would be to create bind-runes).

How to Create Your Own Lønnruner

1. Choose which runic set to use.
2. Divide the runic system into its aettir.

In this example, we will be using the Elder Futhark.

ᚠᚢᚦᚨᚱᚲᚷᚹᚺᚾᛁᛃᛇᛈᛉᛊᛏᛒᛖᛗᛚᛜᛞᛟ

* **First Aett:** ᚠᚢᚦᚨᚱᚲᚷᚹ
* **Second Aett:** ᚺᚾᛁᛃᛇᛈᛉᛊ
* **Third Aett:** ᛏᛒᛖᛗᛚᛜᛞᛟ

And, it gets even more complicated than this! In some ciphers, the aettir are reversed, so the first aett would be the third and vice versa.

For some Lønnruner:

- **Third Aett:** ᛏᛒᛖᛗᛚᛜᛞᛟ
- **Second Aett:** ᚺᚾᛁᛃᛇᛈᛉᛊ
- **First Aett:** ᚠᚢᚦᚨᚱᚲᚷᚹ

In order to explain the different methods and make things easier, I will use the classification pictured above, but feel free to explore other alphabets (such as the Younger Futhark)!

Choose Your Method

There are many ways to create your own Lønnruner. We can get the best-preserved knowledge in Icelandic manuscripts from the seventeenth and eighteenth centuries.

Here is a selection of the easiest and most straightforward styles, so you can start experimenting at home:

Branch or Twig Style

This style consists of a vertical trunk with a number of twigs on the left and right sides. The number of strokes on the left side indicates the aett, and the ones on the right signify its position within it.

Aett	Lines to the left	Runes (lines to the right)
First Aett	1	ᚠ(1) ᚢ(2) ᚦ(3) ᚨ(4) ᚱ(5) ᚲ(6) ᚷ(7) ᚹ(8)
Second Aett	2	ᚺ(1) ᚾ(2) ᛁ(3) ᛃ(4) ᛇ(5) ᛈ(6) ᛉ(7) ᛊ(8)
Third Aett	3	ᛏ(1) ᛒ(2) ᛖ(3) ᛗ(4) ᛚ(5) ᛜ(6) ᛞ(7) ᛟ(8)

Or:

Aett	Lines to the left	Runes (lines to the right)
Third Aett	1	ᛏ(1) ᛒ(2) ᛖ(3) ᛗ(4) ᛚ(5) ᛜ(6) ᛞ(7) ᛟ(8)

Second Aett	2	ᚺ(1) ᚾ(2) ᛁ(3) ᛃ(4) ᛇ(5) ᛈ(6) ᛉ(7) ᛊ(8)
First Aett	3	ᚠ(1) ᚢ(2) ᚦ(3) ᚨ(4) ᚱ(5) ᚲ(6) ᚷ(7) ᚹ(8)

You can get as creative as you want with the branches. In some examples, the branches are simply a straight line; in others, there is a curve to them that also serves as a way to differentiate each word.

Let's work with the first example table:

Thus:

ᚠᚢᚦᚨᚱᚲ =

Or:

ᚠᚢᚦᚨᚱᚲ =

Or:

ᚠᚢᚦᚨᚱᚲ =

Homework

Decipher the following branch style Lønnruner (remember that you can swap the first and the third aettir). Hint; I worked in Elder Futhark with a direct English translation.

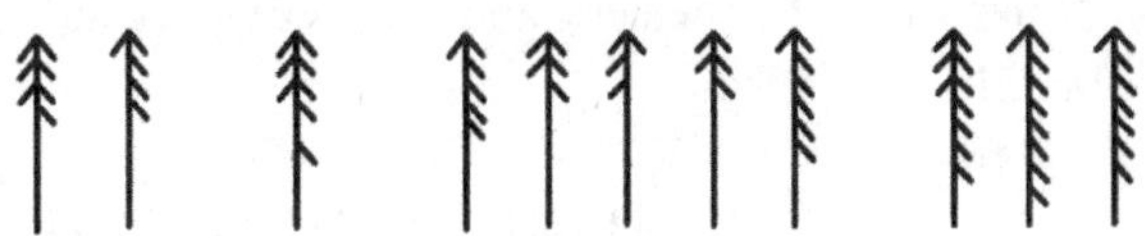

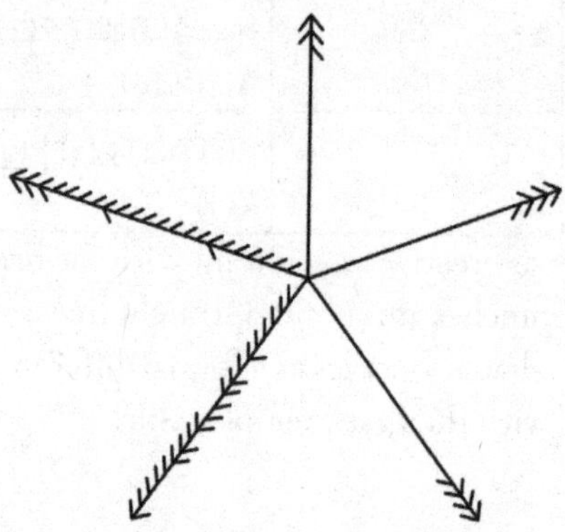

Now, just for fun, we can arrange the same message in a radial bind-rune form without changing the meaning.

Tent Style

The tent style starts with an X shape, which has room for two runes. We read these runes clockwise, so the first arm (upper-left) is the aett and the second is the position within the aett.

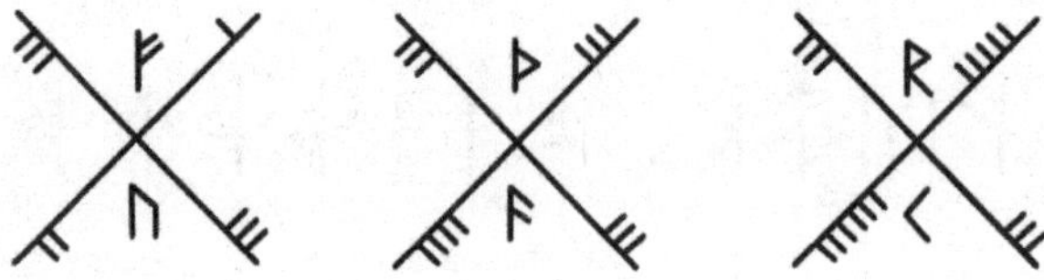

Lines

This method is also known as the Isa rune system because the strokes are similar to the Isa rune. It's the easiest method of them all: the first long lines would be the aett, and the short lines indicate the position within it.

ᚠᚢᚦᚨᚱᚲ =

Using a Specific Rune

I'm sure that, after reading the methods listed previously, you've already got the hang of this! There are some examples that use a specific rune, so the one facing to the left would indicate the aett, and the ones facing to the right the position.

Let's take the Eihwaz rune, for example:

ᛇᛇ ᛇᛇᛇ ᛇᛇᛇᛇ ᛇᛇᛇᛇᛇ ᛇᛇᛇᛇᛇᛇ

Be Creative with Your Lønnruner

Cryptography is an art in itself and has been used by many cultures for thousands of years with different purposes. In the same way, a Lønnruner can be as intricate or as simple as you want, and it can have many uses as well.

On Ghost Runes

Ghost runes are runes hidden within a bind-rune that you can't see easily. Ghost runes can be intentional or created by accident.

Example of intentional ghost rune creation:
Say you create a simple bind-rune by placing ᛟ, ᛝ, and ᚷ. In the resulting bind-rune, the ᚷ will be hidden, but the ᚷ ghost rune was intentional.

Example of accidental ghost rune creation:
By creating a bind-rune with just ᛟ and ᛝ, we might get a similar lookingbind-rune as above. However, the ᚷ hidden in there will be an accidental ghost rune that may influence the meaning of your creation *without* your intention.

Overview of Bind-Rune Creation:

1. Write down name/phrase/selected runes—literal or figuratively.
2. Translate into Old Norse (optional).
3. Omit vowels (optional).
4. Translate into runes (if not already).
5. Delete duplicate runes.
6. Create desired form.

Book of Divination

Would you, that I tell you,
wise and knowing I am?
I hold back from speaking
until you have prepared yourself.
(*Poetic Edda*, "Hávamál," 158)

In the Ancient Norse poem "Völuspá," Odin, the venerable Allfather, fervently summons a wise woman adept in the art of divination to glean insights into both his storied past and the veiled contours of his future. This poignant exchange unfolds as a testament to the profound significance Odin attributes to divination in his ceaseless pursuit of wisdom and foreknowledge.

The act of invoking the wise woman serves as a poignant portrayal of Odin's recognition of the transformative power inherent in divination. In the quest for enlightenment, Odin acknowledges that the ability to peer into the future unveils the intricate tapestry of destiny.

The poem beautifully encapsulates the sacred ritual of seeking glimpses beyond the present, underscoring divination as a venerable tool for unraveling the mysteries that shroud the unfolding epochs.

Odin's appeal to the wise woman not only elevates the importance of divination in Norse mythology, but also resonates with a broader human fascination with the cosmic forces shaping our destinies. The "Völuspá" thus becomes a timeless ode to the indomitable spirit of inquiry, wherein Odin's pursuit of foreknowledge echoes the eternal human quest to decipher the enigmatic script of fate.

The Norns are powerful and mystical beings in Norse mythology who govern the destinies of gods and humans alike. They are often depicted as three sisters, Urðr ("Wyrd"), Verðandi ("Becoming"), and Skuld ("Necessity"). These entities are responsible for weaving and shaping the threads of fate, determining the course of events for every being in the cosmos. The wellbeing and actions of individuals, as well as the fate of the world, are intricately tied to the weaving of the Norns.

Seiðr (seidr), on the other hand, is a form of Norse magick or sorcery associated with certain gods, particularly the goddess Freyja, and practiced by skilled individuals known as seidr-workers, many of whom were women. Seiðr involves the manipulation of the unseen forces of the world to achieve various outcomes, such as foretelling the future, influencing events, or healing. It is a complex and mysterious practice that requires a deep connection with the spiritual realm.

Both the Norns and seiðr highlight the Norse belief in the interconnectedness of fate, magick, and the unseen forces that shape the world. The Norns represent the overarching destiny that governs all, while seiðr reflects the mortal attempt to understand, influence, or navigate that destiny through the practice of magickal arts. Together, they contribute to the rich tapestry of Norse mythology, where the threads of fate and the mysteries of the supernatural intertwine in a complex and fascinating narrative.

Types of Northern Divination

- **Runes:** Perhaps the most well-known form of divination in Northern paganism, runes are ancient symbols representing letters or sounds in runic alphabets. The most common runic system is the Elder Futhark, consisting of twenty-four characters. Practitioners cast or draw runes and interpret their meanings based on the symbols and their positions.

  Though it is the most famous form, it is also a more recent form of divination, and consulting the runes for advice on the future grew out of practices such as...

- **Casting Lots:** Like runes, casting lots involves throwing or casting small objects and interpreting their positions or patterns. In historical contexts, objects like bones, stones, or wood chips were used. Each piece corresponds to a particular meaning, and the interpretation is based on the arrangement and relationships between the lots.

  In ancient times, the most widespread form of divination was commonly referred to as *spá* or *spádómr.* This term encompasses various methods of foreseeing or predicting future events and it is a more general concept that includes practices such as prophecy, visions, or other forms of oracular insight. The Norse people believed in the importance of understanding fate and destiny, and divination played a crucial role in seeking insights into the future, navigating challenges, and making informed decisions. The practice of seiðr, a form of Norse magick, often involved elements of divination, making it a significant aspect of the broader Norse spiritual and mystical traditions.
- **Reading Signs in Nature:** Through the art of útiseta, some Northern pagan practitioners look to nature for divinatory signs. This can include observing the behavior of animals, interpreting the movement of clouds, or paying attention to the direction and shapes of the wind. Such practices often involve a deep connection to the natural world and an understanding of the symbolism embedded in it.

Visions

Runes and lots derive their significance from distinct markings, each carrying its own unique meaning. However, when delving into visions—whether they arise from trances, dreams, or nature-inspired experiences—we can reference this list for the most prevalent interpretations:

- **Animals:** Can represent instincts or aspects of the self.
- **Autumn:** Harvest, abundance, or transition.

- **Axes and Swords:** Power, conflict, or protection.
- **Battlefield:** Confrontation or inner strife.
- **Beards:** Wisdom and masculinity.
- **Being Chased:** Avoidance of an issue or fear.
- **Being Late:** Anxiety about missed opportunities.
- **Being Lost:** Feeling directionless in life.
- **Being Naked in Public:** Fear of exposure or vulnerability.
- **Birdsong:** Messages from nature or joy.
- **Books:** Knowledge, wisdom, or hidden secrets.
- **Boar:** Courage and strength.
- **Bridge:** Transition or connection between phases.
- **City:** Community, social interactions, or complexity.
- **Comet:** Change or celestial influence.
- **Death:** Change or transformation.
- **Desert:** Isolation, introspection, or arduous journeys.
- **Dragon:** Transformation or a powerful force.
- **Drowning:** Overwhelmed by emotions or situations.
- **Dwarf:** Hidden strengths or talents.
- **Earthquake:** Disruption or transformation.
- **Eagle:** Vision, freedom, or perspective.
- **Falling:** Loss of control or fear of failure.
- **Falling Teeth:** Concerns about appearance or aging.
- ***Fenrir* (Wolf):** Uncontrolled power or danger.
- **Festival:** Celebration, community, or joy.
- **Fire:** Passion or destructive forces.
- **Fireplace:** Warmth, comfort, or hearth.
- **Fishing:** Seeking insights or abundance.
- **Flying:** Freedom and liberation.
- **Forest Clearing:** Clarity or revelation.
- **Freyja's Cats:** Independence and mystery.
- **Garden:** Cultivation, growth, or harmony.
- **Giant:** Challenges, external forces, or dominance.
- **Goblet or Chalice:** Ritual, celebration, or Communion (the sacrament).
- **Gold:** Wealth or spiritual significance.

- **Gods in a Dream:** Divine guidance or intervention.
- ***Gungnir* (Odin's Spear):** Focus and determination.
- **Helm of Awe (Ægishjálmr):** Invoking awe and protection.
- **Horse:** Power, freedom, or journey.
- **Houses:** Symbolic of the self or aspects of life.
- **Key:** Unlocking potential or access to hidden aspects.
- **Labyrinth:** Complexity, confusion, or finding one's way.
- **Lake:** Reflection, depth, or inner emotions.
- **Landscapes (Mountains, Forests):** Nature's influence on the soul.
- **Longship:** Journey or adventure.
- **Mask:** Concealment, deception, or hidden identity.
- **Mead or Ale:** Celebration or social connection.
- **Mirror:** Self-reflection or self-perception.
- **Mist or Fog:** Uncertainty, confusion, or mystery.
- **Money:** Represents value or self-worth.
- **Moon:** Feminine energy, mystery, or cycles.
- **Mountains:** Challenges or aspirations.
- **Music:** Harmony, emotions, or expression.
- **Northern Lights *(Aurora Borealis)*:** Spiritual energy or magick.
- **Nudity:** Vulnerability or fear of exposure.
- **Pregnancy:** Creativity or new beginnings.
- **Rainbow Bridge *(Bifröst)*:** Connection between realms.
- **Reflection:** Self-awareness or introspection.
- **Runes:** Messages from the spiritual realm.
- **Running:** Escape from a situation or confrontation.
- **Sacrifice:** Letting go for a greater purpose.
- **Sailing on a Calm Sea:** Smooth journey ahead.
- **Sailing on a Stormy Sea:** Facing challenges or turmoil.
- **School or Exam:** Anxiety or fear of being unprepared.
- **Sea Creatures:** Deep emotions or unconscious forces.
- **Shield:** Protection or defense.
- **Snake:** Transformation or hidden fears.
- **Snow:** Purity, stillness, or coldness.
- **Sorcerer or Wizard:** Magic, wisdom, or hidden knowledge.

- **Spider:** Creativity, patience, or entanglement.
- **Spring:** New beginnings, renewal, or fertility.
- **Square:** Stability, order, or groundedness.
- **Star:** Hope, guidance, or inspiration.
- **Statue:** Solidity, permanence, or idolization.
- **Stone Circles:** Spiritual energy and connection.
- **Storm:** Turmoil, emotional upheaval, or cleansing.
- **Summer:** Growth, abundance, or vitality.
- **Sun:** Masculine energy, vitality, or enlightenment.
- **Teeth:** Concerns about appearance or communication.
- **Thor:** Courage, strength, and protection.
- **Throne:** Authority, power, or leadership.
- **Tower:** Ambition, goals, or a desire for achievement.
- **Valkyrie:** Guidance or protection in battle.
- **Völva *(Seeress)*:** Prophecy and intuition.
- **Volcano:** Passion, transformation, or inner turmoil.
- **Water:**
    - **Calm Water:** Tranquility and peace.
    - **Turbulent Water:** Emotional turmoil.
- **Whirlpool:** Being drawn into a situation or emotions.
- **Wolf:** Instincts, guardianship, wild nature, or connection to Fenrir.

Always remember that visions are a subjective and personal process influenced by individual experiences and perspectives. These symbols offer general insights, but the true meaning of a dream depends on personal associations and feelings.

Historical Context

There is much controversy as to whether runes were used as a tool of divination historically, or if it is merely a modern invention. Tacitus wrote in AD 98:

"They attach the highest importance to the taking of auspices and casting

lots. Their usual procedure with the lot is simple. They cut off a branch from a nut-bearing tree and slice it into strips, which they mark with different signs and throw at random onto a white cloth. Then the state's priest, if it is an official consultation, or the father of the family, in a private one, offers prayer to the gods and looking up towards heaven picks up three strips, one at a time, and, according to which sign they have previously been marked with, makes his interpretation. If the lots forbid an undertaking, there is no deliberation that day about the matter in question. If they allow it, further confirmation is required by taking auspices." (Germania, 10)

This lends to the belief of casting lots, which were marked by the inscription of a rune on each "stick."

Let's look at this from a step-by-step perspective, piecing together what might have been the original procedure:

1. **Gathering Materials:** Begin by carefully selecting and cutting twenty-four twigs, ensuring each one measures precisely 14 cm in length. The ideal thickness for these twigs is like that of an index finger, providing a balanced and tactile quality to your rune staves.
2. **Crafting the Runes:** With a sense of reverence, embark on the creative process of carving one Elder Futhark rune onto each twig. As you breathe life into these symbols, envision the ancient wisdom they carry and the connections they forge with the unseen forces.
3. **Creating the Ritual Space:** Lay out a ritual cloth, designating it as a sacred canvas for your divination practice. The choice of cloth may be significant, as it sets the stage for a connection between the earthly realm and the spiritual energies invoked through the runes. You may mark it with a circle/realm/sigil/etc.
4. **Casting the Lots:** Cast carved rune staves upon the ritual cloth in one quick, fluid motion, forming a (seemingly) random pattern. The alignment and placement of each twig contributes to the energetic flow of the divination space.

5. **Selection of Three Runes:** With intention and focus, gently pick up the three rune staves positioned at the top layer of the arrangement. These three runes will serve as the focal point for your divination reading.
6. **Holistic Interpretation:** Embrace a distinctive approach to rune reading, departing from the modern past/present/future structure (which we will explore later in this chapter). Instead, view all three selected runes as an interconnected triad, weaving a story that encapsulates the present moment and its potential unfolding.
7. **Exploring Symbolic Relationships:** As you read the combined meanings of the three runes, observe how they interact and influence each other. Delve into the nuances of their symbolic language, considering the dynamic relationships that emerge in this holistic reading.

"Each word led me onto another word, Each deed to another deed" (*Poetic Edda*, "Hávamál," 142).

8. **Reflecting on Guidance:** Take the time to reflect on the insights revealed through the interconnected meanings of the runes. Consider how their collective wisdom provides guidance and clarity, offering a profound understanding of your current circumstances and the paths that lie ahead.

Spreads and Layouts

In the realm of Norse divination, the art of casting runes lacks a singular historical method, leading practitioners to draw inspiration from diverse sources, such as Tarot spreads and, more authentically, bone-casting techniques.

Rune layouts and spreads serve as interpretive frameworks, enabling individuals to decipher the messages conveyed by the runes. While the intrinsic meanings of individual runes provide insight, the structure and placement of these symbols in layouts offer a nuanced understanding of their relevance to specific questions and aspects of life.

Distinguishing between a *layout* and a *spread* is, in essence, a matter of semantics, with both terms often used interchangeably. The adoption of Tarot card spreads for rune casting is not uncommon, as some authors seamlessly integrate these structures. However, the distinction lies in terminology, designating those adapted from Tarot as "spreads," rather than rune-specific "layouts."

Selecting an appropriate layout or spread hinges on the depth of information sought. Inquiries demanding comprehensive insights benefit from layouts with more runes, ensuring specificity and detailed guidance. Conversely, more general questions align with smaller layouts that provide a succinct overview. Most modern practitioners use the Elder Futhark for divination, but nothing is stopping you from using any runic system.

Noteworthy rune layouts:

- One-Rune Layout
- Past, Present, and Future (Three-Rune) Layout
- Four Directions
- Five-Rune Layout
- Grid of Nine
- Casting All the Runes—Shamanic Rune Reading

One-Rune Layout

The most basic layout involves one stone. You can cast the runes and pick one, or just reach into your rune pouch and pick a stone. This rune is read as the general feeling and overall attitude toward the question. It also represents the outcome to your question.

Past, Present, and Future (Three-Rune) Layout

Reflecting the linear progression of time, this layout assigns the past, present, and future roles to sequentially chosen runes, unveiling the influences at each stage.

The first one you choose (left) will represent the past. The second one you pick (middle) will be the present and the last one (right) is the future.

- **The Past:** Influences that have had an effect on the past in relation to the question being asked.
- **The Present:** Things presently happening that have an effect on your current situation in relation to the question being asked.
- **The Future:** The outcome of the question being asked.

Four Directions Layout

Since the runes have a solid base in Norse Mythology, each of these positions are named after each of the dwarves that are said to hold up the sky, which was the skull of the giant Ymir. (Sturluson, *Prose Edda*).

The idea for this layout is simple: just a North, South, East and West pattern to place your runes in. The meaning for each position is just as simple...

- ***Nordri* (North):** The past; influences that have had an effect on the past in relation to the topic of the cast.
- ***Vestri* (West):** The present; things presently happening that have an effect on the present in relation to the topic of the cast.
- ***Austri* (East):** The future; possible obstacles to watch for that may hinder the outcome or goal you have set.
- ***Sudri* (South):** The possible outcome of the rune cast.

Things to be aware of for this cast:
This cast is very similar to a three-rune layout because we have the past, present, and future involved with it. However, be aware that the third rune (*Austri*) is not the one that predicts the future for you. Its mission is to try to make sure you're aware of any obstacles that may come your way as you try to reach your goal. The last position (*Sudri*) takes on the role of the usual future position for a three-rune layout.

Another thing you should be aware of is that, regarding the outcome, position is only one possible indicator. You may end up with a rune that, by itself, makes little or no sense in relation to your topic. If this is the case, you need to make sure that you look at the reading as a whole and see what the runes are trying to tell you.

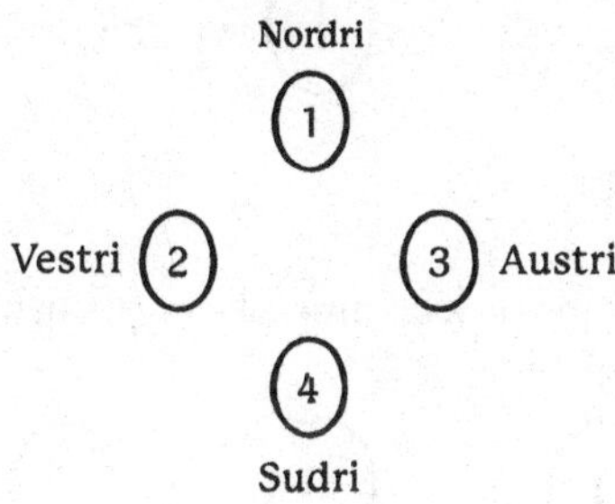

Five-Rune Layout

With this reading, you will form a plus sign with the five runes you pick after you cast them on the cloth. The first will be the bottom of the cross and represents the basic influences that underlie the question. The second one is placed to the left of the centre position and represents the obstacle to overcome. The third rune is at the top and represents beneficial processes. The fourth is to the right of the centre and represents the outcome of the question. The last rune is placed at the centre and shows all the future influences. The layout looks like the following:

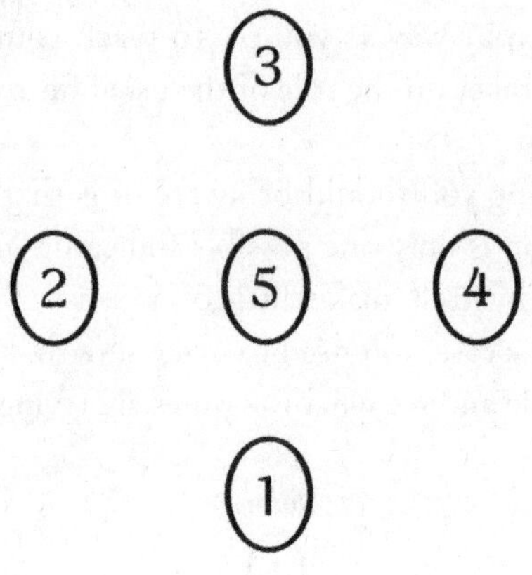

Grid of Nine Layout

Cast out your runes and pick up nine, placing them in a grid as follows:

If you add up the numbers from any row or column (or even diagonally), they add up to the number fifteen. In order to read this, you should do the following:

Read the lowest horizontal line first—it represents the past factors that have acted on the matter at hand. The runes go as follows...

- **8:** Hidden influences that acted in the past.
- **1:** Basic past influences.
- **6:** The questioner's present attitude to these past events.

Read the middle row next—it represents the present forces on the question. The runes in this row are read as follows...

- **3:** Hidden influences acting now.
- **5:** Present state of events.
- **7:** Questioner's attitude toward the present events.

Finally, read the top row—it represents the outcome of the question. Read its runes as follows...

- **4:** Represents hidden influences—delays or obstacles that may prevent the outcome.
- **9:** The best possible outcome of the matter at question.
- **2:** Shows the questioner's response to the result.

Shamanic Rune Reading

This method of casting runes, rooted in the timeless principles of bone-casting, echoes the practices of numerous pre-Christian cultures. Across ancient landscapes, people employed methods involving marked bones or lots, often inscribed with runes, as a means of divination. In the rich tapestry of Norse tradition, runes are cast or read in a manner akin to Tarot, with diverse preferences emerging—some favoring traditional Tarot formats, while others embrace a more authentic and Bronze Age shamanic approach.

Bronze Age Shamanic Approach

In the spirit of an authentic Bronze Age shamanic approach, the practitioner casts all the runes of the Elder Futhark onto an animal hide. This method eschews newer rune sets in favor of the Elder Futhark for its resonance with pre-Bronze Age rituals. The casting, performed on an animal hide, introduces an element of primal connection, and the runes are then interpreted in a holistic and somewhat chaotic pattern.

Guiding Through Complexity

Far from a mere tool for fortune-telling, runes serve as guiding companions through life's complexities. They illuminate potential paths and provide insight into likely outcomes. Rather than offering exact answers or advice, runes present different variables, suggesting possible courses of action in the face of anticipated events. The beauty of rune readings lie in their tendency to hint at answers, leaving room for intuitive interpretation.

Empowering Free Will

Fate may be spun, but the future remains unfixed. The runes affirm the individual's agency to shape their own path, make decisions, and alter their course. Rune readings offer guidance, yet the power to embrace or diverge from the suggested path lies squarely with the seeker. If the guidance doesn't resonate, the individual possesses the strength to forge a different route, embracing the malleability of destiny.

The Symbolism of Casting Cloth

The casting cloth, ideally shaped like an animal hide, holds symbolic significance. It serves as the sacred space where the ancient wisdom of the runes converges with the earthly connection to primal energies. Each section of the cloth corresponds to different aspects of the seeker's life, offering a nuanced lens through which the runes land and reveal their insights.

- **Head:** Reflects the seeker's current state of mind.
- **Neck:** Represents external factors influencing the individual or situation.
- **Back:** Unveils the heart's desire and true motivations, often distinct from conscious thoughts.
- **Front Left Leg:** Highlights obstacles or forces working against the seeker.
- **Rear Left Leg:** Delves into the past, exploring factors transitioning into history.
- **Front Right Leg:** Illuminates what is needed to stay on the "right path" and reveals supportive influences.
- **Rear Right Leg:** Portrays the final outcome of the situation.
- **Groin Area:** Symbolizes aspects of sex and sexuality, along with enduring thought and behavior patterns.
- **Tail:** Signifies what can be learned or taken away from the situation, encapsulating the essence of what remains.

In essence, the shamanic art of rune casting unveils a profound connection to ancient wisdom, intertwining fate, free will, and the ever-shifting tapestry of life. The runes cast upon the hide whisper truths that transcend time, offering seekers a timeless guide through the labyrinth of existence.

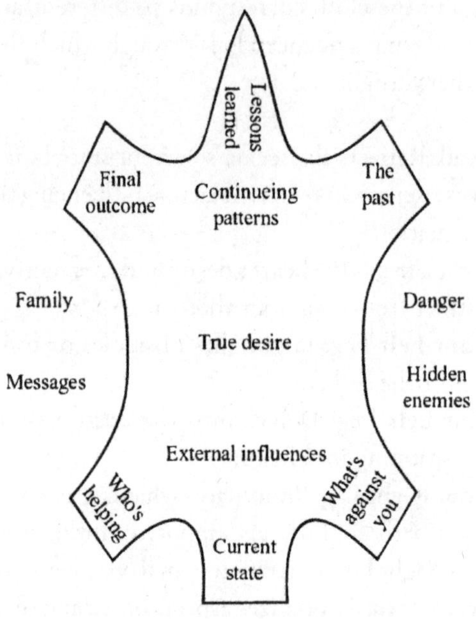

Merkstav

Merkstav refers to the concept of reversed or inverted runes in runic divination. It is similar to the concept of reversed cards in Tarot readings, signifying a potential reversal or negation of the usual meaning of the rune. The term *merkstav* is derived from the Old Norse words *merki,* meaning "sign," and *stafur,* meaning "staff" or "rune."

When a rune appears in a merkstav position, it suggests that the energy or influence of that rune is either blocked, delayed, or distorted in some way. Interpretation of merkstav runes requires careful consideration of the traditional meaning of the rune in its upright position and an understanding of how that meaning might be altered when the rune appears in a reversed or inverted form.

It's important to note that not all runic systems or practitioners incorporate merkstav readings into their divination practices. Some prefer to focus solely on upright rune positions, while others find value in exploring both the direct and inverted aspects of each rune for a more nuanced interpretation.

As with any divination system, the interpretation of merkstav runes is subjective and relies on the intuition and experience of the practitioner. It adds an additional layer of complexity to rune readings, inviting seekers to consider the possibility of obstacles, delays, or reversals in the energies represented by the runes.

If you do choose not to work with them, it is best to ignore them in a reading and not give the value of an upright rune to a merkstav.

Here are some potential merkstav meanings for the Elder Futhark runes:

- **Fehu:** Financial setbacks, loss of wealth, or material instability.
- **Uruz:** Lack of strength, energy depletion, or health issues.
- **Thurisaz:** Reduced conflict, avoiding confrontation, or protection from harm.
- **Ansuz:** Miscommunication, distorted messages, or the need for careful listening.
- **Raido:** Delays in travel, disruptions in journeys, or a lack of progress.
- **Kenaz:** Creative blocks, missed opportunities, or lack of inspiration.
- **Gebo:** No Merkstav.
- **Wunjo:** Emotional discord, dissatisfaction, or lack of joy.
- **Hagalaz:** Temporary setbacks, challenges, or delayed transformation.
- **Nauthiz:** Resistance to change, prolonged hardship, or delayed fulfillment.

- **Isa:** No Merkstav.
- **Jera:** No Merkstav.
- **Eihwaz:** No Merkstav.
- **Perthro:** Lack of insight, uncertainty in outcomes, or hidden influences.
- **Algiz:** Weakened protection, vulnerability, or caution against overconfidence.
- **Sowilo:** No Merkstav.
- **Tiwaz (ᛏ):** Delayed justice, conflicts of interest, or challenges in leadership.
- **Berkana (ᛒ):** Hindered growth, delays in new beginnings, or challenges in nurturing.
- **Ehwaz (ᛖ):** Disruptions in partnerships, communication breakdowns, or challenges in collaboration.
- **Mannaz (ᛗ):** Isolation, lack of community support, or challenges in social interactions.
- **Laguz:** Emotional turbulence, hidden emotions, or challenges in intuitive understanding.
- **Ingwaz:** No Merkstav.
- **Dagaz:** No Merkstav.
- **Othala:** Rootlessness, lack of ancestral support, or challenges in finding one's place.

Blank Runes in Readings

The use of a blank rune in runic divination is a topic of debate among practitioners, as it doesn't have a historical basis in traditional runic alphabets. In traditional runic systems like the Elder Futhark, there is no blank rune.

However, some modern rune sets include a blank rune, often referred to as the *Wyrd* or *Odin* rune. The interpretation of the blank rune varies among practitioners. Some see it as a wildcard, representing the unknown or unexpected, while others view it as a symbol of the void, potential, or a blank slate where anything is possible.

When using a rune set with a blank rune, its meaning in a reading would depend on the specific symbolism attributed to it by the reader or the tradition they follow. It's essential to refer to the accompanying guide or the practitioner's personal understanding of the blank rune in that particular set.

Keep in mind that interpretations of runes, especially when using a blank rune, are subjective and can vary among different practitioners and traditions. If you're using a rune set with a blank rune, it's advisable to explore its meaning within the specific context of the system you are working with.

Birth Runes

The concept of "birth runes" represents a contemporary fusion at the intersection of ancient runic traditions and the celestial wisdom of astrology. This innovative synthesis extends beyond mere runic exploration, encompassing a broader spectrum of eclectic esoteric practices. It is a testament to the evolving nature of metaphysical exploration, where the threads of runic symbology intricately weave with diverse esoteric disciplines, creating a vibrant tapestry of spiritual discovery.

This nascent idea, still in its early stages, heralds a paradigm shift in the world of metaphysics. The dynamic convergence of runes with astrology and various other eclectic and esoteric modalities has sparked a surge of interest, captivating enthusiasts and practitioners alike. Birth runes, as a concept, have rapidly gained momentum, spreading their roots far and wide, like wildfire in the fertile soil of spiritual curiosity.

The marriage of runic symbolism with celestial insights introduces a novel perspective into the intricate dance of fate and cosmic energies. As this innovative concept gains traction, it weaves a narrative that transcends traditional boundaries, offering a fresh lens through which individuals can explore the depths of their spiritual journey.

In the ever-expanding landscape of esoteric exploration, birth runes stand as a testament to the human drive for synthesis and understanding. The blending of ancient runic wisdom with diverse esoteric traditions mirrors the evolving consciousness of those seeking profound insights into the mysteries of existence. This contemporary alchemy of knowledge, spreading rapidly like wildfire, signifies the birth of a new era in metaphysical exploration, where the runes themselves become key players in the cosmic symphony of self-discovery.

Each rune carries a deep meaning and, when you access this oracle, you have direct and accurate information for the question you want to solve or the current moment of your life.

Birth runes are different. They are unique and personal runes tied to your destiny and determined according to your birth. Face the birth runes as fairy godmothers who blesses you and will always protect you no matter what.

Knowing your birth runes will help you to make difficult decisions when you least expect it, especially those that arrive as a simple problem but unfold in much greater things. Like an iceberg, for example. Navigating through the layers of the problem will be easier.

"Birth runes" do not have a historical basis in traditional runic systems or historical runic inscriptions. The idea of "birth runes" is not found in traditional runology and it is generally considered a modern, New Age, or esoteric idea. The system of birth runes is based on numerology, astrology, and other esoteric belief.

The twenty-four Elder Futhark runes are used to determine your birth runes. They were used to determine the personality and life path of every person.

People have always read their fate by the stars. In contrast to one's zodiac sign, birth runes are not intended to reveal fate or which month will bring you great love. They are part of your personality. Fate had a completely different meaning in mythology than it does today. It was believed that a person could change his fate or "rearrange his stars." Today, we accept fate as something final. The view that the path of life is in one's own hands is extremely important, especially with the runes. While each rune shows a path or a course of action, it says nothing about the current state. There is room for individual interpretation. The personally valid runes are calculated according to the date and hour of birth. This makes birth runes very personal. Even if two people were born on the same day, they usually have very different runes due to the hour of their birth. The assumption is that, if you know your own birth runes, difficult decisions can be made easier.

The stories that have been passed down from generation to generation are not fact, but rather a matter of faith. However, that applies to everything that has to do with astrology and the interpretation of fate. The mythology behind Viking birth runes is no exception.

Of particular importance in Nordic mythology are the chariots of Sunna ("the sun") and Manni ("the moon"), which race across the sky, pursued by wolves. The god Odin is constantly searching for heroes who will one day join him in the final battle and avert the terrible doom of Ragnarök. When a child is born, Nornir and Dísir (fate-determining beings and spirits descended from gods, elves, and dwarves) weave all good and bad aspects into the child's fate. They stretch threads across the horizon, with exactly two fixed points. These points are the birthday and the hour of birth. They are called hero-makers. Once the hero-makers are established, the personal dísir takes the reins. Through these, the energy of the planets is drawn into the "soul carpet" of every person. Rune astrology assumes that this is an analogy for the position of the stars and planets.

Compared with the astrology we know, they would be like the planets and the stars, which determine traits of our personality according to the position that they are when we are born.

The Norse still reveal the importance of the cycles of Sunna and Manni through the sky in the writing of our destiny.

There are a few ways to calculate your birth runes, some that even include your birth chart analysis. The most common are the tables that calculate your solar birth rune and your birth hour rune. Compared with our astrology, these runes could be considered similar to our sun sign and rising sign.

The Runic Half-Months/The Solar Rune

We know that the set of runes is composed of twenty-four symbols. Dividing the twelve months of the year for them, we see that each rune governs half a month. The data below is a careful mix of runic astrology:

- **Fehu:** 29 June–14 July; 7.5-22.5 degrees Cancer.
- **Uruz:** 14 July–29 July; 22.5 degrees Cancer to 7.5 degrees Leo.
- **Thurisaz:** 29 July–13 August; 7.5-22.5 degrees Leo.
- **Ansuz:** 13 August–29 August; 22.5 degrees Leo–7.5 degrees Virgo.
- **Raidho:** 29 August–13 September; 7.5-22.5 degrees Virgo.
- **Kenaz:** 13 September–28 September; 22.5 degrees Virgo–7.5 degrees Libra.
- **Gebo:** 28 September–13 October; 7.5-22.5 degrees Libra.
- **Wunjo:** 13 October–28 October; 22.5 degrees Libra–7.5 degrees Scorpio.
- **Hagalaz:** 28 October–13 November; 7.5-22.5 degrees Scorpio.
- **Nauthiz:** 13 November–28 November; 22.5 degrees Scorpio–7.5 degrees Sagittarius.
- **Isa:** 28 November–13 December; 7.5-22.5 degrees Sagittarius.
- **Jera:** 13 December–28 December; 22.5 degrees Sagittarius–7.5 degrees Capricorn.
- **Eihwaz:** 28 December–13 January; 7.5-22.5 degrees Capricorn.
- **Perthro:** 13 January–28 January; 22.5 degrees Capricorn–7.5 degrees Aquarius.
- **Algiz:** 28 January–13 February; 7.5-22.5 degrees Aquarius.
- **Sowilo:** 13 February–27 February; 22.5 degrees Aquarius–7.5 degrees Pisces.
- **Teiwaz:** 27 February–14 March; 7.5-22.5 degrees Pisces.
- **Berkano:** 14 March–30 March; 22.5 degrees Pisces–7.5 degrees Aries.
- **Ehwaz:** 30 March–14 April; 7.5-22.5 degrees Aries.
- **Mannaz:** 14 April–29 April; 22.5 degrees Aries–7.5 degrees Taurus.

- **Laguz:** 29 April–14 May; 7.5-22.5 degrees Taurus.
- **Ingwaz:** 14 May–29 May; 22.5 degrees Taurus–7.5 degrees Gemini.
- **Othala:** 29 May–14 June; 7.5-22.5 degrees Gemini.
- **Dagaz:** 14 June–29 June; 22.5 degrees Gemini–7.5 degrees Cancer.

The Runic Hours/Birth-Hour Rune

As the twenty-four runes are equivalent to the twenty-four hours in a day, the division is perfect, and each rune rules one hour. To know your birth hour rune, just find your birth time in the list below:

- **Jera:** 23:30-00:30
- **Eihwaz:** 00:30–01:30
- **Perthro:** 01:30-02:30
- **Algiz:** 02:30-03:30
- **Sowilo:** 03:30–04:30
- **Teiwaz:** 04:30–05:30
- **Berkano:** 05:30–06:30
- **Ehwaz:** 06:30–07:30
- **Mannaz:** 07:30–08:30
- **Laguz:** 08:30–09:30
- **Inguz:** 09:30–10:30
- **Dagaz:** 10:30–11:30
- **Othala:** 11:30–12:30
- **Fehu:** 12:30–13:30
- **Uruz:** 13:30–14:30
- **Thurisaz:** 14:30–15:30
- **Ansuz:** 15:30–16:30
- **Raidho:** 16:30–17:30
- **Kenaz:** 17:30–18:30
- **Gebo:** 18:30–19:30
- **Wunjo:** 19:30–20:30
- **Hagalaz:** 20:30–21:30

- **Nauthiz:** 21:30–22:30
- **Isa:** 22:30–23:30

Now you are able to determine your two birth runes. Each is considered a puzzle piece of one's personality that leads to a complete picture. A rune, similar to one's zodiac sign, also stands for personal elements, colours, power animals, stones, scents, and medicinal herbs. It is, therefore, worth studying and interpreting the Viking rune meanings in more detail. The following definitions provide a little insight into the interpretation:

- **Fehu:** Fehu is all about success and the winnings you deserve. It is the reward for your hard work and efforts.
- **Uruz**: Uruz predicts good health and physical condition. It means you have great inner strength.
- **Thurisaz**: Thurisaz is ruled by Thor, the god of Thunder. Although it offers protection, it is also about exercising caution. Some important decisions have to be made; it is important to wait for the right moment, and only then act.
- **Ansuz**: Ansuz stands for spoken communication and what you can learn from others. It suggests that you should spend more time with older, wiser people and listen to their advice.
- **Raidho**: This rune is about constant personal development. Think about your goals and the steps you need to take to achieve them. The rune also indicates changes and travel.
- **Kenaz**: Kenaz is a symbol of our intuition. This rune gives clarity in complicated situations. You may not have been aware of the light, but this rune gives you hope that there will soon be a solution.
- **Gebo:** Gebo connects to our relationships and reminds us that it is better to give than to take or receive. It reflects the need to live in harmony with yourself so that you can do the same with others.

- **Wunjo**: Wunjo allows you to enjoy the basic pleasures of life. It stands for happiness, contentment, and well-being. This rune predicts a time of calm and peace.
- **Hagalaz**: Hagalaz is a symbol of confusion and catastrophe. Remember to break bad old habits and change yourself for the best.
- **Naudhiz**: Naudhiz asks you to remain alert. You may have been through difficult times and should now pay more attention to what is happening. You should be patient and not be afraid to face what lies ahead.
- **Isa**: Isa is about patience. A time is predicted where you won't see much progress. Take time to breathe and don't make any hasty, important decisions.
- **Jera**: Jera is the symbol for karma. This rune is about what you planted and harvested with luck. The reward will come, but perhaps with a delay.
- **Eihwaz**: This rune offers protection as you fight for your personal goals. Your imagination will be an important ally.
- **Perthro**: Perthro symbolizes the hidden. Secrets, revelations, and mysteries will be the subject of this time. You may experience some surprises.
- **Algiz**: This is another rune that offers protection. Algiz predicts a good and happy time-frame, but also beware of evil. Lean on friends old and new in times of need.
- **Sowilo**: Sowilo is closely connected to your body and health. You need to relax. The more you allow worries and stress to get to you, the more your body will feel this tension.
- **Tiwaz**: This rune represents success and victory. Fight for what you want, it will be easy for you. In addition to willpower, it is also a symbol of romance. A new affair with good intentions may appear in your life.
- **Berkano**: Berkano symbolizes family and a strong female presence. It predicts family events, such as weddings and births. Everything that is new has a good chance of growing.

- **Ehwaz**: This is another rune related to movement and change. It is a symbol of travel, new jobs, and a new home. Trust that the changes will be for the best.
- **Mannaz**: *Mannaz* means "teamwork." It shows that you receive help and support from others. Think about building partnerships and expanding your contacts.
- **Laguz**: This is another feminine rune. It refers to our intuition and imagination. You will easily feel connected to the divine and be able to handle anything.
- **Ingwaz**: Ingwaz is an important rune that symbolizes graduation. It means you are ready to end something and move on in a new direction. You won't be afraid of it. On the contrary, you will feel fulfilled.
- **Daeg**: Daeg refers to rebellion and constant growth. A new and strong time will come, full of hope and optimism.
- **Othala**: The last rune stands for material goods and inheritance. This heritage can refer to physical or character traits. Older people and an old friend can come into your life to give advice and help.

Book of Spells

Do you know how to write,
if you want to be good,
and learn magic, before you go to sleep?
That is what you must be able to want.
(*Poetic Edda,* "Hávamál," 138)

Within this eclectic blend of mystical practices, the ancient art of útiseta, the enigmatic gand, and the multifaceted tapestry of Nordic magick converge seamlessly. It is a testament to the fluidity of the arcane, transcending the artificial boundaries that humans have imposed upon it. As the Norns weave the threads of fate, as the gods themselves traverse the realms, and as the unseen forces shape our world, they all bear witness to the interconnectedness of magick.

The idea that distinct schools of magick remain separate and compartmentalized is a notion defied by the very essence of these mystical arts. In the eyes of the cosmic forces and the spiritual realm, all magick is a unified force, interwoven like the roots of Yggdrasil, the "World Tree." It is not confined by the limitations of human classification.

The practitioner who delves into this harmonious convergence finds that the boundaries blur and the wisdom of útiseta , the secrets of gand, and the Ancient Nordic traditions become complementary aspects of a broader, more universal magick. It is the recognition that magick transcends cultural distinctions and its essence flows through the veins of existence, connecting all that is seen and unseen.

In this holistic approach, the seeker embraces the entirety of the magickal spectrum, allowing the energies to intermingle and manifest in their purest forms. It is an acknowledgement of the vast and intricate web of energies that shape our reality, where labels and divisions hold no sway, and the practitioner stands on the threshold of boundless potential.

What is Magick?

Magick is a term that is often used to refer to the practice of ceremonial or ritualistic actions with the intention of influencing events or outcomes through supernatural, mystical, or paranormal means. It is a term that has been adopted by various occult traditions and practitioners to distinguish it from *magic,* which is often associated with illusion or sleight of hand.

Magick, as practiced in occult and esoteric traditions, involves the use of symbols, rituals, gestures, and other elements to tap into unseen or metaphysical forces. Practitioners of magick believe in the existence of a spiritual or energetic realm that can be manipulated to bring about change in the physical world.

Aleister Crowley, a British occultist, ceremonial magician, and founder of the religious movement known as Thelema, had a significant influence on the modern practice and understanding of magick. In his seminal work, *Magick, Book 4,* Crowley defined magick and provided insights into its nature, defining *magick* as "the Science and Art of causing Change to occur in conformity with Will."

What is a Spell?

A spell is a magkical action or ritual performed with the intention of bringing about a specific result or effect.

Types of Nordic Magick

Runic spells can take on various forms, from simple meditation to runic yoga, to bind-runes and ever-complex rituals.

In Nordic magick, there is mainly five arbitrary terms for magick (as discussed):

1. Seidr
2. Galdr
3. Runes
4. Útiseta
5. Gandr

On Seidr

Seidr is closely linked to shamanistic work, focusing on trance and evocations. Seidr concentrates on the intake of external energy. It is the gathering of power from a source that is greater than your own.

The "Book of Spirits" should be the Seidr worker's best friend.

Seidr spell example: Any invocation from the "Book of Spirits."

On Galdr

Galdr is ritualized poetry or song. It is the vocalisation of your true intent.

Galdr spell example: Galdralag or Galdr sound vibration from the "Book of Songs."

On Runes

Runes and all sigils form a concentration point for both your intent and your focus. Runes form a bridge between your conscious and subconscious mind while working with the archetypes and rune spirit created by the collective consciousness of likeminded people for centuries.

Rune spell example: Single runes, rune bands, or bind-runes from the "Book of Runes."

On Útiseta

Útiseta, colloquially known as "sitting out," is a practice employed by Norse magicians. It is a cross between meditation and a Native American vision quest, as it puts you in the place to bridge the constraints of the limited earthly world view and the Utgard of the spirit(s).

Shamans have always served as intermediaries, bridging the gap between our everyday human existence and the realms inhabited by various beings, including nature denizens and spirits. Facilitated by trance, these spiritual guides travel between worlds, benefiting the human community while maintaining harmony with the environment, ancestors, and other entities. This ancient practice stands as one of humanity's oldest spiritual traditions.

Útiseta was practiced to receive visions or perform divination. During this vision-questing, the Vitki connected with elements, animals, birds, and transcendental nature spirits called *landvættir.* These spirits, considered guardians, protected and enriched their surroundings, serving as founts of wisdom. Útiseta immersed practitioners in the natural world, fostering inspiration and insights into both the macro and microcosms.

The term útiseta traces its origin to a thirteenth-century Icelandic law prohibiting "sitting out to provoke/wake up trolls and practice paganism," akin to shamanic traditions isolating practitioners in nature for spiritual connection or visions.

Wilderness vision questing, a cross-cultural practice, involves solitary time in nature with fasting. This spiritual tradition practiced for millennia seeks revelation, reconnection to nature and spirits (especially ancestors), and a deeper understanding of the self. Deep introspection in nature yields profound psychological and spiritual benefits.

During the Viking Age, útiseta, or "sitting out," specifically served shamanic practitioners, allowing communion with the spirits of the natural world and the deceased for divination.

Wilderness-questing offers manyfold benefits, including connections to self, personal empowerment, and a heightened bond with others, particularly the natural world and its spirits. Even those outside shamanic practices experience these benefits, as we are inherently part of the natural world.

Reintroduction to this context fosters a renewed sense of vitality, awareness, and wakefulness.

An útiseta involves an overnight stay outdoors, holding a magickal staff (*seiðstafr*), wearing a cloak and hood, and merging with protective spirits—fylgia, dís, or familiar ancestral spirits. The seið worker sings and chants, harmonizing with elements, animals, birds, and landvættir. In forest settings, contact with the *skogsrå* enhances the quester's connection, presenting an offering to land wights for their participation and wisdom.

Varðlokur, "shamanic songs," play a vital role during útiseta, awakening the staff, gathering helpful spirits, and inducing a shamanic state of consciousness. This ceremonial aspect highlights the intentional and immersive nature of Norse magick where shamanic songs connect practitioners with unseen forces in Norse cosmology.

The concept of awakening the staff in seiðr and Norse magick is symbolic, signifying the staff as a ritual tool or focus point, rather than possessing sentience. Objects in Norse mythology often carried symbolic or metaphysical significance, acting as conduits for spiritual energy. The awakening process involved chanting "varðlokur," infusing the staff with magickal energy or attuning it to specific spiritual forces. The staff represented a link between the earthly and spiritual realms, facilitating the practitioner's interaction with mystical energies.

Varðlokur refers to songs or chants in seiðr, translating to "songs of the guardian spirits" or "chants to invoke protective spirits." These songs played a crucial role in Norse magickal rituals, especially during útiseta. Varðlokur were believed to awaken and invoke spirits, guiding seiðr practitioners in their magickal work. While specific examples are scarce due to oral transmission and esoteric practices, varðlokur likely involved rhythmic chanting, symbolic phrases, and poetic language, inducing an altered state of consciousness and connecting with the spiritual realm.

A varðlokur might have involved rhythmic and repetitive chanting, accompanied by words that invoke the presence of protective spirits or beings. The practitioner may have used poetic and symbolic language, drawing upon Norse cosmology, mythology, and the natural world. The goal would be to create a trance-like state, establishing a connection between the earthly realm and the spiritual dimensions. It is likely that a varðlokur would have featured alliteration and kennings, taking on a form similar to a galdralag.

Útiseta is the journey of the soul to the Utgard. Midgard is "the middle yard"—that which is familiar, that which is home. The Utgard is that outside of the Midgard. It is the forest, the wild. The Utgard is that of the trolls, the spirits, and the outlaws. Utgard is where neither the plough nor the law reaches...and, from there, you bring the knowledge back to your Midgard. Odin brought the runes to the gods and mankind via útiseta.

During the course of the útiseta, the quester would continue to sing their experiences and offer galdr (incantations or poetic songs) to the spirits. These periods of singing and chanting would be alternated with long periods of silence to receive the spirits' wisdom and to feel the connections being woven with the unseen and the natural worlds.

Preparing for útiseta involves clarifying one's purpose and finding a safe space in nature. The seið worker offers songs and prayers, allowing inner and outer visions to unfold. While discomfort is expected, suffering is unnecessary. Útiseta concludes at sunrise with practitioners recording and assimilating their experiences. Balancing discomfort without hindering the ceremony, this ritual offers profound insights anchored in one's being.

Caution: Do not undertake an útiseta if you have mental health issues or disorders. Consult your therapist first, as it can be an intense experience and may act as a trigger. Additionally, avoid performing an útiseta in areas with potentially dangerous wildlife or venomous animals.

Duration: One night (traditionally, up to three)

Requirements: Warm clothing, a designated powerful natural location, a pillow for sitting, a small instrument for the starting ritual, and a potential offering for spirits at the end. Phones, lights (such as torches), and watches are not permitted.

Let's begin:

1. **Preparation:** Choose a place in nature where you feel secure. While traditionally performed in the forest, it can be elsewhere, like a clearing, field, beach, or even your backyard. The more natural, the better; ensure it's a place where you truly feel safe—your special place of power.
2. **Diet:** Traditionally, abstain from eating or drinking on the day before, but it's not mandatory, especially if you're inexperienced with abstinence or fasting. During útiseta, refrain from food and drinks.
3. **Timing:** For your first útiseta, consider a night with a full moon for added illumination. Opt for warm seasons to prevent discomfort (dress appropriately and use insect repellent). Choose a night with shorter hours, such as summer.
4. **Arrival:** Reach your place of power before sundown. Get comfortable, avoiding chairs to stay physically connected to the earth while connecting with its spirits.
5. **Initiation:** Start útiseta at sundown with a small ritual—perhaps a prayer, song, dance, or using a drum, bell, or rattle. Follow your intuition.
6. **Nighttime Experience:** As the sun sets, remain calm and focused on breathing. Initial hours may be intimidating, with the nightlife appearing more intricate than daylight. You might perceive creatures and faces in trees, resembling the spirits of ancient times.
7. **Endurance:** Stay in your place until sunrise, even though it may seem prolonged. Eventually, your mental state will ease and become enlightened. Traditionally, express gratitude to natural spirits with a modest offering, like bread or a natural item like a beautiful rock.

8. **Conclusion:** After sunrise, return home. Some may feel energized, while others may feel tired or exhausted. Listen to your body, take time to process, and smoothly reintegrate into your regular life.

On Gandr

Gandr is the exact opposite of *seidr,* as it is the channelling and sending forth of magickal energy towards a selective target.

This is not done by invoking the spirits (at least not as a final product), but rather by evocation and the sending forth of energy.

A great modern example will be the creation of egregores or spell bind-runes and sending it forth by releasing the bind-rune via meditation, exhaustion, sex, or fire (much like the form of sigil magick created by Austin Osman Spare).

Thus, runes and galdr are the two tools that can (and arguably should) be used in both the two main forms of Nordic magick, namely the seidr trance invocation and the gandr evocation, with útiseta being the meditation force that strengthen the body—both physical and astral—of the Vitkar.

Hence, I suggest that it is not two main forms, but ultimately one. It is seidr and gandr, male and female, passive and active, hard and soft. While working with both the microcosms and macrocosms, you will realise that they are but one. One form of magick can't truly exit without you, the practitioner, embracing and blending all.

Egregores

In the realm of magick and occult practices, the phenomenon known as "thought forms" is often explored and articulated through the concept of egregores. An egregore represents a unique aspect of Western esotericism and occultism, embodying the idea of a collective, autonomous psychic entity formed and sustained by the thoughts, emotions, and intentions of a group of individuals.

Egregores, in essence, are believed to manifest as distinct entities with a certain degree of autonomy, influenced by the shared consciousness of those who contribute to their creation. This intriguing concept suggests that the collective psyche of a group can give rise to a thought form that takes on a life of its own, independent of the individual contributors.

The process of egregore creation involves the collective energetic input of a group. This collective energy, generated through shared experiences, rituals, or focused intentions, acts as the life force that animates the egregore. It is the embodiment of the group's combined will and consciousness taking on a symbolic form that encapsulates the essence of the shared thought energy.

Crucial to the understanding of egregores is the idea of autonomy. Once brought into existence, an egregore is thought to have a certain level of independence. It can influence the group that gave rise to it and, in some beliefs, may even act autonomously, carrying out tasks or exerting influence according to its intended purpose.

Symbolic representation plays a significant role in the concept of egregores. The thought form often adopts a symbolic image, sigil, or other representations that serve as a focal point for the group's concentration and connection to the egregore. These symbols act as a conduit for the flow of collective energy, providing a tangible form through which the group can interact with and channel their intentions toward the egregore.

Purpose and intent are fundamental aspects of egregore creation. Groups intentionally create egregores with specific objectives, such as enhancing their magickal workings, protecting a designated area, or embodying certain qualities or virtues. The egregore becomes a tool through which the group can collectively manifest their desires and intentions on a metaphysical level.

Egregores require continuous energetic feeding to remain active and influential. The ongoing thoughts and actions of the group serve as sustenance, ensuring the continued existence and potency of the egregore. Neglect or waning attention from the group may lead to the gradual dissipation of the egregore.

The concept of egregores provides a fascinating lens through which to explore the intersection of collective consciousness, symbolism, and metaphysical manifestations within the realms of magick and occultism. It invites practitioners to delve into the collaborative nature of thought form creation, recognizing the potential for autonomous entities to emerge from the collective psyche of a group.

As with many aspects of magick, the concept of egregores involves a blending of symbolic, psychological, and metaphysical elements, offering a rich tapestry for exploration within esoteric traditions.

In the vast expanse of the Nordic cosmos, a profound tapestry unfolds—a tapestry that encompasses the entirety of their worlds. This intricate fabric of existence weaves together the diverse realms into a singular, harmonious design. At the heart of this cosmic textile stands a majestic tree, its roots delving into the depths of the universe and its branches reaching out to touch every corner of reality.

The symbolism of this central tree reflects the interconnectedness of all aspects of life within Norse mythology. It serves as a metaphor for the convergence of energies from distant realms, a meeting point where the threads of fate are intertwined. Each thread represents a unique aspect of existence—be it the domains of gods, mortals, or other mystical entities—all converging and contributing to the rich and complex narrative of the Norse worldview.

This interwoven tapestry is not just an abstract concept, but finds tangible expression in Nordic artwork. The intricate knotwork adorning artifacts and manuscripts mirrors the complexity of life itself. These knots, with their convoluted patterns, are visual representations of the interconnected relationships between beings, events, and energies. They capture the essence of the Web of Wyrd, illustrating how every individual thread is essential to the overall fabric of destiny.

Within this expansive lake of energies, emotions, and symbols, the shaman emerges as a pivotal figure. Like a skilled weaver, the shaman navigates the currents of this ethereal lake, tugging at the threads of fate. A subtle pull in one direction has a ripple effect, setting the entire weave into motion. The shaman understands the delicate balance within this cosmic tapestry, recognizing that influencing one thread inevitably moves others, creating a dance of energies that shapes the unfolding narrative of life.

The Web of Wyrd

The *Web of Wyrd,* also known as the "Matrix of Fate," is a concept in Norse mythology and runic traditions. It represents the interconnectedness of past, present, and future events. The web is often depicted as a matrix or grid of interlaced runes, symbolizing the threads of fate woven by the Norns, the Norse goddesses of destiny. The Norns are responsible for shaping the destiny of both gods and mortals.

The Web of Wyrd emphasizes the idea that all events and actions are interconnected, forming a complex tapestry of fate. Each individual's destiny is woven into this cosmic web, and the choices made in the present can influence the unfolding of future events. It reflects the cyclical nature of time and the belief that fate is inescapable.

The concept of the Web of Wyrd is closely tied to the runic alphabet, as each rune can be seen as a symbol carrying spiritual and mystical significance. Some believe that, by understanding and working with the runes, individuals can gain insights into their destiny and navigate the threads of fate.

In contemplating the symbolism of the Nordic tapestry, one finds a profound philosophy that embraces the interconnectedness of all things. It invites individuals to recognize their place within the intricate weave of existence, understanding that each action, emotion, and symbol contributes to the unfolding story of life in the grand tapestry of the Norse cosmos.

On Energy Flow in Norse Magick

Magickal energy, often referred to by various names in different cultures throughout history, reflects the profound recognition of a universal force that connects us to the mystical realms. In Chinese culture, it's known as *chi,* while the Japanese call it *ki.* India acknowledges it as *prana,* and, in the islands, it goes by the name *mana.* Yet, the Norse people, with their unique perspective, speak of this energy as *megin,* pronounced "may-gin." Megin, in essence, embodies the fundamental building block of Nordic magick.

The direction of megin, akin to the flow of a river, holds the key to magick in the Nordic tradition. It dictates the very form and essence of the magick being woven. It is a subtle, yet powerful current that weaves its way through the intricate tapestry of rituals and practices, carrying with it the potential for transformation, insight, and transcendence.

Another facet of this magickal tapestry is odr. *Odr* represents the rush of emotions and consciousness that surges through many Norse rituals. It is the ephemeral bridge between the material world and the ethereal realms, uniting the practitioner with the forces beyond ordinary perception.

Within the domain of Nordic magick, you will encounter the intriguing concept that certain magickal forms are better suited for specific genders. For instance, seidr, a particularly enigmatic and versatile branch of magick, is often perceived as *ergi*. This term has been interpreted by various scholars as "unmanly" or "homosexual." However, it's important to note that Viking culture did not stigmatize homosexuality; rather, it held a nuanced view.

In the Viking cultural context, *ergi* was associated with the passive role in a sexual relationship, a role seen as feminine. In contrast, the active role was deemed masculine and muscular. By partaking in the passive role, one embodied the feminine aspect.

In seidr, practitioners open themselves to the spirits and receive energy, taking on a submissive, yielding role, much like the "bottom" in a relationship. In essence, seidr entails relinquishing control, letting go of the ego, and allowing the unbridled power of life to flow through one's being—a potent act of being a vessel for external energies.

This "ergi" aspect in seidr was not to be taken in a literal sense, but rather served as a way of conveying the flow of energy to an audience that existed a thousand years ago. In those times, such a social term held deeper significance.

In contrast to *seidr, gandr* is viewed as a distinctly male form of magick. Those who practiced gandr, known as *Gandrmannen,* enjoyed great reverence in Viking society. In gandr, the practitioner sends out energy, exhibiting a kind of control that was perceived as the proper, manly form of engagement—a demonstration of authority and dominance, as understood in that era.

The intricate dynamics of these magickal forms, their gender associations, and the profound significance of megin and odr enrich the tapestry of Nordic magick, unveiling a multifaceted world view deeply rooted in Ancient Norse traditions.

Invocation and Evocation

Invocation and evocation are two distinct ritualistic practices that involve summoning or calling upon external forces, energies, or entities. While they share some similarities, they differ in their primary focus and the direction of the interaction.

Invocation

- **Focus:** The main focus of an invocation is to invite or call upon a deity, spirit, or divine energy into oneself or a particular space. The practitioner seeks to establish a connection with the invoked entity, often for guidance, assistance, or communion.
- **Direction:** In an invocation, the flow of energy or presence is directed inward, towards the practitioner. The goal is to embody or channel the invoked entity, allowing its influence to manifest within the individual or the ritual space.
- **Purpose:** Invocations are often performed for personal transformation, spiritual growth, or to receive blessings and insights from the invoked presence.

Invocation in seidr is the bringing of something external (or internal) into your subconscious.

Invocations are often associated with spiritual or ritualistic practices and can vary widely depending on the specific tradition or belief system. It's important to note that the following instructions are meant for entertainment purposes only and should not be taken as a serious or genuine invocation. Always respect the beliefs of others and be mindful of cultural sensitivities.

Here's a simplified and generic version of an invocation ritual:

Materials Needed:

- Quiet and undisturbed space
- Candle
- Incense
- The corresponding bind-rune for that which you are invoking (e.g., a deity, spirit, or energy)
- A clear intention or purpose for the invocation

Instructions:

1. **Set the Space:** Choose a quiet and comfortable space where you won't be disturbed. Cleanse the area by physically cleaning it or using incense, sage, or other purifying methods.
2. **Prepare Yourself:** Take a moment to center yourself. Relax through deep breathing or meditation to clear your mind and focus your intention.
3. **Arrange the Tools:** Place the candle, incense, and the bindrune in a central location. You may also want to create a simple altar.
4. **Light the Candle:** Light the candle as a symbol of illumination and the presence of the divine or the energy you are invoking.
5. **Light the Incense:** Light the incense, allowing the smoke to rise. This is often seen as a way to purify the space and connect with the spiritual realm.
6. **Invoke with Intention:** Clearly state your intention for the invocation. You can speak aloud or silently, expressing your purpose and inviting the presence or energy you seek.
7. **Offering:** You may gift an offering to strengthen the energy.
8. **Focus on the Symbol:** Concentrate on the representation or symbol of what you are invoking. Visualize the energy or presence surrounding you.
9. **Communicate:** If you feel comfortable, engage in conversation with the entity or energy you are invoking. Ask questions, seek guidance, or simply express your thoughts and feelings.
10. **Express Gratitude and Close:** Thank the entity or energy for its presence. Express gratitude for any guidance or assistance. Blow out the candle to signify the end of the ritual.

Evocation

- **Focus:** An evocation, on the other hand, is focused on summoning or calling forth external entities, spirits, or energies to appear or manifest in the external world, separate from the practitioner. The emphasis is on establishing a presence or interaction outside of oneself.
- **Direction:** The flow of energy in an evocation is directed outward, towards the external world or a specific location. Practitioners aim to establish a connection with the summoned entity without necessarily embodying or internalizing it.
- **Purpose:** Evocations are often performed for various purposes, including seeking information, requesting assistance, or even commanding the presence of entities for specific tasks. It is a more externalized form of interaction with spiritual forces.

Evocation in gandr is the bringing of something external (or internal) into your conscious mind.

The following steps provide a simplified and generic guide for a basic evocation ritual:

Materials Needed:

- Quiet and undisturbed space
- Candle(s)
- Incense
- Symbols or representations of the entities you wish to evoke
- A clear intention or purpose for the evocation

Instructions:

1. **Set the Space:** Choose a quiet and clean space where you can perform the ritual without interruptions. Cleanse the space using incense, sage, or other purifying methods.

2. **Prepare Yourself:** Center yourself through meditation or deep breathing. Clearly define your intention for the evocation and ensure your mindset is focused and respectful.
3. **Arrange the Tools:** Place the candles, incense, and symbols or representations of the entities in a central location. Create an altar if you wish, arranging the items in a way that feels sacred to you.
4. **Light the Candles:** Light the candles to symbolize illumination and the presence of spiritual forces. The number of candles may vary based on your tradition or personal preference.
5. **Light the Incense:** Light the incense, allowing the smoke to fill the space. This is often done to purify the environment and create a conducive atmosphere for the ritual.
6. **State Your Intention:** Clearly articulate your intention for the evocation. Speak aloud or in your mind, expressing why you are calling upon these entities and what you seek to achieve through the ritual.
7. **Focus on the Symbols:** Concentrate on the symbols or representations of the entities you are evoking. Visualize their presence and imagine a connection being established between you and them.
8. **Request Presence:** Politely and respectfully request the presence of the entities you are evoking. Be clear in your communication and open to any messages or guidance they may offer.
9. **Receive Communication:** Pay attention to any signs, symbols, feelings, or thoughts that may come to you during the evocation. Entities may communicate in various ways, and being open to subtle messages is important.
10. **Express Gratitude and Close:** Thank the entities for their presence and any guidance they have provided. Blow out the candles to signify the conclusion of the ritual.

Ritual Equipment

As mentioned earlier, you, the magician, poet, and ultimate author (*odr*), only need a true intent and a space to perform all and any magick...but we as humans do need a little help from time to time.

Here is a list of ritual equipment that will make wielding the forces easier:

In the Nordic tradition of magick and ritual, practitioners may use a variety of equipment and tools to perform their rituals and connect with the spiritual aspects of their practice. Here is a list of common equipment and tools used in the Nordic tradition:

- **Altar:** A dedicated space or surface used as the focal point for rituals and offerings.
- **Runes:** Runic symbols or stones used for divination, casting, or inscriptions.
- **Staff:** Of major importance in all forms of Nordic magick from seidr trance work to active gand, directing energy, and creating sacred boundaries.
- **Thor's Hammer *(Mjölnir)*:** A symbol of protection, often worn as an amulet or pendant.
- **Blót Bowl:** A bowl used for offering libations, typically filled with mead or other beverages.
- **Offering Plate:** A plate or dish for placing food or other offerings for deities and spirits.
- **Drinking Horn:** A traditional drinking vessel, often used to toast and make offerings.
- **Sword, Seax, and Carving Knife:** Used primarily for cutting, but can also be used for directing energy, as well as for creating sacred boundaries.
- **Cloak or Ritual Garb:** Special clothing worn during rituals, often incorporating traditional Norse designs.
- **Seiðr Rod:** A wand or staff used in seiðr magick for channeling energy and communication with spirits.

- **Bowl of Water:** Represents the element of water and is often used for purification.
- **Candle Holders:** Used for holding candles, which may represent various intentions or deities.
- **Sacred Symbols:** Bind-runes and Galdrastafir, used to invoke or represent specific aspects of Norse mythology.
- **Drums and Drumming Tools:** Used in shamanic and seiðr practices for trance work and journeying.
- **Stones and Crystals:** Used for grounding, meditation, and energy work.
- **Amulets and Talismans:** Jewelry or charms imbued with protective or magickal properties.
- **Shamanic Rattles:** Used in shamanic practices for journeying and connecting with the spirit world.
- **Ritual Rope:** Used for binding and knot magick in some traditions.

So Mote it Be, Amen, and Herrlof

People employ "Amen" and "So mote it be" as concluding phrases in various rituals and prayers, each rooted in distinct cultural and spiritual traditions. "Amen," originating from Hebrew and commonly used in monotheistic religions like Christianity, Judaism, and Islam, serves as a solemn affirmation or agreement, expressing a collective acceptance of the spoken words or prayers. On the other hand, "So mote it be" has its origins in Wiccan and Neopagan practices, representing a declaration that the stated intention or spell will come to fruition.

Both phrases encapsulate a sense of finality and commitment, anchoring the spoken words with a powerful affirmation. "Amen" tends to be more prevalent in religious settings, while "So mote it be" is often favoured in contemporary pagan and magickal traditions, illustrating the diverse ways in which people seek to imbue their words with resonance and significance in spiritual and ritualistic contexts.

As a spell concludes, Norse pagans often utter *Herrlof*—a term resonant with the spirit of triumph in warfare, meaning "praise" or "victory," is a fitting conclusion to affirm the success and triumph that you seek. In the Norse worldview, life is perceived as an unending battle, making Herrlof a fitting affirmation that embraces the ongoing struggle and the pursuit of victory in every aspect of existence.

Rune Activation

Activating runes for use in amulets and talismans is a topic of great intrigue and often garners a multitude of questions among those delving into the realm of bind-runes. the process of activation is a fundamental aspect of Northern magick and is not something that can be easily condensed into a brief paragraph. However, in this chapter, we will embark on a deeper exploration of this intriguing topic, shedding light on the foundations of Nordic magick that often get overshadowed by the rune craft aspect of galdr.

Quick Activation Method

One of the swiftest ways to activate any sigil, including runes, involves a simple three-step process:

1. Print or draw the sigil or rune on paper, or you may choose to print it out.
2. Concentrate your focus on the rune for the appropriate duration, channeling your intention and energy into it.
3. Set the paper bearing the rune on fire and release the rune into the world.

While this method provides a straightforward means of activation, there are numerous other approaches, each offering a unique depth and intensity of energy.

Traditional Method

An ancient and traditional approach to charging runes is to *rist* ("carve") the runes, then stain them. Historically, the staining process often involved the use of blood, either that of the shaman or from a sacrificial animal. Notably, Berserkers would carve the Tyr rune on their shields and weapons, staining them with their own blood before heading into battle. In the *Grettis Saga,* blood staining was employed on runes for the purpose of cursing.

The use of blood carries a potent symbolic and emotional connection, channeling the practitioner's intent and linking it with the runes. This connection, forged through sacrifice, serves as a means of transferring energy to the spirits and the runes themselves.

It is essential to note that, while the blood of the sorcerer can be used for this purpose, it is not an absolute requirement. An ancient substitute for blood was red ochre, seen as the blood of the earth. Any red pigment can be utilized, emphasizing the importance of the practitioner's intent and connection to the energy, rather than the source of the substance. The effectiveness of blood is not necessarily superior; other bodily fluids can also be employed for specific intentions:

- **Saliva:** for art and science.
- **Urine:** for destruction and storms.
- **Sweat:** for growth and health.
- **Tears:** for love and emotions.
- **Semen or Menstrual Blood:** for matters pertaining to love and sexuality.

Activation of a Known Rune or Bind-Rune

The activation of a single rune or a bind-rune, whether obtained from a reputable source or a reputable Vitki, essentially follows the charging phase of a magickal spell. The intent is already imbued within the acquired rune. To activate the bind-rune, hold it in your hand and direct your energy and intention toward your desired outcome. You can charge the rune by vocalizing your intention, visualizing energy infusing the symbol, or exposing it to various sources of energy, such as moonlight or other elements.

Activation of runes can be achieved through several alternative methods:

- **Meditation:** Hold the bind-rune in your hand or place it in front of you. Focus your intention on the desired outcome and visualize the energy of the runes flowing into the symbol, enhancing its magickal power.
- **Charge with Energy:** Hold the bind-rune and visualize energy entering the symbol. You can also employ various methods to charge the symbol with energy, such as exposing it to moonlight, sunlight, submerging it in water, anointing it with oil, or infusing it with the smoke from incense.
- **Elements:** Use the elements for activation. Fire, for instance, involves burning the rune, while water entails casting it into an ocean or lake. Earth requires you to bury the rune, while air involves writing the rune on a piece of paper that you release in a gust of wind.
- **Charge with Emotion:** Staining the rune with blood or tears is a means of infusing it with emotion. However, laughter, too, can charge the rune with energy.
- **Use Sound as a Galdr:** Sound can take on various forms, including traditional galdralag poetry, rhythmic shamanistic drumming, singing, humming, or any form of ritualistic music.

The rune can also be charged through visualization, sunlight, moonlight, water, fire, earth, air, oil, incense, herbs, or simply by carving or drawing it, as the act alone can activate the rune to some degree.

Once the rune is imbued with energy through any of the above methods, it is fully activated. If the rune is intended to serve as an amulet or talisman, this marks the culmination of your journey.

However, if the rune is destined for use in a spell, you may proceed to the construction of your magickal working, harnessing the energies you've skillfully awakened within the runic symbol.

Carving the Runes

In the spells described below, the traditional instruction involves carving the runes onto a candle and observing the ritual until the candle burns out. However, it is important to note that the flexibility of rune magick allows for various alternatives to this conventional method. Beyond the confines of wax, runes may be intricately carved onto a wooden or stone surface, offering a connection to the grounding energy of these materials. Engraving the runes onto a metal amulet introduces an additional layer of permanence and portability, allowing the wearer to carry the runic energies with them throughout the day. Moreover, for practitioners who employ a ritual staff, inscribing the runes onto its surface can infuse the staff with the intended magickal properties, enhancing its potency as a tool for channeling energy during spellwork. In some instances, experimenting with diverse mediums can yield unique and potent effects, granting the practitioner the opportunity to tailor the spell to their preferences and the specific energies they wish to invoke.

Whether etched on candle wax, wood, stone, metal, or staff, the act of carving runes serves as a tangible manifestation of intention, connecting the practitioner to the runic forces and enabling a more personalized and versatile approach to rune magick.

Types of Rune Spells

Within the realm of rune craft, three distinct categories of magick spells emerge: single-rune spells, runic band spells, and bind-rune spells. The augmentation of these spells in various scenarios is achieved through the utilization of galdr (word spells) and evocations/invocations.

Single-Rune Form Rituals

Runes are not just mere letters or even representations of concepts, but full-blown spirits in their own right. Invoking/evoking a separate god will definitely add to the power and megin of a spell, but it is not always necessary, or even conducive, to your outcome. Let's explore the world of single-rune form magick by going through the Elder Futhark. Spell can obviously be written for any of the runes, in any of the systems.

FEHU

A Runic Spell for Wealth and Prosperity:

Time of Day: Perform this spell during the waxing phase of the moon, preferably on a Friday, the day associated with wealth, prosperity and the Vanir.

Materials Needed:

- **Fehu Rune-Carving Tool:** A consecrated tool, such as a ritual knife, or inscribing tool for carving the Fehu rune into the candle wax. Ensure the tool has been cleansed and dedicated for magickal use.
- **Gold or Green Candle:** Representing the energy of wealth and prosperity, choose a candle in either gold or green. The candle should be large enough to burn through the duration of the spell.
- **Incense:** Select a fragrance associated with abundance and prosperity, such as frankincense, cinnamon, or patchouli. The incense will help create a magickal atmosphere during the ritual.

- **Candle Holder:** Place the candle in a holder that is stable and safe for burning candles. This ensures a secure setting for the spell.
- **Symbols of Abundance**: Gather symbols that represent wealth, such as coins, gemstones, or grains. Arrange these around the Fehu rune as a visual representation of the prosperity you seek.
- **Daily Meal Offering:** Prepare a small portion of your daily meal to offer as a token of gratitude to the spiritual forces that will assist in manifesting wealth. This offering symbolizes your willingness to share in the abundance you seek.
- **Quiet and Comfortable Space:** Choose a space where you won't be disturbed during the ritual. Arrange the items in a way that creates a serene and focused environment for spellcasting.
- **Candle and Incense Holders:** Ensure you have appropriate holders for both the candle and incense. This not only contributes to the aesthetics of the ritual, but also promotes safety.
- **Rune Poem Printout or Memorization:** Have the Fehu rune poem printed or memorized to recite during the invocation of the rune spirit. This connects you with the traditional wisdom associated with the rune.
- **Lighter or Matches:** Use a lighter or matches to ignite the candle and incense. Have these on hand for a seamless and uninterrupted spellcasting experience.

Instructions:

1. Begin by finding a quiet and comfortable space. Light a candle and some incense to create a serene atmosphere. Sit or lie down, close your eyes, and focus on your breath. Inhale deeply, allowing relaxation to envelop you with each exhale. Visualize a radiant golden light surrounding you, representing the wealth and abundance you seek.

2. Recite the Fehu rune poem, connecting with the energy and essence of the rune:

"Wealth is a comfort to all men;
yet must every man bestow it freely,
if he wish to gain honour in the sight of the Lord."

3. With a consecrated tool, carve the Fehu rune into a piece of gold or green candle wax. Place the carved rune in the center of your ritual space, surrounded by symbols of abundance such as coins or grains. Offer a small portion of your daily meal as a token of gratitude for the prosperity you are about to receive.
4. Speak your intent clearly and confidently. For example: *"By the power of Fehu, I attract wealth and prosperity into my life. May my endeavors be fruitful, and abundance flow towards me effortlessly. As I release this intention, so shall it manifest."*
5. Ignite the candle with the Fehu rune, focusing on the flame as it dances with the energy of wealth. As the candle burns, visualize your life overflowing with prosperity, envisioning the positive changes that wealth will bring. Once the candle has burned completely, release the energy into the universe by saying, "Herloff."
6. Allow the remnants of the spell, such as the carved rune and any offerings, to remain undisturbed for a lunar cycle to amplify the energy. Trust in the power of Fehu to work on your behalf, bringing abundance and prosperity into your life.

URUZ

A Runic Spell for Invoking Physical Strength

Time of Day: Conduct this spell during the early morning, preferably at sunrise. The first light of day symbolizes the emergence of strength and vitality.

Materials Needed:

- **Uruz Rune-Carving Tool:** A consecrated tool, such as a ritual knife or inscribing tool, for carving the Uruz rune. Ensure the tool has been cleansed and dedicated for magickal use.
- **Red Candle:** Representing the fiery energy of physical strength, choose a red candle. The candle should be large enough to burn throughout the spell.
- **Earth Element Representations:** Gather materials that symbolize the grounding and stabilizing energy of the earth, such as stones, soil, or a potted plant.
- **A Symbol of Personal Strength:** Select an object that holds personal significance and represents physical strength to you. This could be a piece of jewelry, a small weight, or any item that embodies power.
- **Incense:** Choose an invigorating scent like cedar, pine, or sandalwood to enhance the ritual atmosphere.

Instructions:

1. Begin by finding a quiet space where you won't be disturbed. Sit or lie down in a comfortable position. Close your eyes and focus on your breath. Inhale deeply, imagining the life force entering your body with each breath. As you exhale, release tension and let go of any physical or mental burdens. Visualize yourself surrounded by a vibrant, pulsating energy, ready to tap into the strength within.
2. Recite the Uruz rune poem to establish a connection with the rune spirit:

"Aurochs, primal strength,
Earth's sinew, wild and untamed.
Mighty force, unstoppable flow."

3. With the consecrated tool, carve the Uruz rune into the red candle. Place the candle at the center of your ritual space, surrounded by the earth element representations. Offer a small amount of soil or a symbolic gesture representing your connection to the earth.
4. Clearly articulate your intent with statements such as: *"By the essence of Uruz, I call forth the primal strength within. May my body be filled with vitality and resilience. As I carve this rune and make my offering, I open myself to the unstoppable flow of physical power."*
5. Light the red candle, allowing the flame to symbolize the awakening of your physical strength. As the candle burns, meditate on the sensation of power coursing through your body. Once the candle has fully burned, release the energy into the universe by saying, "Herrlof."
6. Embrace the renewed vigor and physical strength that Uruz brings into your life.

THURISAZ

A Runic Spell to Invoke Thurisaz for Overcoming Obstacles

Time of Day: Perform this spell during the late afternoon, as the day transitions into evening, to align with the strength and power associated with Thor.

Materials Needed:

- **Thor's Hammer Symbol:** Acquire or craft a representation of Thor's hammer, Mjölnir, to serve as a focal point for the spell. This can be a pendant, a small figurine, or a drawn image.
- **Red Candle:** Symbolizing Thor's fiery strength, use a red candle as a source of illumination during the spell.
- **Incense:** Select an incense with a grounding and empowering

fragrance, such as cedar or pine, to enhance the ritual atmosphere.

- **Thunderstorm Sounds:** Play or simulate the sounds of a thunderstorm during the spell to invoke the energy of Thor.

Instructions:

1. Find a quiet and undisturbed space. Light the red candle and incense, allowing the scents to fill the air. Close your eyes and focus on the simulated sounds of a thunderstorm. Envision yourself standing in an open field, feeling the electrifying energy of the storm. Let this energy envelop you, heightening your senses and connecting you to the primal power of nature.
2. Recite the Thurisaz rune poem to invoke the spirit of Thor and the jötnar:

"Thorn is extremely sharp,
for every man who grabs it,
it is harmful,
and exceedingly cruel to every man who rests among them."

3. Using a consecrated tool, carve the Thurisaz rune onto the red candle. Place the Thor's hammer symbol near the candle. Offer a small portion of hearty food, like grains or meat, to invoke the strength of Thor and the jötnar.
4. Clearly state your intention, such as: *"By the might of Thor and the power of Thurisaz, I call upon the strength to smash through all obstacles in my life. Just as Thor wields Mjölnir to conquer challenges, so too shall I triumph over adversity."*
5. As you release the energy, utter the word "Herrlof" with conviction.
6. Feel the surge of strength and power coursing through you, propelling you toward victory over obstacles. As the

candle burns, visualize Thor's hammer smashing through barriers, clearing the path for your success and triumph.

ANSUZ

A Rune Spell to Invoke Ansuz for Divine Inspiration

This spell can be used as a stand-alone ritual or as a precursor to grander spell work.

Time of Day: Perform this spell during the late evening, under the soft glow of moonlight, to tap into the mystical and reflective energies associated with Odin.

Materials Needed:

- **Ansuz Rune-Carving Tool:** Use a consecrated tool, such as a ritual knife or inscribing tool, for carving the Ansuz rune. Ensure the tool has been cleansed and dedicated for magickal use.
- **Blue Candle:** Representing the ethereal and communicative qualities of Odin, use a blue candle as the focal point of the spell.
- **A Chalice or Cup:** Symbolizing the well of inspiration, use a chalice or cup filled with clear water as an offering to Odin
- **Incense:** Choose an incense with a scent that resonates with the ethereal, such as lavender or frankincense, to elevate the ritual atmosphere.

Instructions:

1. Find a quiet and dimly lit space. Light the blue candle and incense, allowing their presence to create a serene

ambiance. Sit comfortably, close your eyes, and focus on your breath. Imagine a tranquil pool of water before you, representing the well of inspiration. With each inhale, draw in the essence of the calming water, and with each exhale, release any mental barriers. Allow your consciousness to sink into a meditative state.

2. Recite the Ansuz rune poem to invoke the spirit of Ansuz/Odin:

> *"The mouth is the source of all language,*
> *a pillar of wisdom and a comfort to wise men,*
> *a blessing and a joy to every knight."*

3. With the consecrated tool, carve the Ansuz rune onto the blue candle. Place the candle in the center of your ritual space, surrounded by the chalice filled with water. Offer a few drops of your favorite essential oil into the water as a symbol of your personal essence and dedication to the well of inspiration.
4. Articulate your intent clearly with statements such as: *"By the power of Ansuz, in the sight of Odin I call forth waves of odr, the divine inspiration that bridges realms. May this well of inspiration flow through me, enhancing my spellwork and guiding me in situations where divine insight is needed."*
5. As you release the energy, utter the word "Herrlof" with conviction as an acknowledgment of the triumph of inspiration over obstacles and challenges.
6. Feel the waves of inspiration flowing through you, connecting you to the realms beyond, and embrace the heightened consciousness that Ansuz has bestowed upon you. As the candle burns, visualize the well of inspiration overflowing with wisdom and guidance.

RAIDHO

A Runic Spell to Embrace the Path of Enrichment

Time of Day: Perform this spell during the early morning, as the sun rises to symbolize the beginning of a new day and the potential for personal growth.

Materials Needed:

- **Raidho Rune-Carving Tool:** Employ a consecrated tool, such as a ritual knife or inscribing tool, to carve the Raidho rune. Ensure the tool has been cleansed and dedicated for magickal use.
- **Green Candle:** Representing the color of growth and renewal, use a green candle as the focal point of the spell.
- **A Symbol of Personal Growth:** Choose a small item that symbolizes your personal journey of growth, such as a sprouting seed, a leaf, or a small potted plant.
- **Incense:** Select an incense with a rejuvenating fragrance, such as eucalyptus or mint, to create an invigorating atmosphere.

Instructions:

1. Begin in a quiet space with the green candle and incense burning. Sit comfortably and focus on your breath. Inhale deeply, envisioning the air bringing revitalizing energy into your body, and exhale, releasing any stagnation. Picture a path stretching before you, bathed in the soft light of the rising sun. As you step onto this path, feel a sense of anticipation for the personal growth that lies ahead.

2. Recite the Raidho rune poem to invoke the spirit of Raidho:

   "Riding is easy for warriors
   while they are in the hall
   but very strenuous for those
   who have to dismount
   and lead the horses on foot."

3. With the consecrated tool, carve the Raidho rune onto the green candle. Place the candle in the center of your ritual space, surrounded by the symbol of personal growth. Offer a handful of fertile soil or a few drops of water onto the soil, symbolizing the nourishment and care you dedicate to your personal journey.
4. Say your Intent: Clearly state your intent with phrases such as: *"By the essence of Raidho, I embrace the path of personal growth and enrichment. May this journey lead me to new horizons and opportunities, strengthening me along the way."*
5. As you release the energy, utter the word "Herrlof" with conviction.
6. Feel the energy of Raidho guiding you on your path, supporting your growth and transformation. As the candle burns, envision your journey expanding, flourishing, and leading you to new heights of personal development.

KENAZ

A Runic Spell for Knowledge and Enlightenment

Time of Day: Perform this spell during the twilight hours, as day transitions into night. The liminal space between light and darkness aligns with Kenaz's transformative energy.

Materials Needed:

- **Kenaz Rune-Carving Tool:** Utilize a consecrated tool, like a ritual knife or inscribing tool, for carving the Kenaz rune. Ensure the tool has been cleansed and dedicated for magickal use.
- **Yellow Candle:** Representing the colour of intellect and illumination, use a yellow candle as the central focus of the spell.
- **A Quill or Pen:** Symbolizing the act of recording and acquiring knowledge, use a quill or pen as a representation of the seeker's quest for wisdom.
- **Incense:** Select an incense with a scent that evokes clarity and mental acuity, such as sandalwood or lavender, to enhance the ritual atmosphere.

Instructions:

1. Find a quiet space and light the yellow candle and incense. Sit comfortably, focusing on the flame of the candle. Inhale deeply, allowing the scent of the incense to sharpen your senses. Picture a door before you, symbolic of the threshold between mundane knowledge and the hidden realms of enlightenment. Open the door in your mind and step through, entering a space where wisdom flows freely.
2. Recite the Kenaz rune poem to invoke the spirit of Kenaz:

> *"Torch is known to every living man*
> *by its pale, bright flame;*
> *it always burns where princes sit within."*

3. With the consecrated tool, carefully carve the Kenaz rune onto the yellow candle. Place the candle in the centre

of your ritual space, alongside the quill or pen. Offer a small handful of dried herbs, such as sage or rosemary, into the flame as a symbol of your dedication to gaining knowledge.

4. Clearly state your intent, such as: *"By the light of Kenaz, I seek knowledge and understanding. May the flame of wisdom illuminate the path before me, granting insight and clarity in my pursuits of learning."*
5. As you release the energy, utter the word "Herrlof" with conviction.
6. Feel the transformative energy of Kenaz infusing your space, bringing clarity and understanding to the subject of your focus. As the yellow candle burns, visualize the illumination of wisdom casting its light upon your chosen area of study, revealing hidden insights and fostering intellectual growth.

GEBO

A Rune Spell for Cultivating Reciprocal Energies

Time of Day: Perform this spell during the evening, as the sun sets, and the day transitions into the calm of dusk. The quiet moments between day and night are conducive to invoking the harmonious energies of Gebo.

Materials Needed:

- **Gebo Rune-Carving Tool:** Utilize a consecrated tool, such as a ritual knife or inscribing tool, specifically dedicated for magickal work, to carve the Gebo rune.
- **Two Candles (one white, one gold):** Representing the dual aspects of giving and receiving, use a white candle for the giver and a gold candle for the receiver.

- **Offering of Incense:** Select a sweet and balancing incense, like frankincense or myrrh, to create an atmosphere of harmonious exchange.

Instructions:

1. Light both candles and the incense. Sit comfortably, focusing on the flames of the candles. Inhale deeply, allowing the calming scent of the incense to center your mind. Close your eyes and visualize a luminous thread connecting you to the recipient of your harmonious exchange. Feel the energy flow between you and the other party, creating a sense of interconnectedness.
2. Recite the Gebo rune poem to invoke the spirit of Gebo:

"Generosity brings credit and honor,
which support one's dignity;
it furnishes help and subsistence
to all broken men
who are devoid of aught else."

3. Using the consecrated tool, carve the Gebo rune onto each candle. Place the white candle on the left side and the gold candle on the right side of your ritual space. Offer a small token of your generosity on a plate between the candles, such as a piece of fruit, a coin, or a symbolic item that represents a gift.
4. Clearly state your intent; for example: "*Through the balanced energies of Gebo, I invoke the spirit of reciprocal giving and receiving. May this spell foster harmony and mutual benefit in the exchange between myself and [recipient's name or a general term like "others" or "the universe"]. May the flow of generosity be a source of credit, honor, and support.*"
5. As you release the energy, utter the word "Herrlof" with conviction. This Old English term, meaning "praise" or

"victory," signifies the acknowledgment of a successful and harmonious exchange.

6. Feel the balanced energies of Gebo resonating in your space, creating a harmonious exchange of energies. As the candles burn, visualize the reciprocal flow of energy between you and the intended recipient, fostering a sense of mutual support, honor, and dignity.

WUNJO

A Runic Spell to Invite Harmony and Bliss

Time of Day: Perform this spell during the morning, as the sun rises and bathes the world in its gentle light. The dawn symbolizes the awakening of new possibilities and the potential for joy.

Materials Needed:

- **Wunjo Rune-Carving Tool:** Employ a consecrated tool, such as a ritual knife or inscribing tool, dedicated for magickal workings, to carve the Wunjo rune.
- **Yellow or Gold Candle:** Reflecting the radiant energy of joy, use a yellow or gold candle as the centerpiece for this spell.
- **An Offering of Sweet Fragrance:** Choose a sweet and uplifting incense, like jasmine or vanilla, to enhance the joyful atmosphere of the ritual.

How to Get into Trance State:

1. Begin in a quiet space, lighting the yellow or gold candle and the chosen incense. Sit comfortably, focusing on the flame of the candle. Inhale deeply, allowing the soothing scent of the incense to envelop you. Close your eyes and imagine a golden aura of light surrounding you, representing the warmth and joy you seek to invoke.

2. Recite the Wunjo rune poem to invoke the spirit of Wunjo:

   "Joy is for him who has understood,
   felt in his heart,
   and experienced how to listen;
   it is proper to speak of it.
   It makes a man cheerful on a journey."

3. Using the consecrated tool, carve the Wunjo rune onto the chosen candle. Place the candle at the center of your ritual space. As an offering, present a small bowl of honey or a piece of sweet fruit, symbolizing the sweetness of joy you wish to attract.
4. Clearly state your intent, such as: *"By the radiant energy of Wunjo, I invite joy and harmony into my life. May this spell illuminate my path, infusing my days with cheerfulness and a sense of fulfillment. As I carve this rune and make my offering, I open myself to the joyous energies that surround me."*
5. Finish by saying "Herrlof."
6. Feel the uplifting and joyous energy of Wunjo filling your space, creating an atmosphere of positivity and harmony. As the candle burns, visualize the golden light expanding, radiating joy and fulfillment throughout your being and the environment. Allow the essence of Wunjo to bring a sense of cheerfulness to your journey and experiences.

Homework

For most spells, I have devised this simple "template," if you will. Following this template (or deviating from it), continue to create rune spells for the remaining second and third aett of the Elder Futhark.

1. Trance
2. Invoke/Evoke

3. Carve
4. Offering
5. Intent
6. Herrlof

Rune Band Spells

Runic bands represent one of the oldest forms of rune magic. To craft them properly requires not only a deep understanding of each individual rune, but also of how multiple runes interact and how Germanic numerology influences their combined power. Most of the rune spells recorded in the old sagas take this form.

Germanic Numerology

Exploring the realm of "numerical significance," let's now venture into the intriguing world of Viking numerology. Numerology, the study of the meaning and significance of numbers, goes beyond the physical and delves into fringe sciences or metaphysical realms.

Among the Vikings, a belief persisted that numbers held particular significance, evident throughout their legends and stories. Take the tale of Drapnir, Odin's golden arm ring, which every nine days would "drip" eight identical arm-rings, being itself the ninth. Parties of three gods (or any combination of gods, mortals, or giants) were often seen competing or questing in groups of three. The number four also made frequent appearances, such as the four dwarves supporting the sky and the four branches of Yggdrasil, the "World Tree."

Viking mythology of numbers from low to high can be classified as such:

The Number Three: "Sacred" or "Divine"

- Odin, in his pursuit of godhood, sacrificed himself for three days, emerging as a god.

- Yggdrasil boasts three roots nurtured daily by three Norns, weaving fate for all living beings.
- The first humans were created by three gods: Odin, Vili, and Vé, each bestowing three gifts upon humanity.
- Loki, the mischievous deity, has three notable children: Hel, ruler of death; the Midgard Serpent, and Fenrir, the harbinger of Ragnarök.
- Binding Fenrir to subdue his fate required three attempts.
- Norse mythology features three dragons, one being a man transformed into a dragon.

The divine association with the number three is evident in sacred beasts, objects, gods, and various aspects of human life throughout Norse mythology.

The Number Four: "Order" or "Balance"

- Audhumla, the great cow, created Odin's grandfather Buri, and four rivers of milk flowed from her utter.
- Four dwarves, representing the cardinal directions, support the corners of the sky.
- Among the branches of Yggdrasil, four deer dwell, embodying a sense of order and balance.

The Number Seven: "Longsuffering" or "Endlessness"

- Great Vikings were said to have fought in seven wars.
- Great sea voyages would often confront hardships for seven days at a time:

> *"For seven days we rode across the cold land,*
> *but other seven days we hit the waves;*
> *the third seven days we went onto a dry land."*
> ("The First Lay of Guðrúnarkviða")

The Number Eight: "Insufficient" or "Unfavorable"

- Sleipnir, Odin's eight-legged horse, resulted from one of Loki's tricks gone awry.
- Numerous sagas depict parties of eight Vikings facing defeat or encountering obstacles due to unforeseen circumstances or unfavorable luck.
- Ships attacking in groups of eight were defeated in the *Grettis Saga,* even when outnumbering the enemy with only five ships.

The Number Nine: "Magickal Power" or "Mystical"

- Odin hanged from the world tree for nine days before the magick of runes was revealed to him.
- Drapnir, Odin's golden arm-ring, produced eight copies of itself every nine days, increasing Odin's horde for eternity.
- The branches of Yggdrasil support nine realms, each with its unique significance.
- Heimdall, the guardian of Bifrost (the Rainbow Bridge), was born from nine sisters.
- In the climactic battle of Ragnarök, Thor takes nine steps before succumbing to death, highlighting the mystical power associated with the number nine.

These numbers intricately intertwine with Viking numerology, influencing the outcomes of sagas and imbuing the realms of gods and mortals with symbolic significance.

For example, a runic band spell to summon the Thurses will look like this:

ᚦᚦᚦᚢᛏᚱᛟᛚᛟᚲᛁᚾ
Thursa Thursa Thursa (three to summon the sacred)

Uruz (unstoppable wild force)
Trollaukinn (Old Norse; "possesion by spirits")

Homework

Create a short (three or four different runes) runic band spell based on numerology for each of the five important Germanic numbers.

Rune Spells in the Sagas

Let's delve into the runic spells mentioned in historical contexts, particularly those detailed by Sigrdrífa in the "Sigrdrífumál." While magick is frequently alluded to in the Eddas and Ancient Norse texts, comprehensive spell formulations are scarce. In this exploration, we will elaborate on the runic spells highlighted by Sigrdrífa, providing additional insights.

It seems that these charms were all in Elder Futhark.

Alu

The term *Alu* functions as a charm word discovered on artifacts from the Germanic Iron Age in Central and Northern Europe. It is a prevalent early runic charm, appearing alone or as part of a larger formula. Scholars debate its origin and meaning, with consensus leaning toward its representation of amulet magick or serving as a metaphor for it.

The sequence "alu" appears in numerous runic inscriptions of the Elder Futhark in Germanic Iron Age Scandinavia, and occasionally in early Anglo-Saxon England, spanning the period from the third to the eighth century. This word is often found in isolation, as seen on the Elgesem runestone, or as part of a formula, as observed on the Lindholm "Amulet" (DR 261) in Scania, Sweden. The symbols in "alu" correspond to the runes Ansuz, Laguz, and Uruz. While the origin and meaning of *alu* remain subjects of debate, scholars generally agree that the term signifies a manifestation of historical runic magick.

Interestingly, *alu* disappears from runic inscriptions shortly after the Migration Period, predating the Christianization of Scandinavia. However, it persists beyond this era, becoming increasingly associated with ale.

Delving into the ale brewing process, it represents a magickal transformation, turning ordinary ingredients into something extraordinary—grains into alcohol. This transformative process is reflected in its inscription on various amulets, mundane objects, and weapons, imbuing them with sacred significance.

While the literal meaning of *alu* is commonly accepted as "ale" or an "intoxicating beverage," scholars have delved deeper into its significance. Previous etymologies suggested a connection with Proto-Germanic *aluh,* meaning "amulet" or "taboo," derived from *alh,* meaning "protect." Cognates in Germanic dialects include Old English *ealh* ("temple"), Gothic *alhs* ("temple"), and Old Norse *alh* ("amulet)". Edgar Polomé proposed an etymological link between Germanic *alu* and Hittite *alwanza,* meaning "affected by witchcraft."

In Raetian and North Etruscan dedicatory votive objects, *alu* has been discovered to signify dedication. Connections have been suggested between these objects and the term alu found in runic inscriptions. Therefore, the act of carving "ALU" onto an object signifies a transformative process, turning the mundane into the sacred and the ordinary into the magickal.

By examining the runes Ansuz, Laguz, and Uruz individually in an esoteric manner, momentarily setting aside linguistic considerations, one arrives at the essence of "wisdom to undergo energetic, emotional, and material transformation."

Victory Runes

In the *Poetic Edda,* specifically in the Sigrdrífumál, "victory runes" are mentioned to be engraved on a sword, emphasizing the significance of carving them on both the grasp and inlay, naming Tyr twice.

Gladness Runes

Sigrdrífa, the valkyrie, presents Sigurd with a memory-draught charmed with "gladness runes." This ale, is imbued with strength, mighty fame, charms, healing signs, spells, and gladness-runes: "Beer I bring thee, tree of battle, Mingled of strength and mighty fame; Charms it holds and healing signs, Spells full good, and gladness-runes" (*Poetic Edda,* "Sigrdrífumál," stanza 5).

The description provided suggests a combination of runes associated with positive attributes, strength, fame, charms, healing, spells, and, most importantly, gladness. While there isn't a direct one-to-one correspondence between English words and runic symbols, you can choose Elder Futhark runes that embody the essence of the qualities mentioned.

Here's a suggestion for runes to use for "gladness runes" based on their symbolic meanings:

- **Strength:** *Uruz—Uruz* is associated with physical and mental strength, endurance, and primal power. It is a representation of the raw and untamed strength.
- **Mighty Fame:** *Kenaz—Kenaz* is often linked to knowledge, creativity, and controlled fire. In the context of mighty fame, it represents the illuminating fame achieved through skill, artistry, or transformative endeavors.
- **Charms:** *Gebo—Gebo* symbolizes the concept of exchange

and gifts. In the context of charms, represents the giving and receiving of positive energies and blessings.

- **Healing Signs:** *Algiz—Algiz* is a rune associated with protection and higher spiritual connection. It signifies a shield or a guardian presence, offering healing and protective energies.
- **Spells:** *Ansuz—Ansuz* represents divine communication, wisdom, and inspiration. In the context of spells, it symbolizes the connection to higher knowledge and the channeling of divine energy for magickal purposes.
- **Gladness:** *Wunjo—Wunjo* is the rune of joy, happiness, and fellowship. It embodies the idea of positive emotions, harmony, and the joyous aspects of life.

ᚢᚲᚷᛉᚨᚹᚹᚹ

Ale-Runes (Ølrunar)

In stanza 7 of the Sigrdrífumál, ale-runes are introduced as a protective spell against bewitchment through ale served by the host's wife. The runes Naudiz and Laukaz are recommended to be marked on one's fingernails and the cup, respectively.

"Ale-runes learn, that with lies the wife Of another betray not thy trust; On the horn thou shalt write, and the backs of thy hands, And Need shalt mark on thy nails. Thou shalt bless the draught, and danger escape, And cast a leek in the cup" (*Poetic Edda*).

ᚾ ᛚ

Birth Runes (Biargrunar)

Stanza 8 introduces birth-runes, a spell to aid childbirth. These runes are to be written on the palms and around the joints, seeking assistance from the fates.

"Birth runes learn, if help thou wilt lend, The babe from the mother to bring; On thy palms shalt write them, and round thy joints, And ask the fates to aid" (*Poetic Edda*).

Start by writing the runes (I use an ordinary black marker) on the palms, running down to the wrist and then continue writing all the way around the arm repeating the six runes, twisting around the arm once or twice or however many times need be. The act of twisting the runes around the arm symbolically reinforces the protective and supportive energy associated with each rune.

- **Berkana:** Berkana is associated with fertility, growth, and nurturing. It symbolizes the protective and nurturing aspects of childbirth, representing the potential for new life and growth
- **Ingwaz:** Ingwaz is often linked to fertility, peace, and inner harmony. It represents the inner strength and balance needed during childbirth.
- **Ehwaz:** Ehwaz is associated with partnership, teamwork, and the bond between a mother and child. It symbolizes the collaborative effort and support involved in the birthing process.
- **Gebo:** Gebo represents the concept of giving and receiving, symbolizing the exchange of energies. In the context of childbirth, it represents the bond between the mother and the newborn.
- **Uruz:** Uruz is linked to physical and mental strength, representing the stamina and endurance required during childbirth.
- **Ansuz:** Ansuz symbolizes divine communication and wisdom. It is to be included to seek guidance and protection during the birthing process.

Wave-Runes (Brimrunar)

In stanza 9, wave-runes are detailed as a spell for ship protection, with instructions to carve runes on the stem and rudder. This enchantment ensures safe passage through treacherous waters.

"Wave-runes learn, if well thou wouldst shelter, The sail-steeds out on the sea; On the stem shalt thou write, and the steering blade, And burn them into the oars; Though high be the breakers, and black the waves, Thou shalt safe the harbor seek" (*Poetic Edda*).

1. **Laguz:** Laguz is the rune associated with water, representing the ebb and flow, depth, and the mysteries of the unconscious. It is highly appropriate for a spell aimed at protecting against the challenges of the sea.
2. **Eihwaz:** Eihwaz is associated with protection and defence. Its strength can be invoked to safeguard the ship from potential harm during its journey.
3. **Ansuz:** Ansuz symbolizes divine communication and wisdom. It can be included to seek guidance and protection during the voyage.
4. **Gebo:** Gebo represents the concept of giving and receiving. It is used to invoke a balanced and harmonious relationship with the sea, seeking the favour and protection of the waves.
5. **Algiz:** Algiz is a rune associated with protection and higher spiritual connection. It can symbolize a shield or guardian presence, offering defence against dangers on the water.
6. **Mannaz:** Mannaz is associated with humanity and cooperation. It is included to invoke unity among the crew members and promote teamwork for a safe journey.

To apply these wave-runes, follow the instructions given in the stanza by carving them on the stem, rudder, and burning them into the oars. The act of inscribing and burning these runes is symbolic of infusing the ship and its components with the protective qualities represented by each rune.

ᛚᛇᚨᚷᛉᛗ

Branch-Runes (Limrunar)

Stanza 10 introduces branch-runes, a healing spell to be carved on trees with eastward-bent boughs. This spell is believed to transfer sickness from the afflicted to the tree.

"Branch-runes learn, if a healer wouldst be,
And cure for wounds wouldst work;
On the bark shalt thou write, and on trees that be
With boughs to the eastward bent."
(Poetic Edda)

- **Sowilo:** Sowilo represents the sun and is associated with healing, light, and positive energy.
- **Algiz:** Algiz is a rune of protection and higher spiritual connection, symbolizing a shield or guardian presence.
- **Berkana:** Berkana is linked to fertility, growth, and nurturing, symbolizing the healing power of nature.
- **Ehwaz:** Ehwaz is associated with partnership and teamwork, representing the cooperative effort in facilitating healing.
- **Othala:** Othala is connected to ancestral heritage and home, symbolizing grounding and stability.

The Jera rune in the runic alphabet is associated with the concept of harvest and cycles. To represent the idea of "switch," Jera can be combined with Raido, the rune associated with journeys and transitions. This combination could symbolize the cyclical nature of transitions or switches in one's journey.

Thus, creating a bind-rune for "switch":

Take the bind-rune for the name of your target (see: "Book of Runes"). Here, we are using the previously created "John Doe" rune and the pictograph for tree:

...plus ᛊᛉᛒᛗᛟ, carve this on the bark of the tree that you choose.

By using the same logic and replacing the pictograph of the tree with another bind-rune, this time of a human victim, an easy (and extremely potent) curse can be created.

Speech-Runes (Malrunar)

Stanza 11, despite its corruption, alludes to speech-runes, a spell possibly aimed at enhancing rhetorical skills at the thing, or assembly.

"Speech-runes learn, that none may seek
To answer harm with hate;
Well he winds and weaves them all,
And sets them side by side, At the judgment-place,
When justice there The folk shall fairly win."
(Poetic Edda)

1. **Ansuz:** This rune is associated with the mouth and communication. It represents divine breath, wisdom, and the power of speech.
2. **Raido:** Raido is linked to the journey and communication. It enhances the ability to articulate thoughts and express ideas clearly.
3. **Gebo:** Gebo signifies the exchange of gifts and partnerships. In the context of speech, it represent the harmonious exchange of ideas through communication.
4. **Wunjo:** Wunjo relates to joy, harmony, and satisfaction. Using this rune contribute to creating positive and uplifting speech.
5. **Thurisaz:** Thurisaz, while associated with strength, can also be applied to powerful and assertive speech, ensuring that your words have impact.
6. **Laguz:** Laguz is associated with water and emotions. Using this rune enhance the emotional depth and resonance of your speech.
7. **Mannaz:** As the rune of humanity, Mannaz is to be employed to promote understanding and empathy in speech, fostering connection with others.

ᚨᚨᚨᚱᚱᚱᚱᚷᚹᚦᛚᛗᛗᛗ

Thought-Runes (Hugrunar)

Stanza 12, although incomplete, discusses thought-runes, suggesting a spell to sharpen one's wit.

> *"Thought-runes learn, if all shall think*
> *Thou art keenest minded of men" (Poetic Edda).*

1. **Ansuz:** This rune is associated with divine breath, wisdom, and communication. Using Ansuz enhances your ability to think clearly and articulate your thoughts with intelligence.
2. **Kenaz:** Kenaz represents knowledge, creativity, and the controlled application of power. It is to be employed to stimulate thought processes and insight.
3. **Raido:** Raido is linked to the journey and can symbolize the mental journey of acquiring knowledge. It aids in expanding intellectual horizons.
4. **Wunjo:** Wunjo relates to joy and satisfaction. Incorporating Wunjo in your runic work will help in cultivating a positive and joyful mindset conducive to clear thinking.
5. **Gebo:** Gebo signifies the exchange of gifts and partnerships. It promotes harmonious thought processes and cooperative thinking.
6. **Isa:** Isa is associated with stillness and concentration. It assists in focusing your thoughts and promoting mental clarity.
7. **Algiz:** Algiz is a rune that aids in connection to higher realms. It is employed to enhance mental awareness and safeguard against distractions.
8. **Eihwaz:** Eihwaz represents the Yew tree, symbolizing endurance and resilience. Using Eihwaz will help in cultivating a resilient and enduring mindset.

ᚨᚲᚲᚲᚲᚱᚹᛁᛉᛊ

In unraveling these semi-historical rune spells, we gain a deeper understanding of the intricate weave of magick in Ancient Norse traditions, as passed down through poetic sources like the "Sigrdrífumál."

Homework

Within the semi-historical spells, gladness runes, birth-runes, wave-runes, speech-runes, and thought-runes are all examples of runic band spells, sometimes intermixed with numerology. You can create a runic band spell incorporating numerology.

The Nine Realms

The Nine Realms are powerful astral spheres of emotion and spiritual archetypical behaviour, as stated in the "Book of Spirits." Each realm can and will add its own nuances to your magickal work.

Let's start with Asgard, the highest of all vibrations within the branches of Yggdrasil.

A Spell to Invoke the Power of Asgard
Channeling the forces of Justice, Order, and War from the Realm of the Æsir.

Time of Day: Twilight, when day meets night in celestial balance.

Materials Needed:

- A small wooden disc or a piece of chalk
- Rune for Asgard (found in the "Book of Spirits")

- A blue or silver candle
- Frankincense or juniper incense
- A bowl of clear water
- An offering of mead or honey
- A piece of white fabric

Instructions:

1. Close your eyes and take deep, intentional breaths. Envision the bridge, Bifröst, connecting the mortal realm to Asgard. Visualize yourself crossing this bridge, feeling the transition from the earthly realm to the celestial splendor of Asgard.
2. Invoke the assistance of your personal spiritual guides or guardians, referred to as your *stíga* in Norse tradition. Request their presence and guidance as you embark on this journey to connect with the forces of Asgard.
3. Create a sacred circle by drawing the rune associated with Asgard in the center. This can be on a piece of wood, drawn in the sand outdoors, or traced with chalk on the floor indoors. As you carve or draw, focus on the qualities of justice, order, civilization, and war associated with Asgard.
4. Place the blue or silver candle at the top of the rune, representing the celestial realms. Light it, symbolizing the connection between the mortal and divine planes. Position the frankincense or juniper incense at the bottom of the rune, representing the sacred connection between realms.
5. Set the bowl of clear water at one side of the circle, representing the harmonious flow of justice and order. Place the offering of mead or honey on the other side, symbolizing the sweetness of civilization and the strength of war.
6. In a steady and reverent voice, declare your intent: "In the realm of Asgard, I stand at the crossroads of justice and war, order and civilization. Asgardian deities, I call upon your wisdom and strength. May the qualities of your

celestial abode infuse my being with the essence of justice, order, and the courage to face the battles of life. As I carve the rune, may the bridge to Asgard be opened, and may the Æsir guide and empower me."

7. Carve (or draw) the victory rune (previous) on a personal amulet; this is to be carried with you indefinably.
8. Finish by saying "Herrlof."
9. Allow the candle to burn completely, absorbing the energy of Asgard. Collect the remnants of the offering and bury them in the earth as a gesture of gratitude.
10. As you re-enter the mortal realm, carry the energy of Asgard within you in the form of the double Tyr rune. Embrace the virtues of justice, order, civilization, and the courage to face the battles of life. May the celestial influence of the Æsir guide you on your path.

Homework

Create a spell for each of the remaining realms of influence:

- **Alfheim:** Ancestor veneration
- **Midgard:** Growth and skills
- **Jötunheim:** Transformation
- **Vanaheim:** Nature and fertility
- **Niflheim:** Cold, darkness, and creation
- **Muspelheim:** Fire and destructive forces
- **Svartalfheim:** Crafting
- **Helheim:** Medicine and disease

The Four Reasons

In the realm of magick, we divide the spells into both categories (healing, love, wealth, weather, defensive, offensive, growth, etc.) and forms (word spells, evocations, rune spells, and combination spells—combing two or more forms into a ritual).

We can further narrow said list into only four, thus streamlining our intentions:

Restorative Spells

- **Healing:** Spells focused on physical, emotional, or spiritual well-being.
- **Growth:** Spells for personal development, learning, and inner growth.

Relational Spells

- **Love:** Spells that foster love, harmony, and connection.
- **Wealth:** Spells related to abundance, prosperity, and financial well-being.

Protective Spells

- **Defensive:** Spells for protection, warding off negativity, and ensuring safety.
- **Offensive:** Spells that may be used for self-defense or to repel harm.

Influential Spells

- **Elemental:** Spells involving natural elements, weather, or environmental influence.
- **Manifestation:** Spells for manifesting desires, intentions, and personal goals.

Regarding wealth, wealth can be approached from both a personal (influential spell) and relational standpoint. For instance:

- **Personal:** Spells focused on attracting financial abundance and prosperity for oneself.
- **Relational:** Spells intended to bring wealth and prosperity

to a family, community, or group, emphasizing shared resources and communal well-being.

This condensed list maintains the essence of various spell categories while simplifying and grouping them into overarching themes. It allows for flexibility and adaptability within each broad category.

Please note that not all spells are necessarily more powerful when combined, sometimes you only need one element. Spell categories and form also do have the tendency to blur the lines a lot.

Restorative Spells

Renewed Vigor: A Nordic Rune Spell for Healing
Tapping into Ancient Energies for Restoration and Well-Being.

Time of Day: Dawn, when the world is reborn in the morning light.

Materials Needed:

- A white candle
- A bowl of pure water
- A healing herb such as chamomile or lavender
- Clean bandages or a piece of sterile cloth
- A blank piece of paper and a pen
- A small cauldron or fire-safe dish
- A secluded and consecrated space for the ritual

Instructions:

1. Begin by walking in a circle around your sacred space (*Ve*), chanting healing runes Thurisaz, Berkano, and Eihwaz. As you move, let the repetitive motion and the resonance of the runes guide you into a meditative trance state. Feel the protective energy of the Ve enveloping you.

2. Invoke the healing energies of the goddess Eir by carving her bind-rune (see: "Book of Spirits") onto a piece of wood. Stain the runes with the healing herb, infusing them with the essence of restoration.
3. Recite the following poem to invoke their presence:

"Eir, healer divine,
With your touch,
let health be mine.
Bind-runes carved,
symbols of might,
Restore my being,
bring forth the light."

4. Feel the presence of Eir as you recite the words and channel her energy into the runes.
5. Cast your rune set onto the same sacred animal cloth utilized for shamanic readings. Observe the spatial distribution of the runes on the cloth—the predominant area of concentration corresponds to the specific region associated with health concerns in your body. Exclude the remaining runes from consideration, focusing exclusively on the ones that have found their place in the identified area. Delve into the nuanced interpretations of these selected runes, unraveling the messages they convey about your health and well-being. This method not only refines your divinatory practice but also deepens your insight into the intricate connections between runic energies and bodily wellness.
6. Look for insights or guidance related to the specific healing needs, allowing Eir to communicate through the runes, ask questions if you have any.
7. Carve the runes Thurisaz, Berkano, and Eihwaz onto a piece of paper and stain them with the healing herb.

8. Ignite the piece of paper with the runic symbols using the white candle. As the paper burns, visualize the flames transmuting any negativity or illness into healing energy. Place the burning paper into a cauldron or fire-safe dish, allowing the ashes to accumulate.
9. Finish by saying "Herrlof."
10. As you exit the sacred space, carry the energy of renewal and well-being with you. Remain open to the healing energies that surround you, allowing the runes and the divine powers invoked to continue their work in your life.

Relational Spells

A Wealth Magick Spell
Bridging the Ancient and Modern Flows of Abundance

Time of Day: Friday—Fair Weather

Materials Needed:

- Seed rune (Saaddoorn)
- Knife/carving Tool
- Wood of a fruit tree
- Untilled field/bowl of soil

The Saaddoorn bind-rune, on a visual level, represents a seedling, forever growing and increasing your financial yield.

The rune Ingwaz ᛝ forms the head of the seedling. As the god Yngvi Freyr standing for fertility and changing the future.

The rune Jera ᛃ represents a good harvest and a positive financial outcome.

The rune Fehu ᚠ represents the power of the Vanir and liquid money

The Gilch ᚲ rune represents money forms the base and the root system of the Saaddorn bind-rune (The Lønnrunerform is used here).

Instructions:

1. Begin the spell by acknowledging the diverse forms of wealth, encompassing both traditional and modern concepts. Recognize the significance of wealth in the bounties of the earth and the currency of today. Embrace the dual nature of wealth as you prepare for the ritual. The inclusion of Macromannic runes, particularly the Gilch rune, symbolizes wealth, not only in harvest and cattle, but also in the form of currency.

2. Carve the bind-rune onto a twig from a fruit-bearing tree, emphasizing the merging of ancient and contemporary wealth symbols. As you carve, recite the galdralag of intent, repeating until the carving is complete: "Money flows to me in abundance, amidst ease. Well-versed in wealth, well-versed in weather."
3. Stain the rune with gold or silver paint/enamel, enhancing its symbolic richness.
4. Call upon Yngvi Freyr, invoking the god of the good year and giver of gold. Acknowledge the interconnectedness of the present and the future, seeking Freyr's assistance in influencing the energies of wealth.
5. "God of the good year and giver of gold, wealth is fair weather, you welcome no woes."
6. To charge the spell with the power of the Vanir, earth, and nature, bury the rune stav in an untilled field. If this is not possible, place it in a bowl of soil on your altar.
7. Sit by the freshly buried rune in the field or next to your

altar. Close your eyes and envision the abundant growth around you—lush green fields, cattle grazing in the distance. Recognize the stav as the seed from which all prosperity grows. Open your eyes with the understanding that you are a magnet for wealth.

8. Say "Herrlof."
9. In this magickal working, the "Wealth Magick Spell" seeks to harmonize the ancient and contemporary aspects of abundance, creating a bridge between the past and the present. The rune, charged with the energies of nature and the Vanir, serves as a beacon attracting prosperity in various forms to the practitioner.

Protective Spells

Let's turn protection into its proactive stage the curse. This curse is not entirely historic but the inspiration for it is straight from the Eddas.

In the poem "Skírnismál" (found in the *Poetic Edda*), Freyr's servant Skírnir is sent to woo Gerðr on Freyr's behalf. Through this exchange, Freyr threathens to curse Gerðr through Skírnir: "I write thee a charm and three runes therewith; longing and madness and lust...that only the frost Thurses may satisfy from time to time."

The exact runes used are lost to history. However, seeing that this is a Vanir god, we might as well reckon that the runes used will be of Elder Futhark.

The runes I have used is all merkstav of:

- Othala ᛟ for Home
- Lagus ᛚ for Emotions
- Thurisaz ᚦ for Sexuality

Thus,

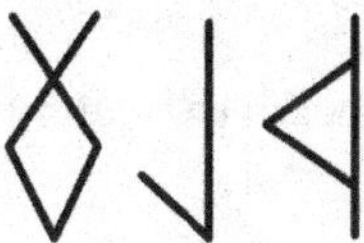

- Othala for Longing
- Lagus for Madness
- Thurisaz for Lust

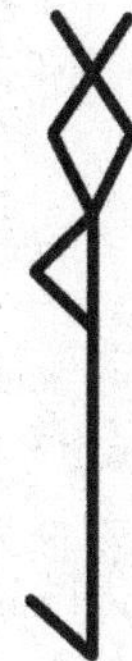

Adding the name of our target, "John."

In sharp contrast with the previous spell, we still call on Freyr showing both the dualistic side of nature but also of all the Norse gods.

Casting Longing, Madness, and Lust on Your Target

Time of Day: Midnight, beneath the watchful gaze of a waning moon

Materials Needed:

- Bind-rune for longing, madness, and lust
- A piece of black cloth
- A quill or sharp object for carving
- Blood (use responsibly and ethically)
- A burial mound or bowl of ashes

Instructions:

1. Begin at the edge of your sacred space, marked by stones or symbols of protection. Chant the names of the runes (Othala, Lagus, Thurisaz) as you walk in a clockwise circle, gradually entering a meditative state. Feel the energy of the runes resonating within you.
    * Stand at the center of your sacred space, facing north. Raise your arms to the sky and call upon Freyr, the god of fertility and desires: "god of grief and giver of cold, an eye for an eye, you welcome no woes."
2. Feel the presence of Freyr embracing your ritual, connecting with the forces of nature. For nature can be both nurturing and cruel.
3. On the black cloth, draw the bind-runes for "longing," "madness," and "lust." As you carve each rune, visualize the essence of longing, madness, and lust intertwining. Focus on the intensity of desires.
4. Prick your finger with the quill or sharp object and allow a few drops of blood to fall onto the bind-rune. As your blood mingles with the symbols, envision your desires becoming a potent force, ready to be unleashed.

5. Place the stained bind-rune in the center of the burial mound or bowl of ashes. As you bury it, imagine the fertile earth absorbing the energies, grounding your desires. Visualize the roots of the burial mound connecting with the core of the earth.
6. Thank Freyr for his presence and guidance. Step back from the burial mound, feeling the energy of the spell sealed within the earth. Close the ritual with gratitude and a sense of fulfilment.
7. Finish by saying "Herrlof!"

Influential Spells

In Norse mythology and magickal practices, the concept of using knots in storm magick is associated with a form of protective and controlling magick. This practice involves tying knots, typically in a specific number, to influence or control natural forces, particularly storms. The use of knots in magickal practices is known as "knot magick" or "knot spellcraft."

Wind knots were purchased from witches and wizards in the seaports of Finland, Norway, Denmark, Ireland, and Scotland. In the days of sailing ships, no prudent sailor left the harbor without his witches' knot stowed in his gear.

Vulnerable to the forces of weather, sailors sought to control the wind with witchcraft. They believed they could carry the wind aboard ship where it would remain secured for a safe voyage. If the wind failed, the sailor untied a knot and released a wind.

A Norse myth tells how Volundr kept a supply of wind knots in his smithy. Hanging there was a long rope with knots at regular intervals. In every knot, a storm wind was bound. Each week he untied a knot. Freeing the wind, he sent it south with his mad song charged with thunder and hail.

To this day, the bitter winds that sweep across the Gulf of Finland are blamed on witches.

The formula for a witch's knot was to tie three knots in a cord while repeating a magick incantation. The spell was sealed by spitting on the knot as it was tied. Untying the first knot brought a gentle breeze. The second knot enclosed a stronger wind. The third contained a hurricane. It was to remain tied to insure a tempest-free voyage.

This is a two-part spell, with the first you harness the power of the storm within your knots and with the second you release it.

At its core, knot magick operates on the principle that the act of tying or untying knots can invoke or release specific energies into the universe. The practitioner, by binding intentions into the knots, creates a tangible representation of their desires. Each knot becomes a focal point for the concentration of energy, making the knot itself a vessel for the spell's purpose.

The number of knots used holds significance, with three being particularly revered in Norse magick for its associations with completeness, balance, and power.

Spell 1: Binding the Storm Winds

Time of Day: Evening, as storm clouds gather.

Materials Needed:

- A sturdy cord
- Three knots
- Outdoor space with a view of the impending storm

Instructions:

1. **First Knot—Mild Gust:** As the storm approaches, tie the first knot in the cord. Focus on the intention of capturing the energy of a mild gust of wind. Visualize the gentle caress of the breeze. Say: "By knot of one, the winds begun, a gentle whisper, the storm's first son."

2. **Second Knot—Medium Wind:** As the storm intensifies, tie the second knot with the intent of capturing the energy of a medium-strength wind. Envision the growing force of the wind. Say: "By knot of two, the tempest grew, a breeze turned to a wind that blew."
3. **Third Knot—Very Strong Wind:** As the storm reaches its peak, tie the third knot, focusing on the intention of capturing the energy of a very strong wind. Visualize the powerful forces of nature. Say: "By final knot, the storm winds bind, a mighty gale, unleashed, confined."

Spell 2: Releasing the Storm Winds

Time of Day: When the winds are calm.

Materials Needed:

- The cord with the three knots
- Outdoor space with a view of the calming storm

Instructions:

1. **First Knot—Gentle Release:** As the storm begins to subside, untie the first knot with reverence, visualizing a gentle gust of wind being released. Say: "By knot undone, the winds now sway, a gentle breeze to end the day."
2. **Second Knot—Natural Flow:** Untie the second knot, allowing the storm's energies to flow naturally. Visualize a harmonious dispersal of the remaining elemental forces. Say: "By knot untied, the course set free, let nature flow in harmony."
3. **Third Knot—Mighty Release:** Untie the third knot, releasing the full force of the storm's energy. Imagine a mighty tempest fading into the distance. Say: "By final knot, the storm is hurled, a mighty dance around the world."

In the intricate dance between the practitioner and the elements, knot magick weaves intentions into the fabric of reality. It serves as a bridge between the physical and the metaphysical, allowing those who wield its art to tap into the primal forces of nature and influence the world around them. The spells presented here demonstrate the delicate balance between binding and releasing, a testament to the wisdom and respect required when working with the untamed energies of storms.

...and now we come to the final spell in this Svartebok. Let's incorporate everything we learned:

The reasons people cast spells can vary widely, as they are often influenced by personal beliefs, cultural practices, and individual circumstances. However, one of the most common reasons people cast spells is to manifest positive changes in their lives. The desire for change propels magick thinking. Many individuals turn to spell casting when they are seeking positive changes in their lives, whether it be in the realms of love, career, health, or personal growth. Spells are often seen as a way to influence and direct energy toward a specific goal or outcome.

Last Spell

Homework

Before continuing onwards with this spell, you are going to create three bind-runes:

Create a bind-rune for your higher self. Start with your name bind-rune and either add runes for higher qualities to it or, in a meditative trance, in order to communicate with your guardians and ancestors. Use the evocation runes in the "Book of Spirits" to aid you in the latter stage.

Then, compose a galdralag poem that encapsulates your intent for spiritual awakening and wisdom. Write that poem in any runic style of your liking (translated into the appropriate language or directly from English). Create a second bind-rune (in any form) for that poem.

So, let's add everything we learned into one Nordic spell for change. This spell will fall into the first category of restorative spells:

A Spell for Spiritual Awakening and Wisdom
Awakening the Inner Light with Odin's Guidance

Time of Day: Dawn, as the world is bathed in the first light of the day.

Materials Needed:

- A white candle consecrated with Othala for Odin
- Rhythmic drumming music or a drum
- Rune for Alfheim
- Rune for Higher Self
- Rune of intent
- Three small wooden disc or a pieces of parchment
- Red ochre or another natural stain
- A bowl of salt
- Your divination rune set tool
- A pen and a piece of paper

Instructions:

1. Find a quiet space and sit comfortably. Close your eyes and begin listening to the rhythmic drumming. Allow the beat to guide your breath, syncing it with the pulse of the drum. Feel the vibrations reverberate through your body, gradually entering a trance state as you become attuned to the rhythmic flow.
2. Carve the bind-rune for Alfheim onto the first wooden disk and place it in the centre of the Ve. This will establish that this Ve is of vibration higher than yourself.
3. Hold the second wooden disc or parchment in your hands. Carve the bind-rune of your higher self onto it, focusing on each stroke with intent. Stain the carved bind-rune

with red ochre, symbolizing the life force and wisdom your higher self imparts.

4. Light the candle dedicated to Odin and invoke him by reciting the following poem: "Wise wanderer, god of wild and wind, grant me thy megin, grant me thy might. Wise Allfather, Odin, seeker of truth, By Othala, Ansuz, and Dagaz, guide my youth. Grant me wisdom's light, in your presence stand, Awaken the spirit, reveal the hidden strand."
5. Feel Odin's presence as you recite the words, sensing the flow of ancient wisdom and spiritual insight.
6. Casting your rune set, communicate with Odin. Pay attention to the symbols and messages revealed, allowing Odin to convey wisdom and direction through the divination.
7. Carve the rune of your intent onto the last wooden disc or parchment. Stain the carved rune with the same red ochre, infusing them with the essence of your aspirations.
8. Choose a sacred space, either outside under a great tree or inside in a bowl of salt. Bury the carved runes, symbolizing the connection between the earthly and spiritual realms. As you cover them, visualize the energy of your intent merging with the natural elements.
9. Release by saying "Herrlof": Conclude the ritual by saying "Herrlof," signifying the completion of the spell. Allow the white candle to burn completely, absorbing the energy of spiritual awakening and wisdom.
10. As you go about your day, carry the energy of the spell with you. Embrace the insights gained from Odin and the symbolic burial of your intent, trusting in the unfolding journey toward spiritual enlightenment and wisdom.

Homework

Write a spell for each of the other categories; relational spells, protective spells and influential spells. use bind-runes of different forms, runic bands and words of power.

GLOSSARY

Æsir: In Norse mythology, one of the two main groups of deities, the other being the Vanir. The Æsir are associated with war, wisdom, and governance.

Aett: A family or clan within Norse culture, often used in the context of runic traditions to refer to one of the three eight-rune sets.

Alfheim: In Norse mythology, one of the Nine Worlds, home to the light elves or "álfar."

Animism: A belief system that attributes spiritual significance to natural elements, objects, and phenomena.

Ancestor Worship: The veneration or reverence of ancestors as a part of religious or spiritual practices.

Anglo-Saxon: Refers to the people, culture, and language of the Anglo-Saxons, who inhabited England from the fifth to the eleventh centuries.

Asgard: In Norse mythology, one of the Nine Realms, the realm of the Æsir gods, and a central location in the cosmology.

Ásynjur Goddess: A collective term for the female Æsir deities in Norse mythology.

Astral: Pertaining to the non-physical realm or dimension beyond the material world.

Audumla: In Norse mythology, the primeval cow that licked the ice, leading to the creation of the first being, Buri.

Berserkers: Norse warriors who fought with intense ferocity and were believed to channel animalistic or supernatural powers in battle.

Bind-Runes: A type of runic magick where two or more runes are combined to create a unique symbol with specific magickal properties.

Blót: A Norse pagan ritual involving the sacrifice of animals to honor deities and seek their favor.

Caster: A practitioner of magickal arts or spells.

Chanting: The repetitive vocalization of words or sounds, often used in rituals or meditative practices.

Deity: A divine being or god.

Dísablót: A specific type of blót dedicated to the female spirits, or *dísir*.

Divination: The practice of seeking knowledge or insight through supernatural or symbolic means, such as tarot cards, runes, or scrying.

Drápa: A form of Old Norse poetry often used to praise kings or heroes.

Drumming: The use of drums in ritualistic or spiritual practices, often to induce trance or altered states of consciousness.

Edda: A collection of Old Norse poems and prose, preserving much of Norse mythology and cosmology.

Egregore: Collective thought-form or psychic entity created and sustained by the shared beliefs and emotions of a group, believed to influence the thoughts and actions of its creators.

Élivágar: Refers to the primal rivers of ice in Norse cosmogony, preceding the creation of the world.

Evocation: The act of summoning spirits or deities.

Fólkvangr: In Norse mythology, a field ruled by the goddess Freyja where half of those who die in battle go after death.

Fornyrðislag: A poetic meter used in Old Norse poetry.

Frost Giant: A type of giant in Norse mythology associated with the cold and ice.

Futhark: The runic alphabet used by Germanic languages before the adoption of the Latin alphabet.

Galdr: Old Norse magick involving chanting or incantations.

Galdrastafir: Magickal staves or symbols used in Norse magickal traditions.

Galdralag: A form of Old Norse poetic meter.

Galdramál: A poetic form focused on magickal themes.

Galdramenn: Practitioners of galdr, skilled in magickal chanting.
Gand: A magickal staff or wand in Norse folklore.
Germanic: Relating to the Germanic peoples or their languages, including the Norse.
Ginnungagap: In Norse cosmogony, the primordial void before the creation of the world.
Goetia: A practice involving the conjuration of demons or spirits.
Grimoire: A book of magick spells, rituals, and symbols.
Hamr: In Norse mythology, the shape or form one takes in the spiritual or astral realm.
Hamingja: A concept in Norse folklore related to personal luck or fortune.
Hávamál: A collection of Old Norse poems, imparting wisdom and advice.
Herrlof: In Norse mythology, the honor or glory gained in battle.
Helheim: In Norse mythology, the realm of the dead ruled by the goddess Hel.
Hof: An Old Norse term for a temple, often used in the context of Norse religious practices.
Hugr: In Norse thought, one's mind or consciousness.
Invocation: The act of calling upon a deity or spirit.
Ironwood: A mythical and sacred type of wood often associated with magick and divination.
Jötnar: Another term for giants in Norse mythology.
Jötunheim: In Norse mythology, the realm of the giants.
Kenning: A poetic metaphor or compound word used in Old Norse poetry.
Kynnfylgja: In Norse folklore, a type of spirit associated with family or lineage.
Landvættir: Guardian spirits of the land in Norse mythology, associated with specific geographic features.
Ljóðaháttr: A poetic meter used in Old Norse poetry.
Macrocosms: The larger, cosmic-scale aspects of existence.
Magick: The use of ritual, symbols, and energy to bring about desired changes.

Magick Circle: A symbolic boundary created for magickal rituals and protection.

Meditation: A practice of focused contemplation or mindfulness.

Megin: A concept in Norse magick, often translated as "might" or "power."

Merseburg Charms: Old High German spells recorded in the tenth century.

Microcosms: The smaller, individual-scale aspects of existence.

Midgard: In Norse mythology, the realm of humans.

Mjölnir: The legendary hammer of the god Thor, often used as a protective symbol and associated with strength and lightning.

Muspelheim: In Norse mythology, the realm of fire.

Nidstang: A pole used in Norse cursing rituals.

Niflheim: In Norse mythology, the primordial realm of ice.

Neopaganism: A modern revival or reconstruction of pagan beliefs and practices.

Nordic: Relating to the cultural and mythological traditions of the Norse people.

Norns: The Norse equivalent of Fates in Greek mythology, responsible for weaving the destiny of gods and humans.

Oðr: In Norse mythology, a concept related to the poetic inspiration and divine frenzy.

Pantheon: A group of deities or gods worshiped in a particular culture or religion.

Paganism: A broad term encompassing various polytheistic, nature-based, and folk religions.

Ragnarök, the End of the World: In Norse mythology, a series of future events including a great battle and natural disasters.

Realm: A distinct or defined domain, often referring to a supernatural or divine space.

Ritual: A set of prescribed actions or ceremonies often performed for religious or magickal purposes.

Runes: The letters of various Ancient Germanic alphabets, often used for magickal or divinatory purposes.

Seax: A type of single-edged knife associated with the Saxons.

Seers: Individuals with the ability to foresee the future or receive divine insights.

Seiðr: A form of Norse magick associated with divination and fate-weaving.

Seiðkonur: Female practitioners of seiðr.

Shapeshifters, reflecting the transformative aspects of these beings: Entities or beings capable of changing their physical form.

Shamanism: A spiritual practice involving communication with the spirit world, often through altered states of consciousness.

Sigils: Magickal symbols created for a specific magickal purpose.

Skáldskaparmál: In Norse mythology, a work presenting the poetic language and its use.

Skalds: Norse poets or bards who composed and recited poetry.

Sorceresses: Female practitioners of magick, often with a connotation of malevolence.

Soul: The spiritual or immortal essence of an individual.

Songs: In the context of Norse culture, often refers to poetic compositions or chants.

Spirits: Supernatural entities or beings.

Stíga: Ethereal beings in this imagined realm, take the form of luminous, animal-like spirits, fostering a profound connection between individuals and their inner strength; as companions on life's journey, they offer guidance and protection, with the bond strengthening through introspection, self-discovery, and alignment with one's true purpose.

Svartalfheim: In Norse mythology, the realm of the dark elves or dwarves.

Svartebok: A black book or grimoire associated with dark magick.

Symbel: A ritualistic drinking ceremony in Norse culture, often accompanied by toasts and oaths.

Trolls: Mythical beings in Norse folklore, often depicted as nature deities and/ forces of chaos.

Theurgy: A form of ritual magick aimed at invoking the presence of deities or divine powers.

Trance: A state of altered consciousness, often induced for spiritual or mystical purposes.

Ulfhednar: Norse warriors associated with wolves, often in a berserker-like manner.

Útiseta: A Norse ritual involving sitting out in nature for spiritual insight.

Valhalla: In Norse mythology, a great hall where heroes slain in battle are taken after death.

Vanir: A group of deities in Norse mythology associated with fertility and prosperity.

Vanaheim: In Norse mythology, the realm of the Vanir.

Vedic: Relating to the ancient scriptures and traditions of the Vedic period in India.

Vikings: Norse seafarers and warriors from the late eighth to early eleventh centuries.

Vision Quests: Rituals or journeys undertaken for spiritual insight or enlightenment.

Vitki: A Norse term for a wise person or magician.

Volur: Norse seeresses or prophetesses.

Valkyries: Warrior maidens in Norse mythology who choose those who may die and those who may live in battle.

Yggdrasil: The "World Tree" in Norse mythology, a sacred, giant tree that connects all of existence.

...and, so, I write and stain the runes.

BIBLIOGRAPHY

Anonymous. *The Poetic Edda.*

Anonymous. *Grettis Saga Ásmundarsonar.*

Crowley, Aleister. *Magick: Book 4.* Weiser Books, 1998.

Foote, Peter Godfrey and David M. Wilson. *The Viking Achievement: The Society and Culture of Early Medieval Scandinavia.* London and New York: Sidgwick and Jackson, St. Martin's Press, 1990.

Rimbert, *The Vita Anskarri.*

Sturluson, Snorri. *Egil's Saga.* 1250.

Sturluson, Snorri. *Heimskringla.* 1230.

Sturluson, Snorri. *The Prose Edda.* 1220.

Tacitus. *Germania.* 98.